TROUBLED WATERS

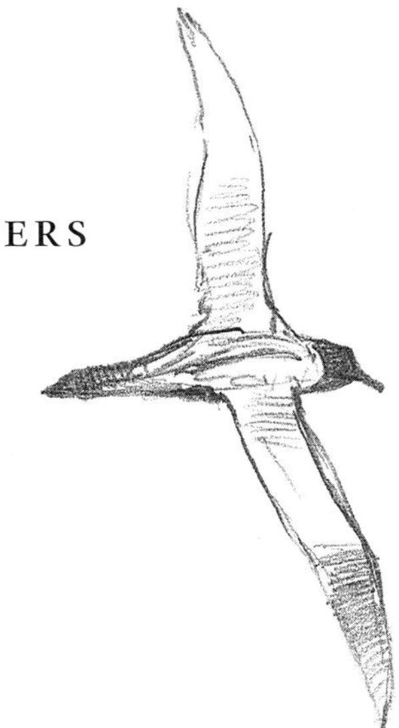

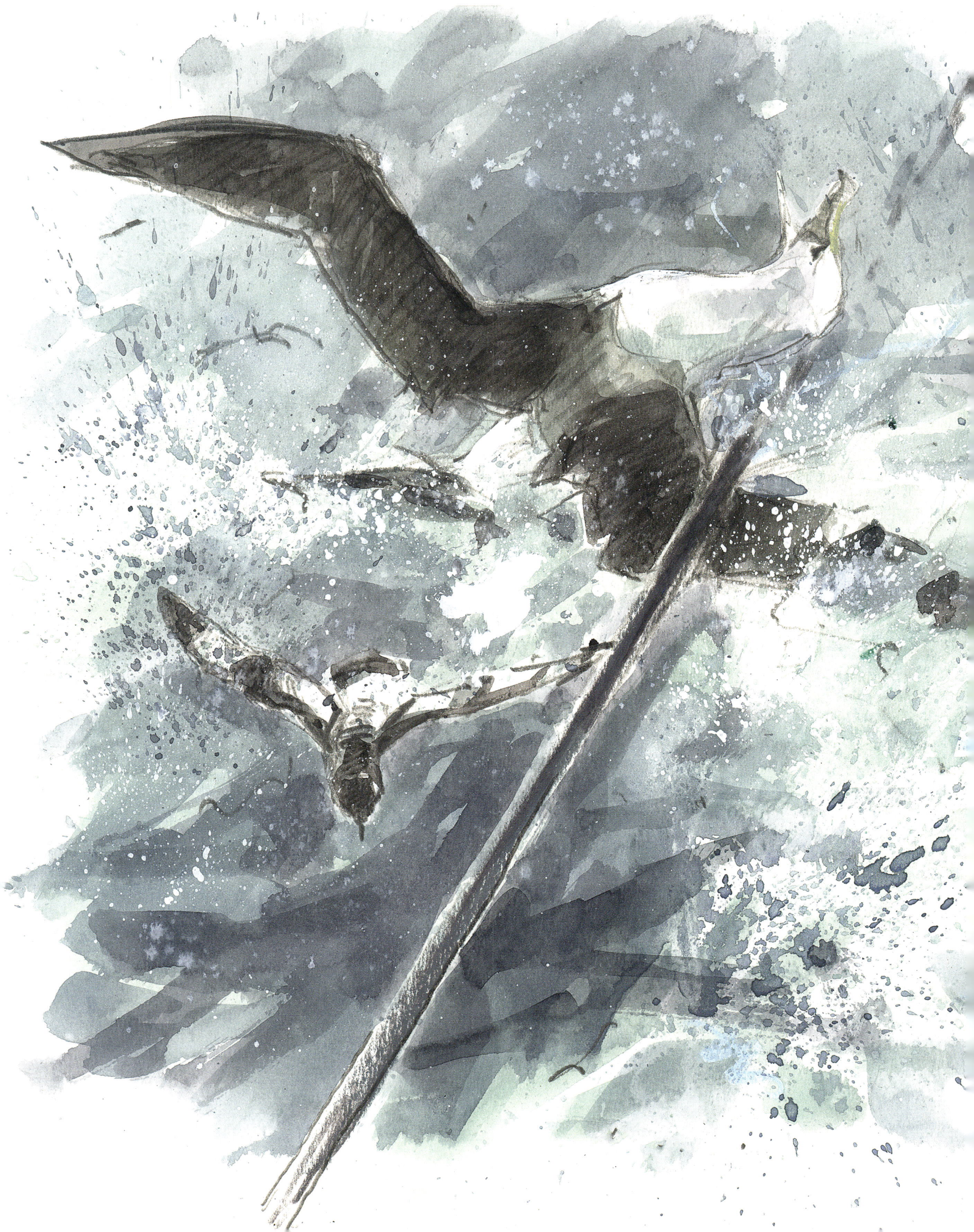

Troubled Waters

Trailing the Albatross, an Artist's Journey

Bruce Pearson

LANGFORD PRESS · 2012

For Peter in the hope he would have approved.
And for Laura who I wish so much was with us
to read it and tease me.

First published in 2012 by
Langford Press, 10 New Road, Langtoft
Peterborough PE6 9LE
www.langford-press.co.uk
Email sales@langford-press.co.uk

ISBN 978-1-904078-48-7

A CIP Record for this book is available
from the British Library

Editorial consultant, Robert Burton
Designed and typeset in Magma and Cycles
by Nye Hughes of Dalrymple, Edinburgh
Origination by MRM Graphics Ltd, Winslow, Bucks
Printed in Spain

Front cover: Detail of *Wanderer and mollymauks off South Georgia.* Frontispiece: *Collision: shy albatross and trawler cable.* Opposite: *South Georgia pipits.*

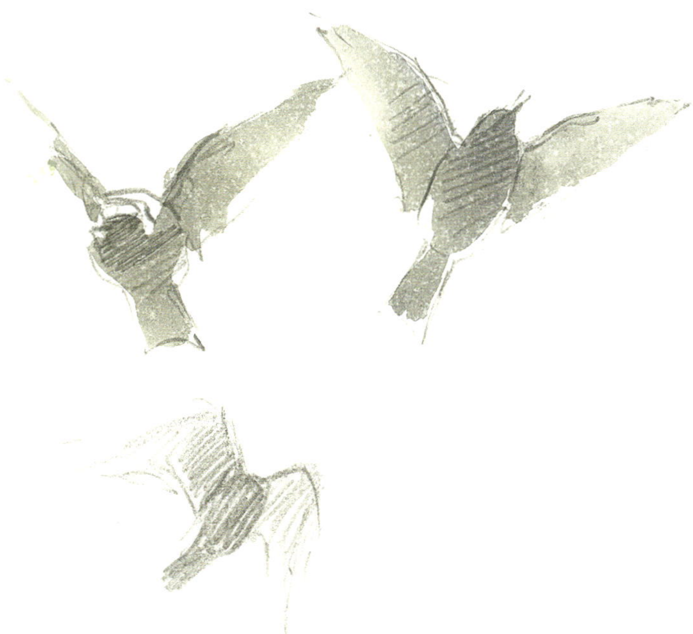

DAME ELLEN MACARTHUR

Preface

'In my head I had thought that the most incredible thing that could happen down there was that I might be able to get close to the albatross, perhaps be able to see the expressions on its face, or look into its eyes as it sat on its nest. Never for a moment did I think that I would be able to sit on a hilltop with possibly the most stunning view in the world, almost able to touch the birds as they flew past. As their perfect feathers were lit by the powerful sun, they looked like polished sculptures, just their eyes and head moving occasionally. They were so clearly enjoying the afternoon warmth and having fun up there: not feeding or fishing, just playing in the up-draught. They banked round so steeply that their wings were almost vertical, and sometimes, as they turned, almost stalling in the sky, they would pedal with their feet as if they were playing on the edge of their balance. Their eyes were always level with the horizon, which is amazing when you watch the speed at which they are able to manoeuvre, but they fly with the utmost precision: whether it's calculating a steep bank perfectly or wandering over the waves with their wingtips just millimetres from the water. I found myself laughing as they flew past. I felt a surge of such pleasure and excitement, and I began talking to them, asking them questions as they passed, sometimes like rockets, and sometimes so slowly and gracefully.'

From *Full Circle* by Ellen MacArthur, published by Michael Joseph, London, 2010

I have been lucky enough during my sailing career to spend months, quite literally, racing through the southern oceans in the company of these astonishing birds. In fact they made such an impression on me, that following my second successful circumnavigation I went down to South Georgia for several months. It was here that all expectations I had were exceeded by the character, personality and scale of these wise and graceful creatures.

PROFESSOR JOHN CROXALL CBE FRS

Foreword

Albatrosses are amongst the most iconic inhabitants of remote islands and distant seas; spectacular travellers across the great waters of our world. Sadly, their fate is now closely linked to our ability to manage sustainably the resources and habitats of the global ocean; it may already be too late to undo the long-term damage of over-exploitation and pollution.

Bruce Pearson is uniquely qualified to portray this paradox, bringing his artist's eye and creative vision to illustrate and illuminate the challenges faced by these charismatic birds; and the challenges they pose for those who wish to save them for posterity.

I am most privileged to be associated with this book, yet my links with Bruce on our journeys with albatrosses make this highly appropriate. Thus my first experience of albatrosses was joining Bruce and Peter Prince at Bird Island, South Georgia in 1976. Peter, one of the great seabird field scientists, had already hired Bruce to help start new albatross research at South Georgia and I had just been employed by the British Antarctic Survey to manage the establishment of these and other new programmes on seabirds (especially penguins and wandering albatross) and marine mammals. Bruce already showed his trademark commitment to his fieldwork and dedication and skill at sketching the incomparable wildlife of South Georgia after the day's fieldwork was complete. It is more than a little nostalgic to see a selection of those sketches in this book and to recollect one's recognition of Bruce's talent at the start of his exceptional career.

Few who encounter albatrosses or visit South Georgia are left unmoved. I was lucky enough to work there for another 30 years and Bruce maintained a close interest in the island and its wildlife until opportunities to revisit could be achieved. The intervening years, however, saw albatrosses in general, and at South Georgia in particular, suffer greatly, especially from interactions with fisheries. As albatross populations declined, the research at Bird Island was central to discovering the mortality in longline fisheries, bringing this to world attention and helping to devise ways of reducing the bycatch of albatrosses in these fisheries. After a decade of advocacy at the Commission for the Conservation of Antarctic Marine Living Resources, effective measures were imposed on longline vessels fishing in the Southern Ocean in 1996; within two years bycatch rates had been reduced by 90% and it is now many years since an albatross was killed in fishing around South Georgia.

Unfortunately, however, similar measures proved much more difficult to implement effectively in the vast areas of albatross habitat to the north of the Southern Ocean and many thousands of albatrosses continued to die each year as bycatch in fisheries. To make progress, BirdLife International recognised that it was necessary to work directly with fishers to show them how to avoid killing albatrosses (and the benefits arising through improved fishing efficiency). This led to the establishment, through the Save the Albatross campaign, of the Albatross Task Force, now involving some 20 people working long-term in 8 countries. This team, working with local fishers, managements and governments, has already achieved some impressive successes, particularly in South Africa, so this was a logical choice of host country when Bruce offered to help BirdLife portray the work of a group of people showing particular dedication to helping save the albatross.

We owe Bruce a considerable debt for his unstinting efforts to bring albatrosses and their plight to the public eye; I commend this powerful and beautiful book to all who care about seabirds and seas.

Professor John Croxall is the Chair of BirdLife International's Global Seabird Programme

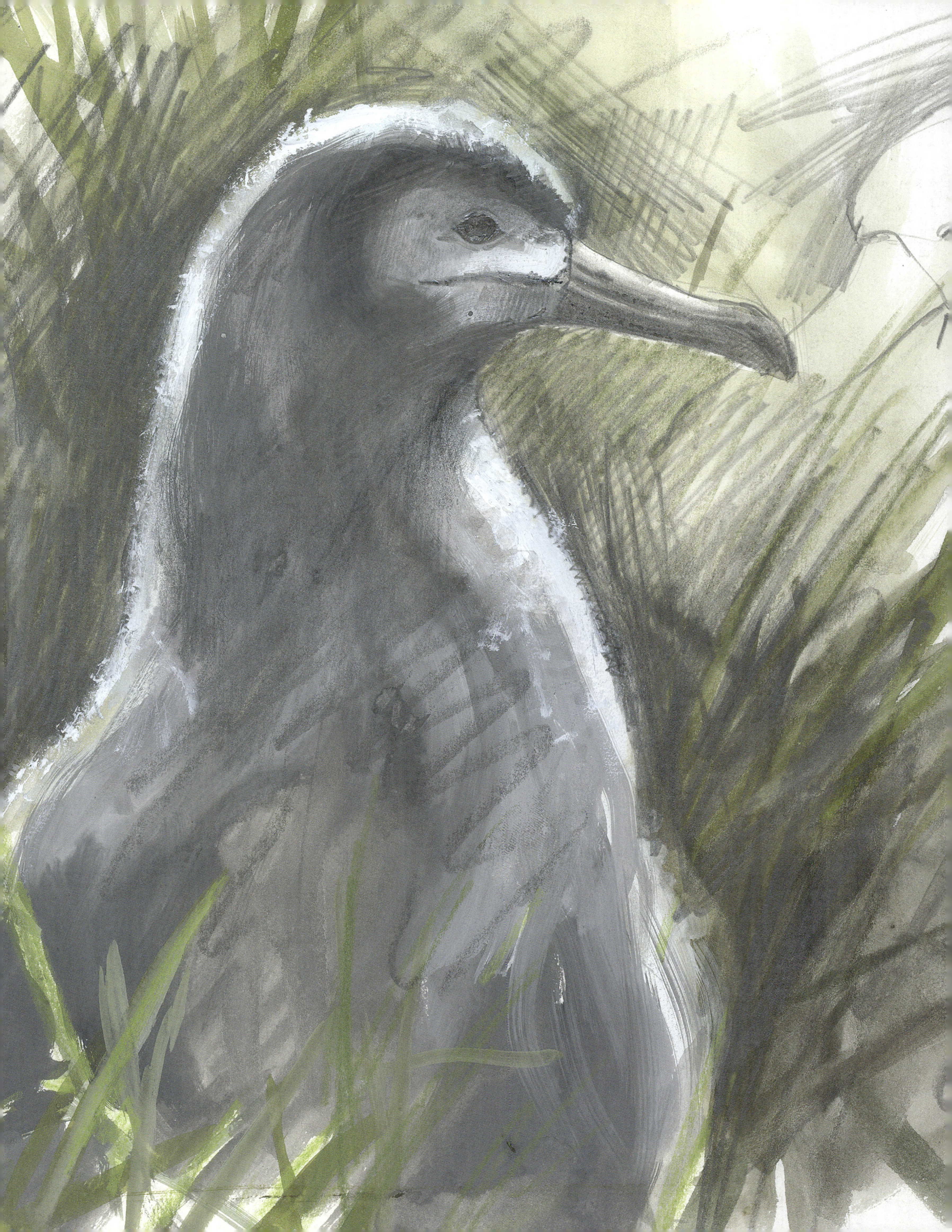

CHAPTER 1

Launching an idea

1 Young black-browed albatross on the nest, Bird Island, 1977
42 × 59 cm · watercolour and pencil

With their vast extent, changing moods of calm and storm; sheer beauty and otherworldly sense of place, the world's great oceans are largely beyond most people's experience and imagination. Home to a small number of hardy professional mariners, merchant seamen, fishermen, and a few oceanic explorers, only a privileged few experience the deep ocean at first hand. Unless great storms blow ashore and strand hapless seabirds on our beaches, most of us are insulated from the sea's true nature, and from the exotic, enigmatic birds that live far beyond the horizon of Coleridge's 'painted ocean'.

But, over thirty five years ago, a privileged encounter with a young wandering albatross on a remote island in the Southern Ocean fired my imagination about albatrosses, and started a life-long journey.

In the summer of 1975 I was recruited to be a field assistant for the British Antarctic Survey (BAS) as part of a research programme on Bird Island, a small island just off the north-west tip of South Georgia. One day I came across a wandering albatross chick collapsed into a boggy hollow. Its soaking wings were spread-eagled supporting a body partly engulfed by mud. It had obviously been trying to struggle out for some time and was exhausted. Managing to extract the bird, I got it onto drier ground – made a note of the identifying number on the ring around its left leg – and started to clean it up a bit. The juvenile plumage showed everywhere except for a few wisps of down. It was thin, but not too weak as it snapped at me and remained alert. What to do? Its weight suggested it had been abandoned by the parent birds a while ago to fledge on its own, but hadn't yet managed to get airborne. It had not been trapped so long that it had exhausted itself to the point of death, but any delay would make it more vulnerable to attack from skuas and possibly giant petrels. Apparently there was nothing broken. I noted the nest location and carried on.

When I returned a few hours later the young wanderer had dried out, but its low weight was still troubling. It clearly needed a feed, but how to nurse a wandering albatross up to full flying weight? There were tubes and a funnel some distance away in the base hut, but how to provide buckets of oily mashed-up squid and fish to pour down the bird's throat? The best hope, I believed, lay in getting it to sea. Out there, at least it would have a chance.

So, feeling the strength of the wind, and seeing the clear weather, I gathered up the young bird and, standing 50 metres back from the cliff edge, held it above my head. Its wings were opened for balance, but quickly it held them more firmly and flapped them. I stumbled forward and began running down the slope. As the wind over the flight feathers began to lift the bird, I felt the weight come and go. It flapped vigorously and began to slip from my hands. Then, like letting go of a large balloon, the young wanderer seemed to float for a moment then was up and away, flying strongly.

I had left art school in the early 1970s with a degree in Fine Art and a long-term and keen interest in natural history stimulated largely by trips through the English countryside and sometimes further afield to places like the Western Isles and Southern Europe. Needless to say, the high seas and the world of pelagic seabirds were completely unknown to me but fate soon saw that change. In 1973 and just finishing art school, I was lucky enough to land a first job working as a trainee production assistant in the film unit at the Royal Society for the Protection of Birds (RSPB). I soon fell in with a group that mixed socially with scientists working at the nearby BAS headquarters in Cambridge.

With regular visits to the pub, I was able to listen to their fascinating tales of adventures 'down south' and began to glean glimpses of the fantastic wildlife and scenery through endless slide presentations. At the same time I was starting to discover the work of the great Edward Wilson from a book compiled by Brian Roberts – *Birds of the Antarctic* – where I gained inspiration at each turn of a page. Wilson was Captain Scott's friend who took part in the *Discovery* and *Terra Nova* expeditions to Antarctica, and died alongside him on the ill-fated expedition of 1910–12. Wilson was primarily a naturalist, with leanings towards zoology and especially ornithology, but he was also a doctor, and an artist of exceptional talent whose output was prodigious. Although convinced he was nothing more than an amateur dabbler, his work in watercolour, crayon and pencil ranged from beautifully simple sketches and line drawings of icy landscapes and icebergs, to colour studies of auroras and anatomical specimens. He also painted albatrosses, petrels and penguins from life, many of them completed in the most extreme weather conditions imaginable. The book hooked me on the whole idea of seabirds and the Southern Ocean. And from what I was seeing and hearing, South Georgia was THE place for anyone with an interest in wildlife and wild places.

For three years a small group of us spent the austral summers studying the food and feeding ecology of grey-headed, black-browed and the magnificent wandering albatross, the largest flying bird in the world! Every day

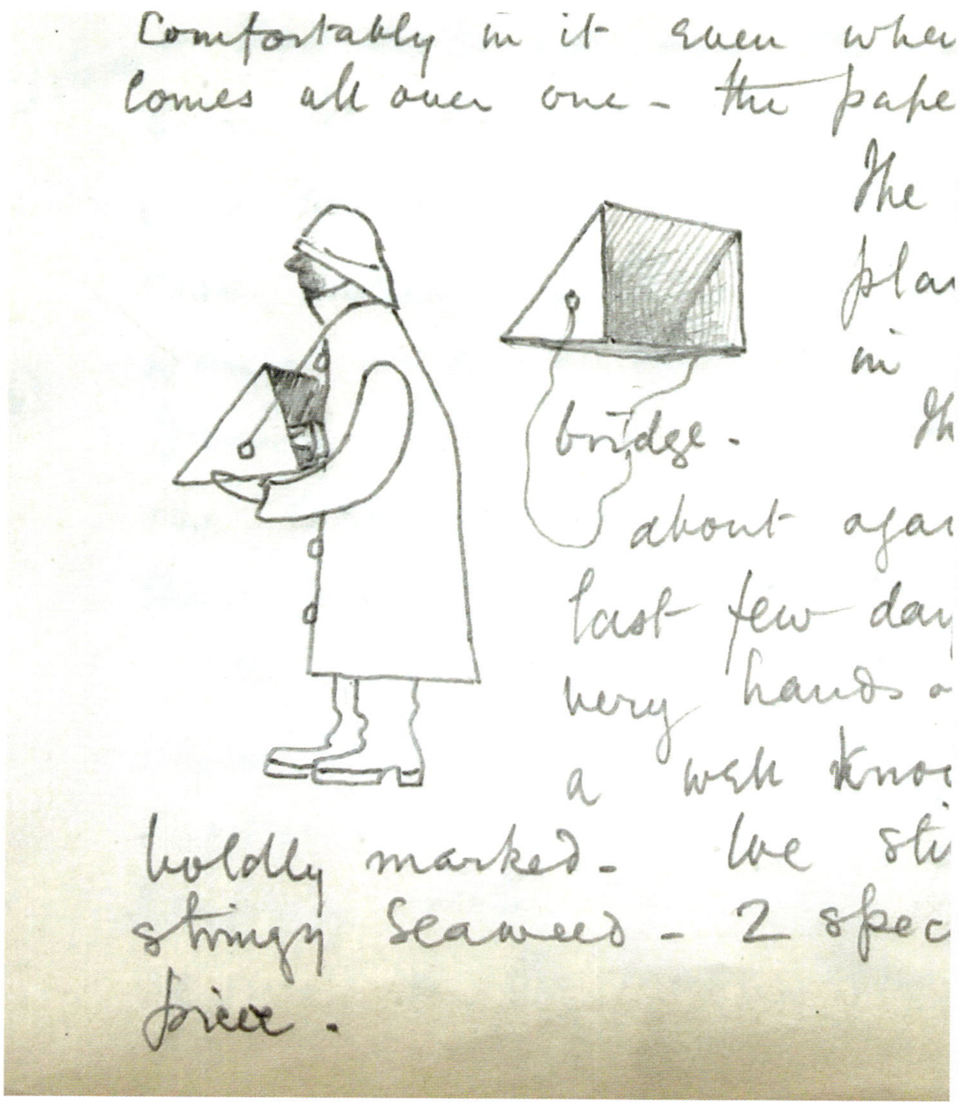

2 E. A. Wilson, 'Bad weather sketching box'. Reproduced by kind permission of the University of Cambridge, Scott Polar Research Institute.

'I have made a bad weather sketching box which I hang round my neck and can sketch comfortably in it even when it rains and blows a gale and spray comes all over one. The paper keeps comparatively dry.'

Nothing I have ever deployed to protect the paper when painting and sketching at sea has worked effectively. Now, unless the rain and spray are horizontal, I tend to let the weather play a part in the work.

we dispersed around the island to weigh and ring albatrosses; we also counted fur seals and macaroni penguins in their vast colonies. Sometimes in the darkness on steep sloping cliffs we mist-netted nocturnal petrels to collect food samples; we pushed our arms deep into nesting tunnels to retrieve the chicks of burrowing petrels; and we covered every square metre of the island to ring all the wandering albatross chicks.

And in our hut in the evenings we took it in turns to invent meals out of dehydrated vegetables, tinned meat and fish, and a range of dried ingredients thrown in – all washed down, especially on Saturday nights, with rum and whisky, tall tales, loud music – featuring mostly female voices – and a tremendous sense of comradeship. Our entire existence 'down south' was a profound experience that shaped the future of all our young lives.

In every moment not required for an assistant's task, I was sketching the movements and behavioural nuances of the wildlife all around me; wandering albatrosses displaying, downy young being fed, and young birds taking to the wing for the first time. I drew fur seal pups being born and adult males ripping each other to shreds for mastery of the breeding beaches. I drew penguins braying, and petrels chattering in the twilight by their burrows. I sat by albatross nests looking closely at the structure of bills and the details of plumage; I noted the colours and patterns of moulting feathers, and one cold day I warmed my hands under the belly feathers of an incubating wanderer! Along with the life studies from Bird Island, I made drawings about the lives of many birds at sea each season while we crossed the Southern Ocean between the Falkland Islands and South Georgia. Then there were opportunities to gather notes and sketches about the colours and shapes of icebergs, the moods of the sea, and to get to know many of the other species of those cold latitudes. It was constantly exhilarating!

But that was over 35 years ago and, at the end of my third summer on Bird Island, I left the seasonal employment with BAS to pursue a freelance career as an artist. Over the following years, I worked on a number of different wildlife and landscape themes for fine art exhibitions, book projects, and television programmes. Although we had not realized it at the time, ours and others' efforts to understand the breeding cycles and biology of albatrosses in the 1970s and early 1980s and protect their island habitats, marked a significant turning point in the fortunes of the species with which we had shared our lives. Then we believed that there were no threats to the seabirds and that their populations were largely stable. In that Southern Ocean paradise, it seemed all was well. After all, many scientists considered the outlook for albatrosses had actually brightened since the sealers and whalers had abandoned their interests in the remote Southern Ocean and stopped their avaricious killing for food. Until the 1960s and '70s optimism abounded about the results of conservation and the restoration of nesting island habitats.

But then a devastating new threat emerged in the ocean habitats where the birds feed. Over the past 35 years, seabirds – particularly albatrosses – have become threatened at a faster rate than all other groups of birds. I followed this depressing and alarming story by staying in close touch my BAS freinds from the Bird Island days. From the continuing long-term albatross population monitoring studies they could see that by the late 1970s wanderer populations on Bird Island and South Georgia were starting to decline. Their concern was echoed by other scientists working elsewhere. At first, the reasons for the declines were not evident. Then one by one the teams of scientists began to ring the same alarm bell. If the losses were not occurring during the relatively short time birds were spending on the breeding grounds, surely, they surmised, factors at sea were most likely to be the principal causes.

So they had to find ways of investigating the birds' pelagic existence. Already, as part of the food and feeding ecology work, BAS scientists and colleagues had developed several kinds of electronic devices that automatically counted how many times the adult birds visited their nests and by weighing the chick how much food it received. To the ever more sophisticated technology they added devices that could track albatrosses by satellite telemetry. Very soon this showed that breeding female wandering albatrosses in particular were travelling from Bird Island to an area off the coast of Brazil where large numbers of fishing vessels also gathered.

Ornithologists elsewhere used satellite technology to provide further evidence that albatrosses and other seabirds were travelling to feed where fishing fleets congregated. It made perfect sense that the birds and fishermen should target the same rich waters. From South Africa and other Southern Ocean fisheries it was soon clear that subtropical longline fisheries for tuna were a major source of albatross mortality. Observers on fishing vessels reported huge numbers accidentally hooked and

MOLLYMAUKS

Mollymauk is a common name still sometimes used for the smaller albatrosses, like black-browed and grey-headed. It is said to derive from a corruption of 'mallemowk' or 'mallemugge' names given by early European sailors to the northern fulmar and meaning 'foolish gull'.

With a curious contemporary irony, Edward Wilson deployed a hooked line on his Southern Ocean voyages and easily caught albatrosses at sea so he could study fresh skins. In today's commercial fisheries it is both baited hooks and entanglement with lines that has resulted in the dramatic decline in albatross populations – mollymauks especially.

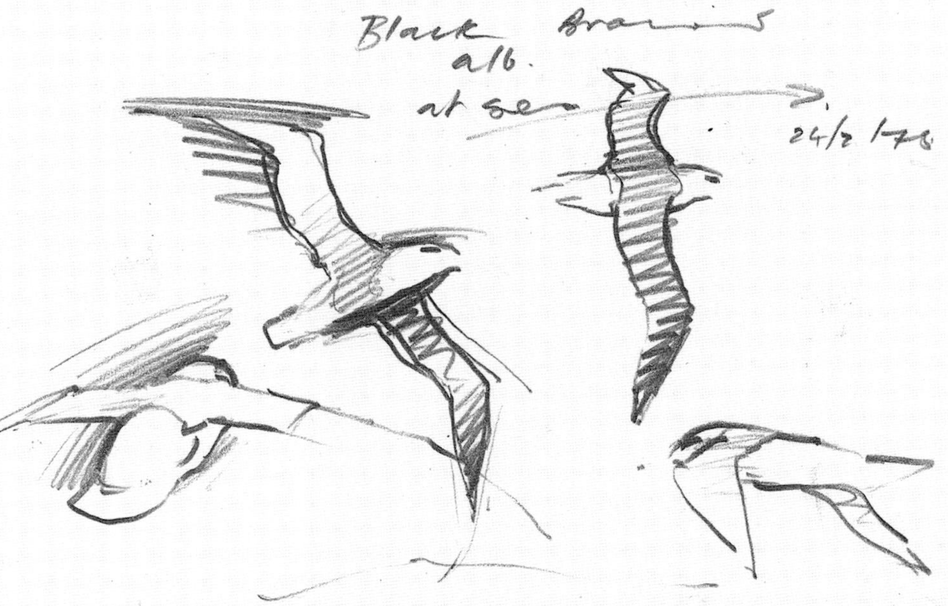

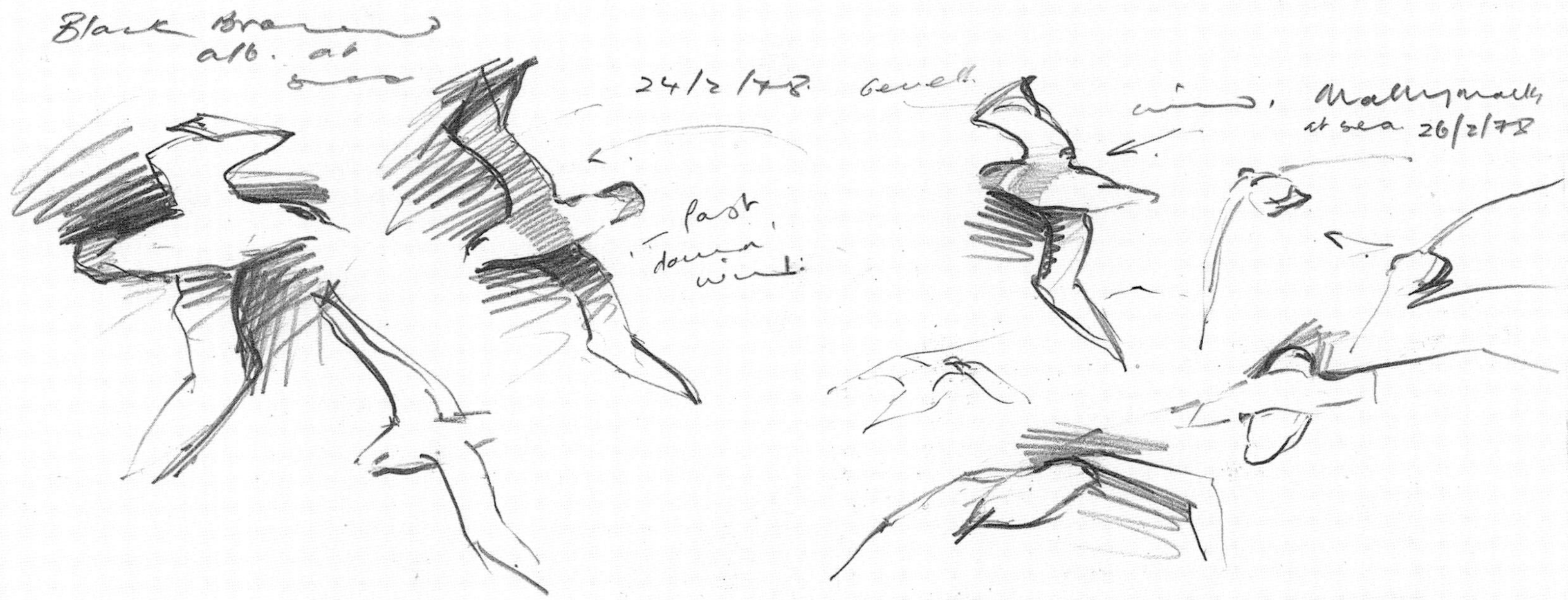

3 Mollymauks at sea, 1978
15 × 21 cm · pencil

drowned on baited lines. Estimates in the early 1990s were that as many as 300,000 seabirds were dying each year – and perhaps one-third were albatrosses. Equally damaging was pelagic trawling where the large numbers of seabirds congregating behind boats discharging offal are vulnerable to collisions with cables and trawl nets.

Although solutions were needed urgently, the international nature of the threat and powerful commercial interests meant they would not be simple. If there was a turning point in seabirds' fortunes, it came in 1995 when over 120 conservationists, seabird and fisheries scientists, and representatives of fisheries worldwide, gathered for the inaugural conference on albatrosses in Hobart, Tasmania. Participants from eleven nations agreed six main recommendations to help reduce albatross mortality at sea.

In 1997 BirdLife International initiated the Global Seabird Programme to mobilize conservation efforts and establish a regulatory framework for reducing seabird losses. In 2000 the Save the Albatross Campaign was launched and an Albatross Task Force assembled in 2005 to work with fishermen and fisheries management authorities and advise on how best to avoid the seabird bycatch, and change began to happen.

At the same time, sadly, unregulated fishing interests – so-called 'pirate vessels' – were, and still are, operating beyond the reach of international treaties and boundaries. Illegal, unreported and unregulated fishing fleets are reckoned to cause around a third of albatross deaths. At its worst, pirate fishing is organised criminal plunder with no regard or respect for regulations, national sovereignty, or conservation. Such fishing often leaves devastation in its wake. Certainly, it means that albatrosses and petrels remain at severe risk of catastrophic losses at sea.

Like so many others, I was aghast at the prospect of these iconic symbols of avian grandeur facing possible extinction. Even more devastating was realizing that some of the deaths must have happened to some of 'my birds' – individuals that I had got to know so well on their colonies in the Antarctic. There were birds that I had ringed and weighed as chicks; birds I had known as adults, recognised their breeding partners and known on which hillside they had nested. Perhaps some of them would have sat for me as I painted their portraits. As well as being highly concerned as a 'birder', the issue was personal. I wanted to know which of 'my birds' were gone, and what – if anything – could be done to prevent any more losses. And so the idea for the Troubled Waters project was launched.

Firstly, I had an archive of drawings, paintings and sketches form the early years on Bird Island that catalogued a key turning point in the fortunes of some of the most beautiful birds in the world. I had exhibited some of my sketches and the paintings developed from them soon after returning from Bird Island, but since then they had been filed away in studio drawers. Perhaps they could be brought out and shown in a different context to support the albatross campaign in some way?

Secondly, working as a freelance artist ever since the formative Bird Island experience, I had been tackling a range of subjects and themes about wildlife and the natural world. Sometimes I focused on where human activity interacts with animals in wild places to create interesting ideas about conservation and our relationship with nature. I tried to imagine a fishermen's perspective on the lives of the birds caught as bycatch, and about the collision, or mingled destinies, of longliners and seabirds on the open ocean. Surely there was no intention among fishermen, illegal or legal, to catch albatrosses? A seabird on the line has no commercial

4 Young black-browed albatross on the nest, Bird Island, 1977
34 × 48 cm · pencil

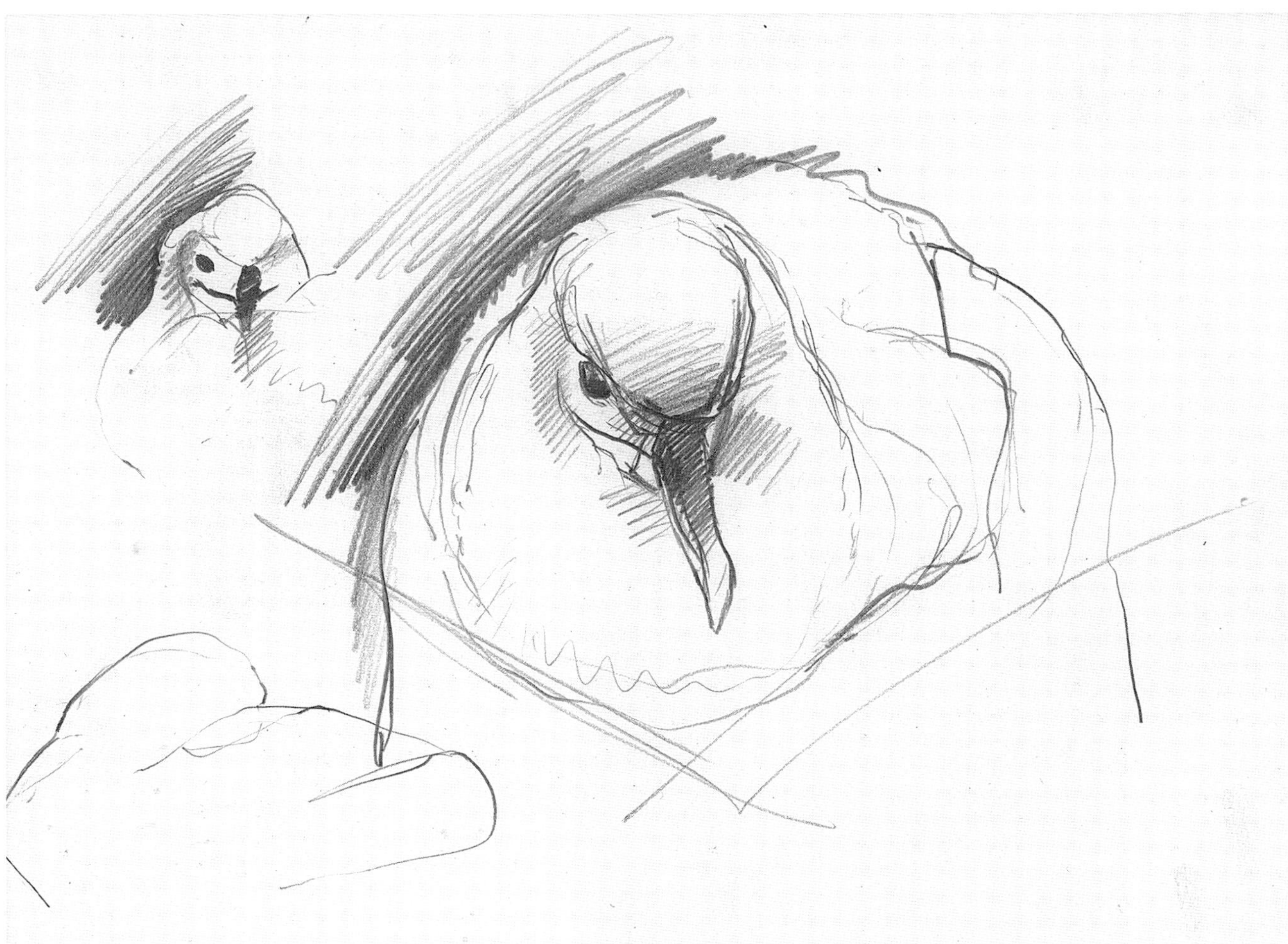

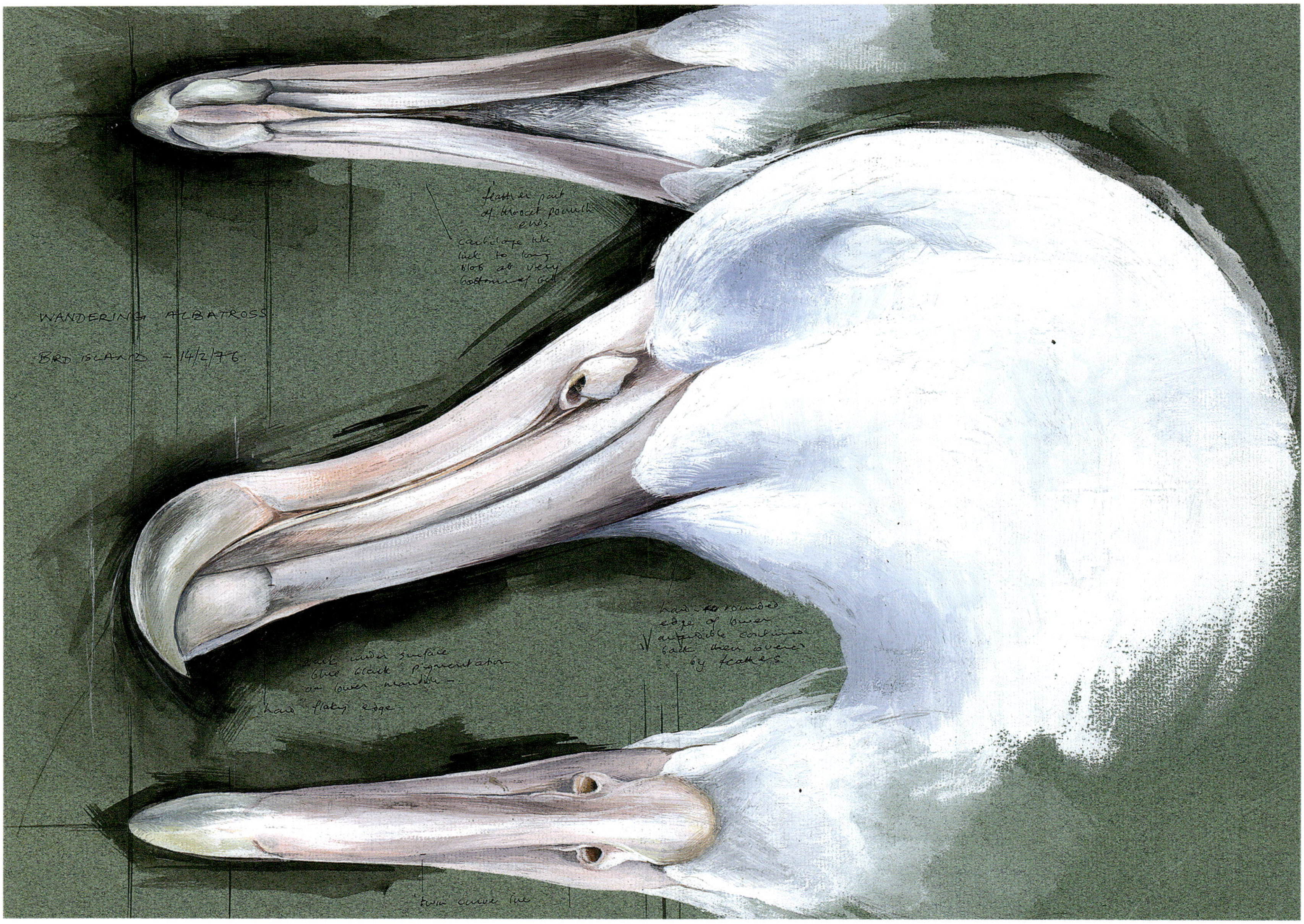

value and wastes their time in untangling and dealing with it. And surely fishermen, who might not necessarily consider themselves as conservationists, must also see the deaths as sad and pointlessly destructive?

What if I could become 'embedded' in the work of the Albatross Task Force and get aboard long-line and trawl vessels to work alongside fishermen and task force observers, to witness the collision of birds and fishing interests at sea? I guessed that getting access to the illegal or pirate vessels would be extremely difficult, and even hazardous. Over a number of years I had been exchanging ideas with BirdLife's John Fanshawe about art and conservation. We had discussed possibilities of bringing them together in a creative partnership that might excite the imagination of new audiences in the support of albatross conservation. Seeing the possibilities in Troubled Waters, John and I worked with the BirdLife Seabird Group, and BirdLife South Africa, to arrange for me to work on-board a long-line fishing vessel, and possibly a trawler as well.

And then, more recently, with two opportunities to return to South Georgia, the third major strand of the Troubled Waters idea fell into place. After thirty five years, seeing everything again, but in light of a new

SEA CHANGES

In the decade from 1995, remarkable results have been achieved to protect not just albatrosses, but seabirds globally. The main conference recommendations in Hobart were: to set lines at night, place streamers over longlines, adopt mechanical bait throwing, discharge offal on opposite side to set lines, use weighted lines, and use thawed bait.

These measures, either singly or in combination, have occurred simultaneously as a consequence of science and engineering, education and training, international conventions and laws, industry innovation, and the policy and action of non-governmental organisations.

Even so, currently 19 out of 21 species of albatross are considered either threatened or vulnerable, and some face the prospect of global extinction.

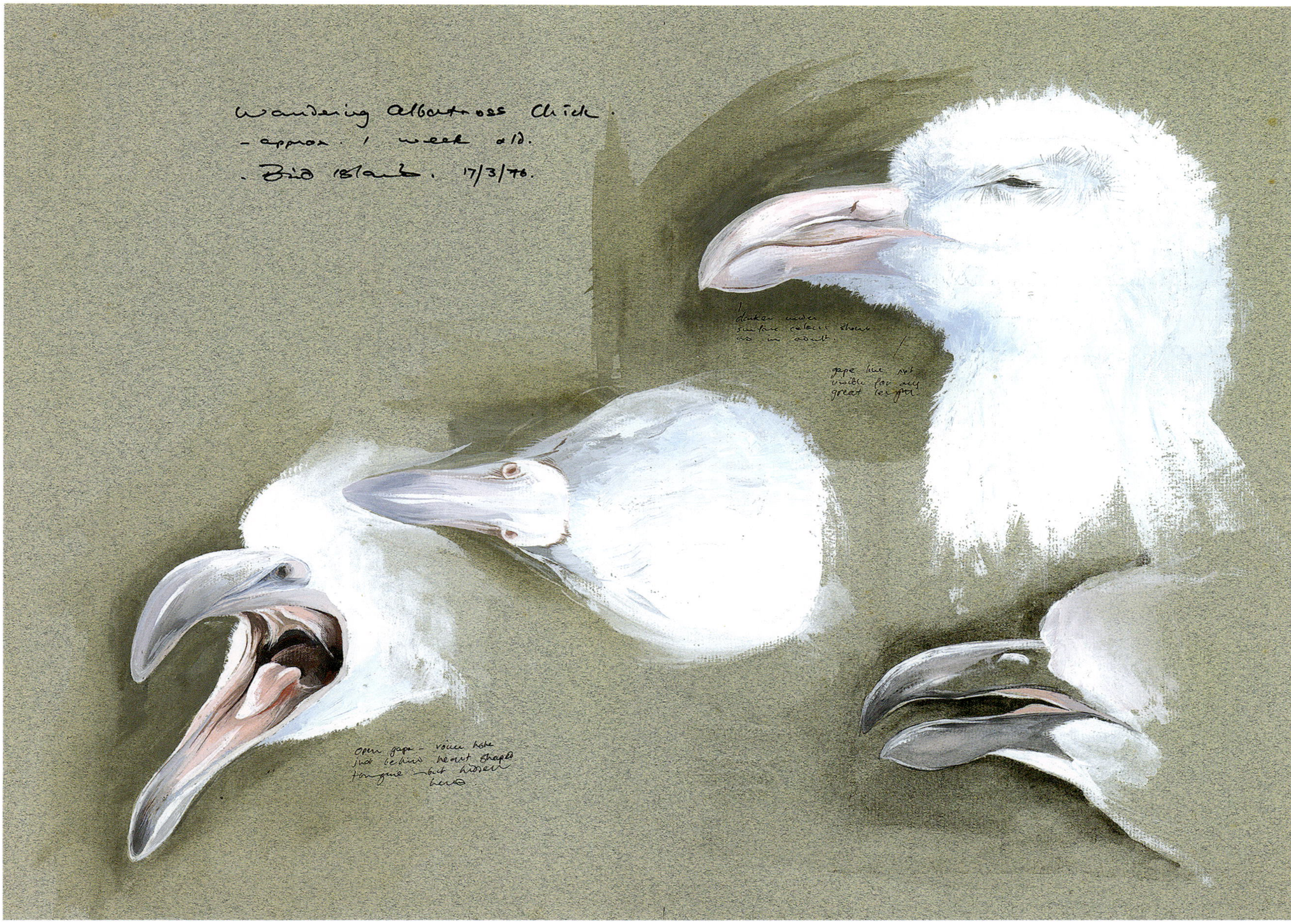

5 Wandering albatross (*Diomedea exulans*), adult, Bird Island, 1976
30 × 42 cm · watercolour and ink

6 Specimen study of wandering albatross (*Diomedea exulans*) chick, about 1 week old, Bird Island, 1976
32 × 47 cm · watercolour and pencil

understanding of conservation, and the threats seabirds were facing, I believed that the return visits could generate a wealth of new visual material and ideas; a fresh perspective on the fate of 'my' albatrosses. Obviously, I could not return to Bird Island and lay my hands on the birds again – even if some of them still survived. The island is now designated a Specially Protected Area, so it is strictly out of bounds without a permit, and the very close contact I had been lucky enough to enjoy with the birds in the 1970s is now much more controlled. The remaining birds are far more precious these days and any threat, including disturbance, has to be avoided.

Nevertheless, landing at Bird Island was not essential. Just to see the birds and experiencing their oceanic world again would generate fresh insights and inspiration. This would then be combined and compared with the intensely personal Bird Island experiences that had been lying dormant for years. If the creative responses to witnessing the conflict between seabirds and fisheries could be woven into the gap between my original and contemporary artwork, the project could surely engage viewers and readers in an experience both visceral and compelling. It would be one that offers insights into our understanding of the oceans, and which inspires engagement and identification with an extraordinarily urgent conservation crisis.

So this book is the result of all these ideas and discussions coming together with the intent of bringing my fascination with these magnificent birds and their environment into people's reach, and generating a powerful visual appreciation and understanding of their pelagic existence. And hopefully, it also provides an insight into the lives of the remarkable people who venture into the ocean wanderers' domain by sharing some extraordinary adventures and experiences trailing in the wake of the albatross.

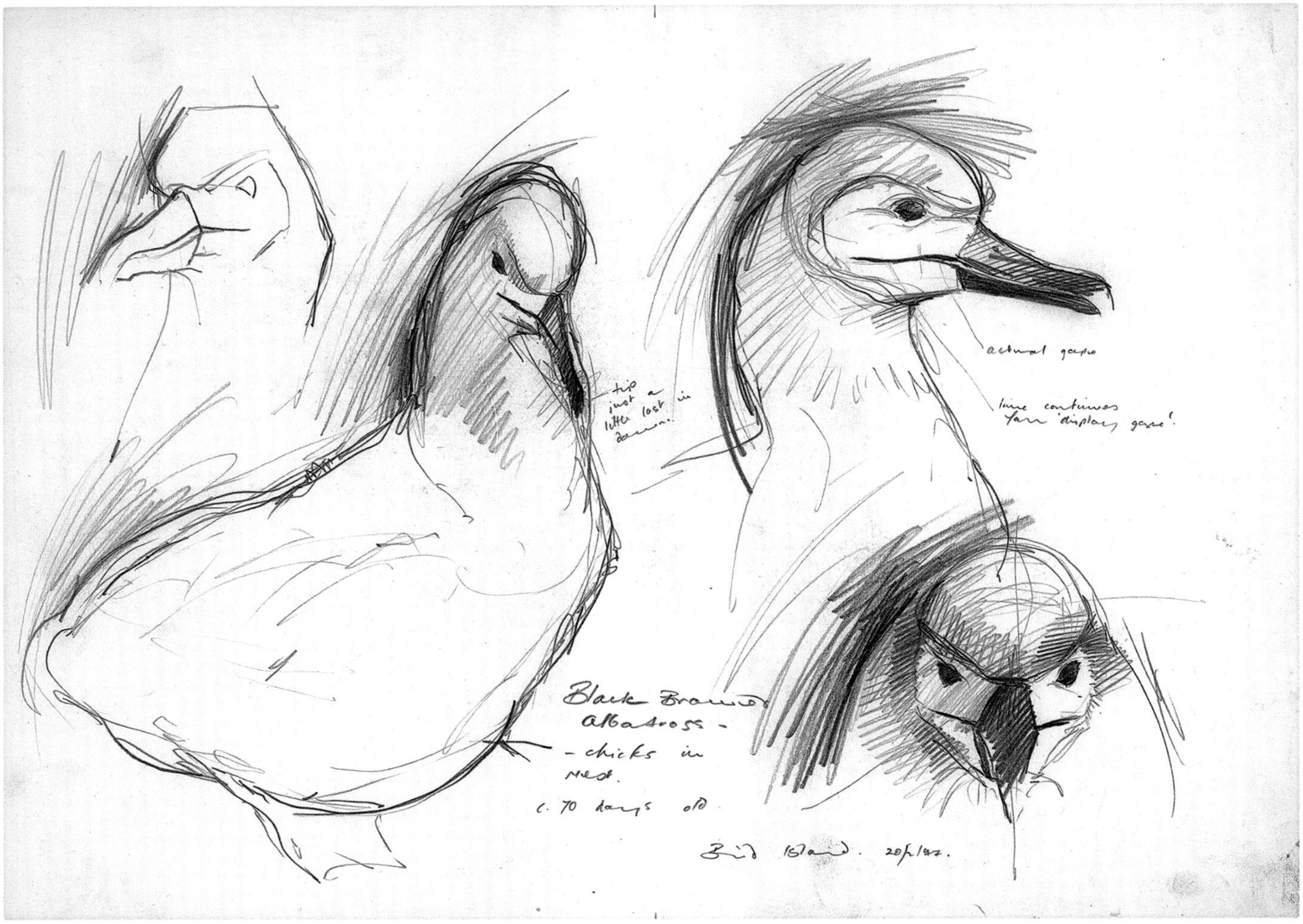

7 Young black-browed albatross chick in the nest, about 70 days old, Bird Island, 1977
42 × 59 cm · pencil

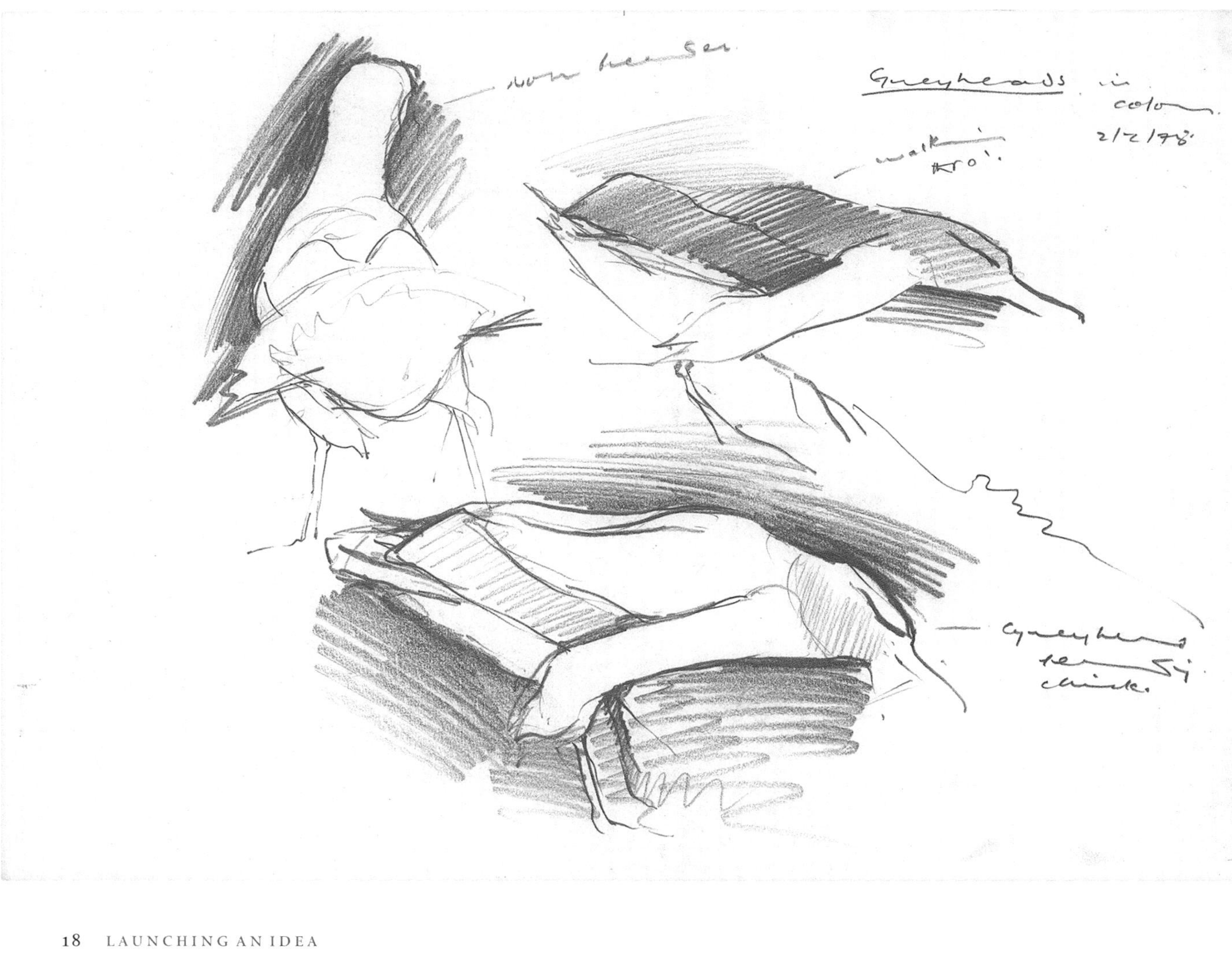

8 Grey-headed albatross, colony activity, Bird Island, 1978
34 × 48 cm · pencil

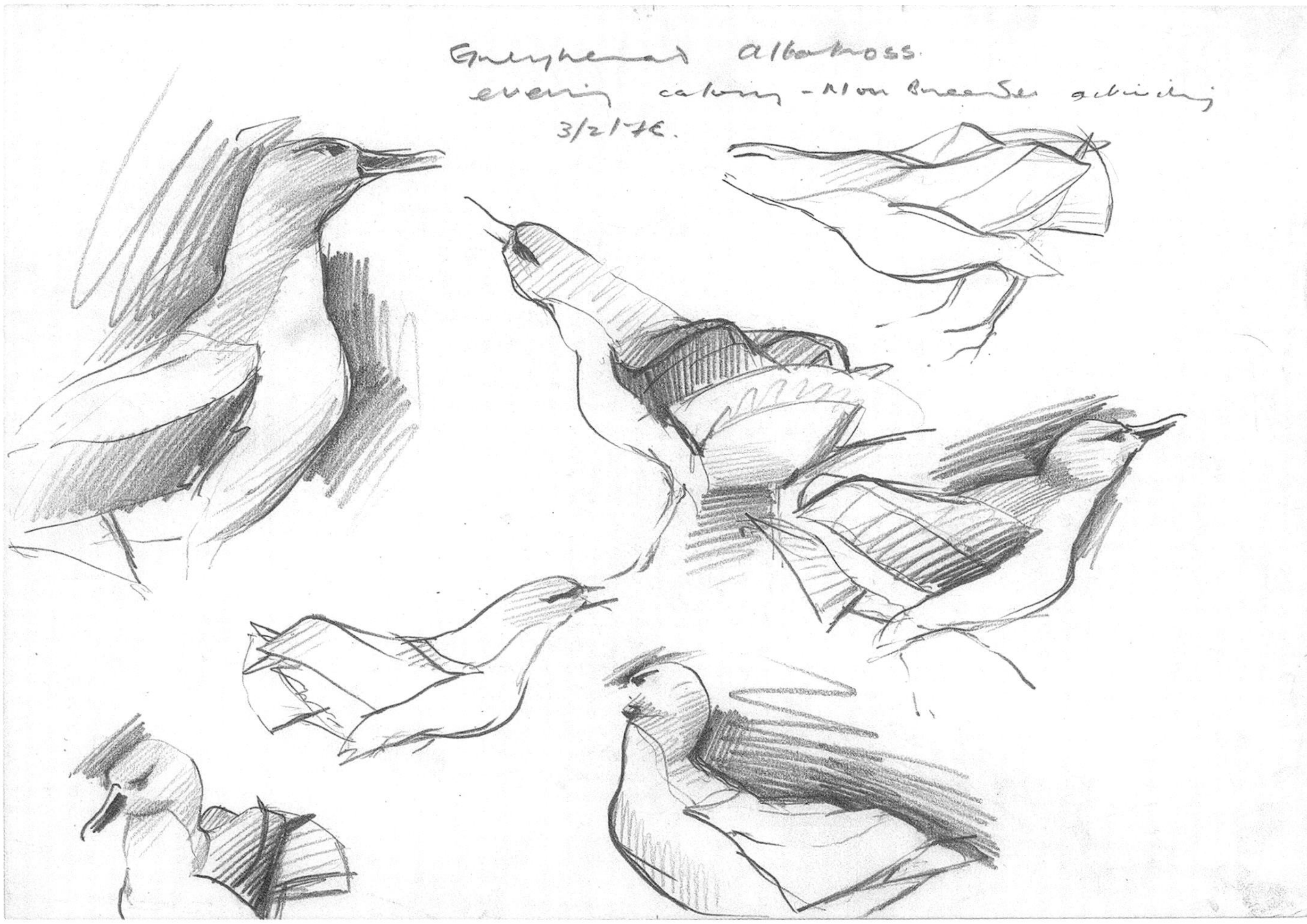

9 Grey-headed albatross, colony activity, Bird Island, 1978
34 × 48 cm · pencil

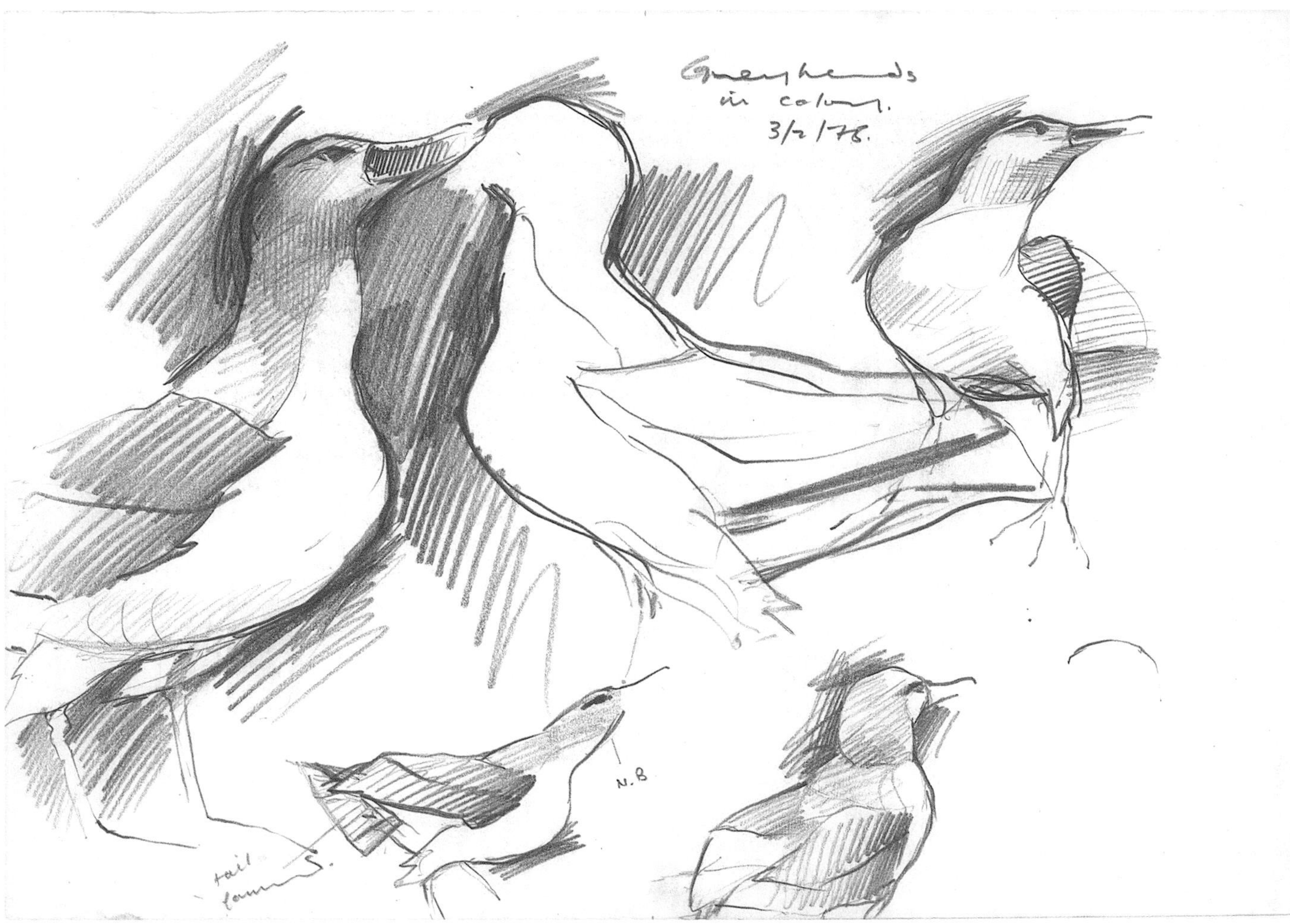

10 Grey-headed albatross, colony activity, Bird Island, 1978
34 × 48 cm · pencil

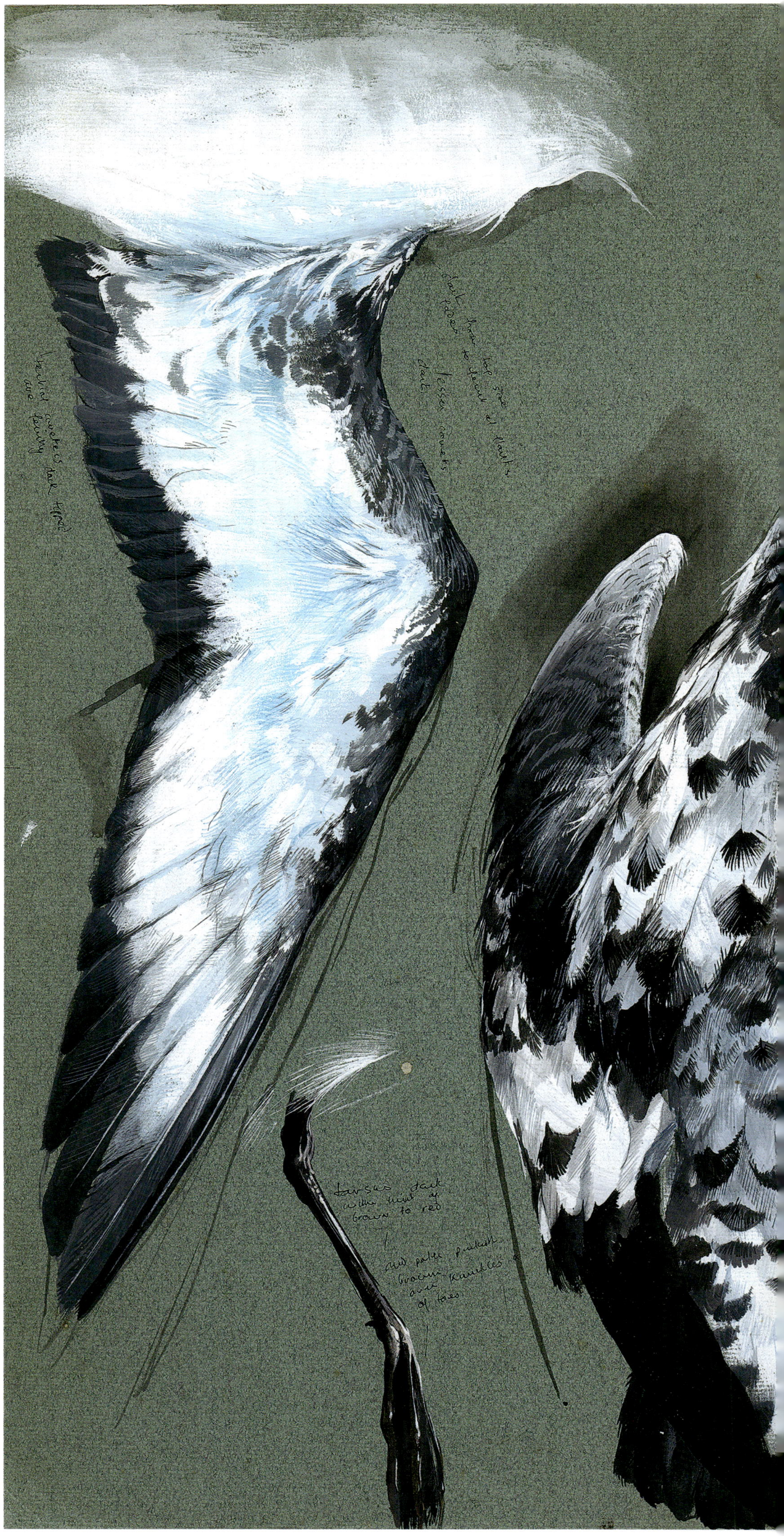

11 Specimen study, Cape petrel (*Daption capense*), Bird Island, 1976
47 × 64 cm · watercolour and ink

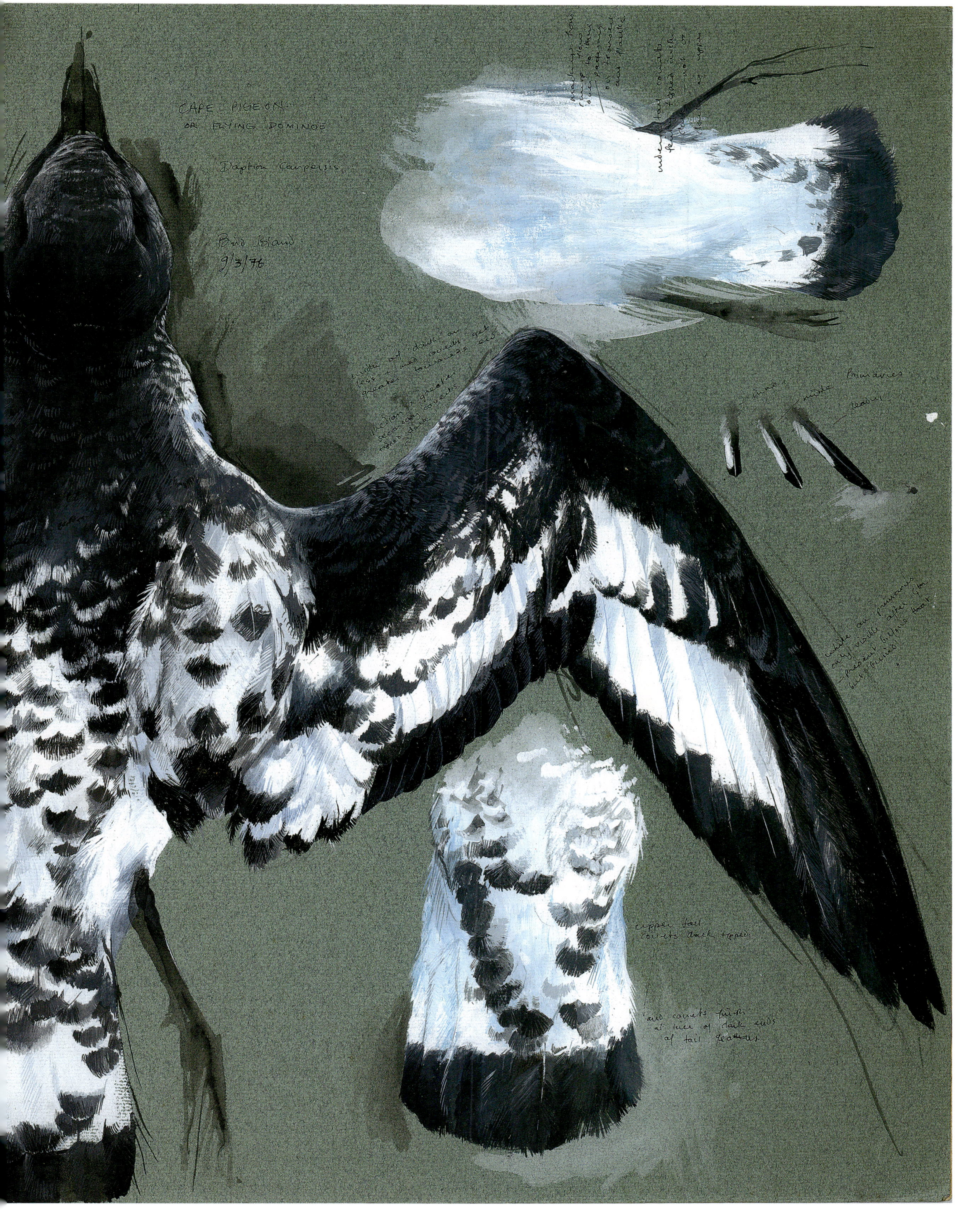
CAPE PIGEON
OR FLYING DOMINOE
Daption capensis
Bird Island
9/3/76
upper tail coverts dark tipped
and coverts finish at line of dark ends of tail feathers.

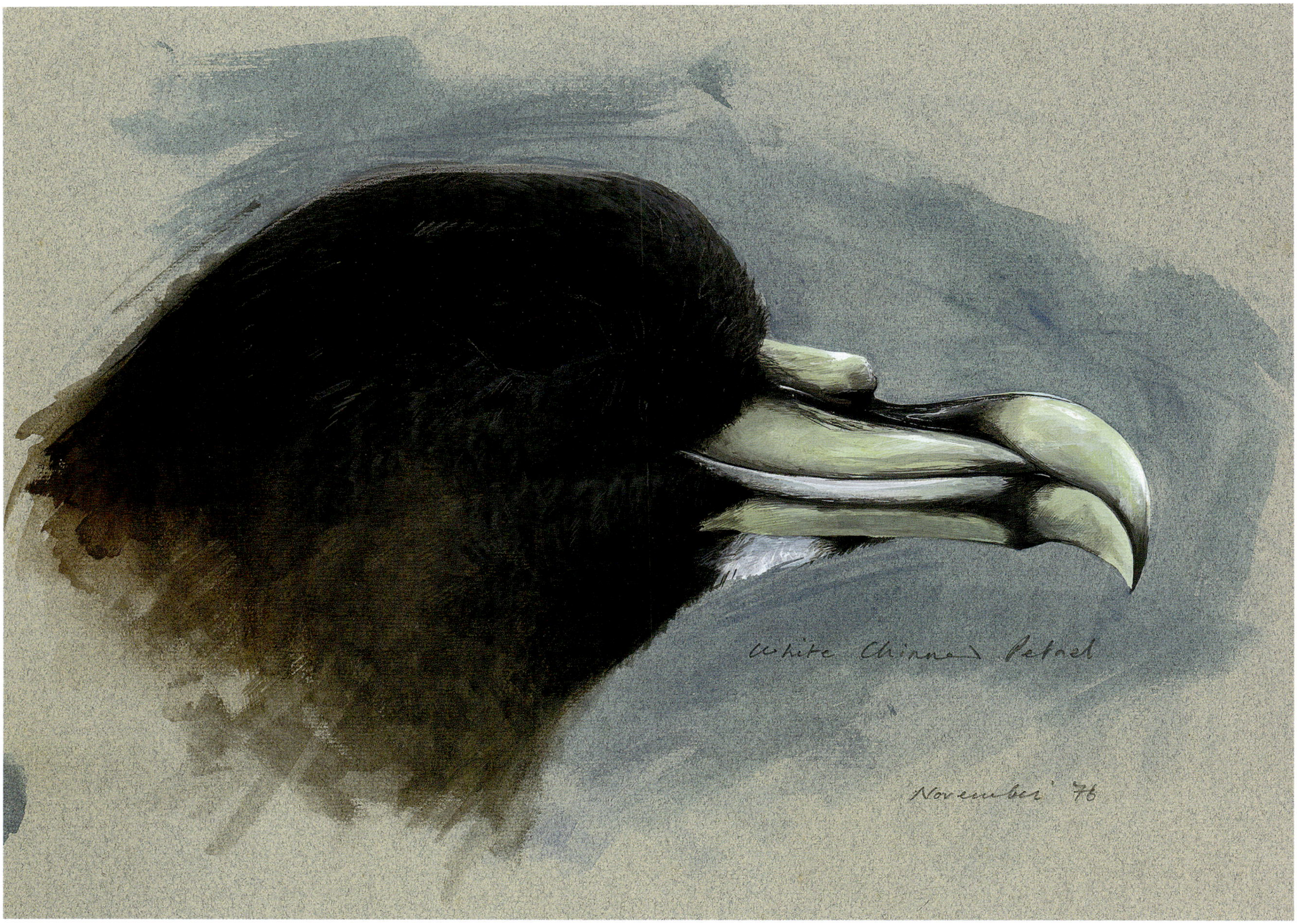

12 Specimen study, white-chinned petrel (*Procellaria aequinoctiali*), Bird Island, 1976
30 × 42 cm · watercolour and ink

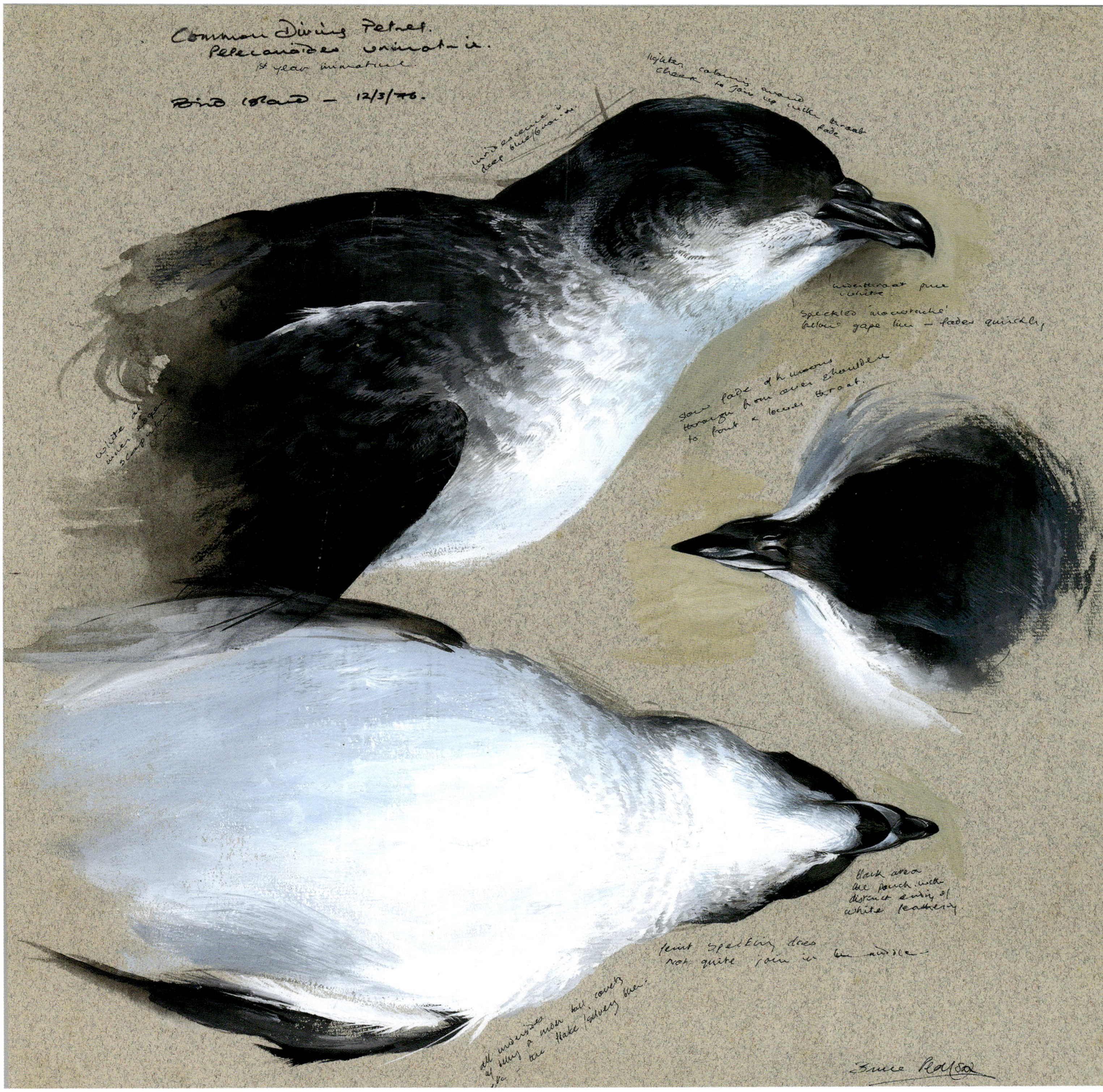

13 Specimen study, common diving-petrel (*Pelecanoides urinatrix*), Bird Island, 1976
40 × 40 cm · watercolour and ink

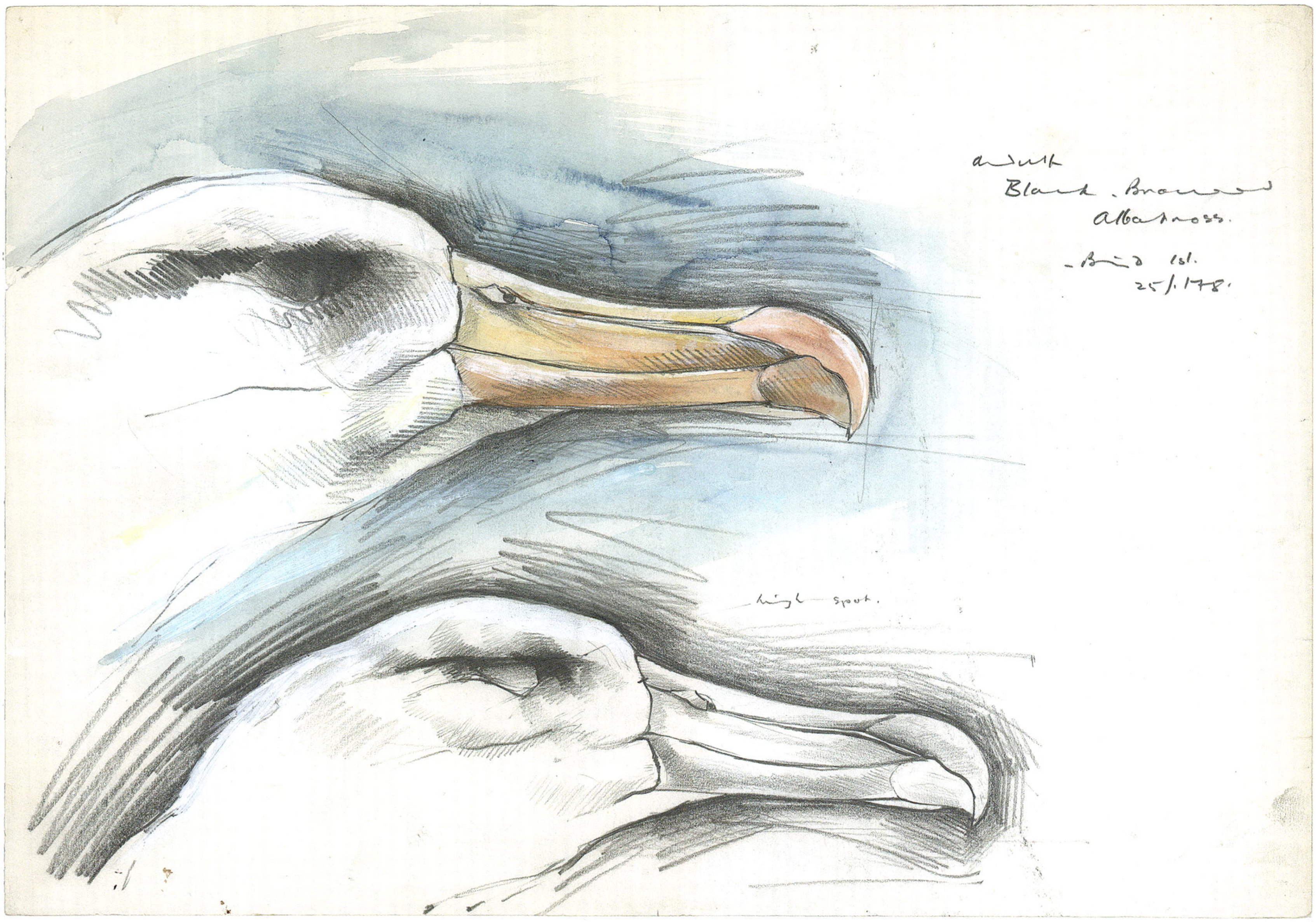

14 Specimen study, adult black-browed albatross (*Thalassarche melanophrys*), Bird Island, 1978
42 × 59 cm · watercolour and pencil

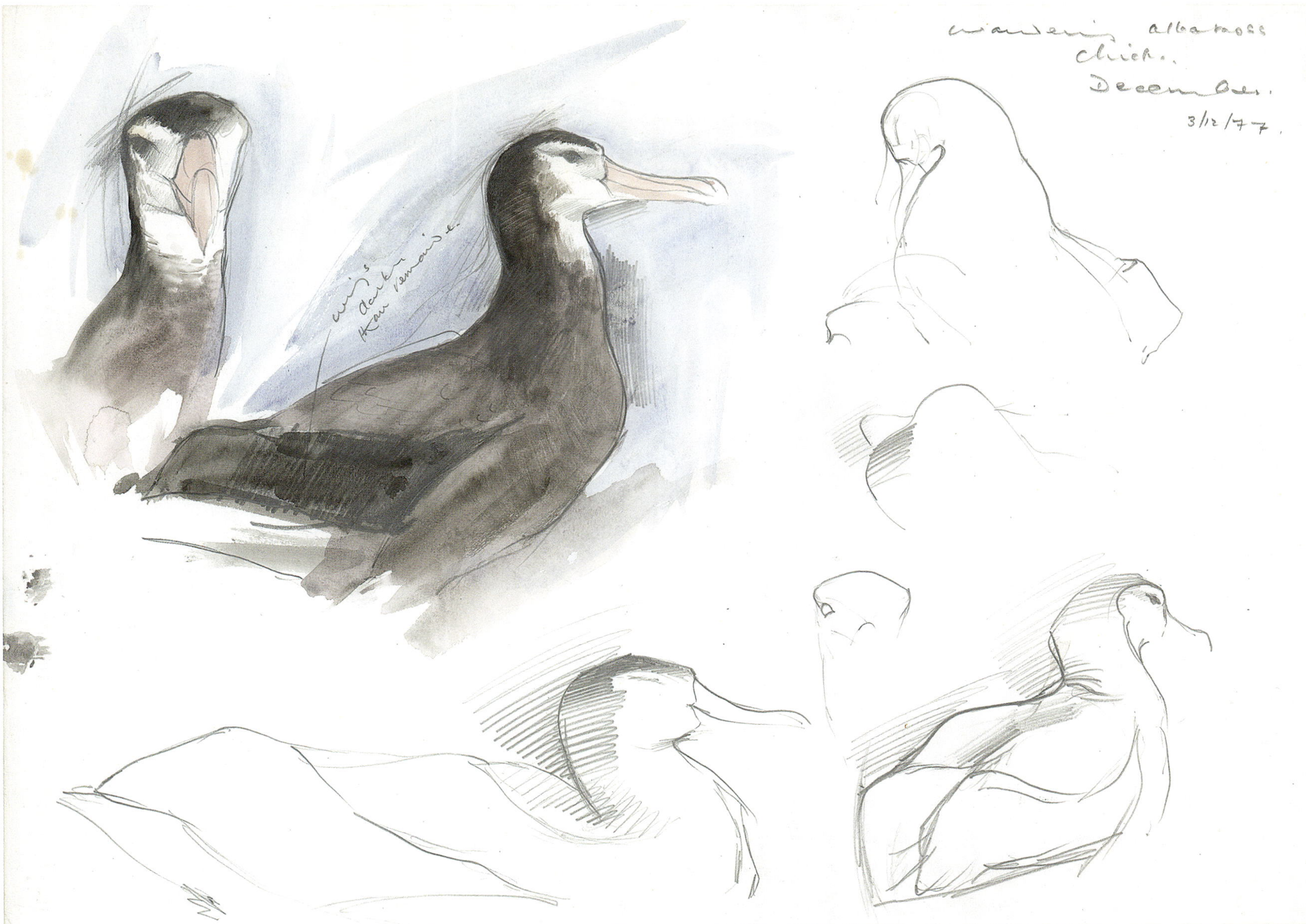

15 Wandering albatross (*Diomedea exulans*), young bird about to fledge, Bird Island, 1977
42 × 59 cm · watercolour and pencil

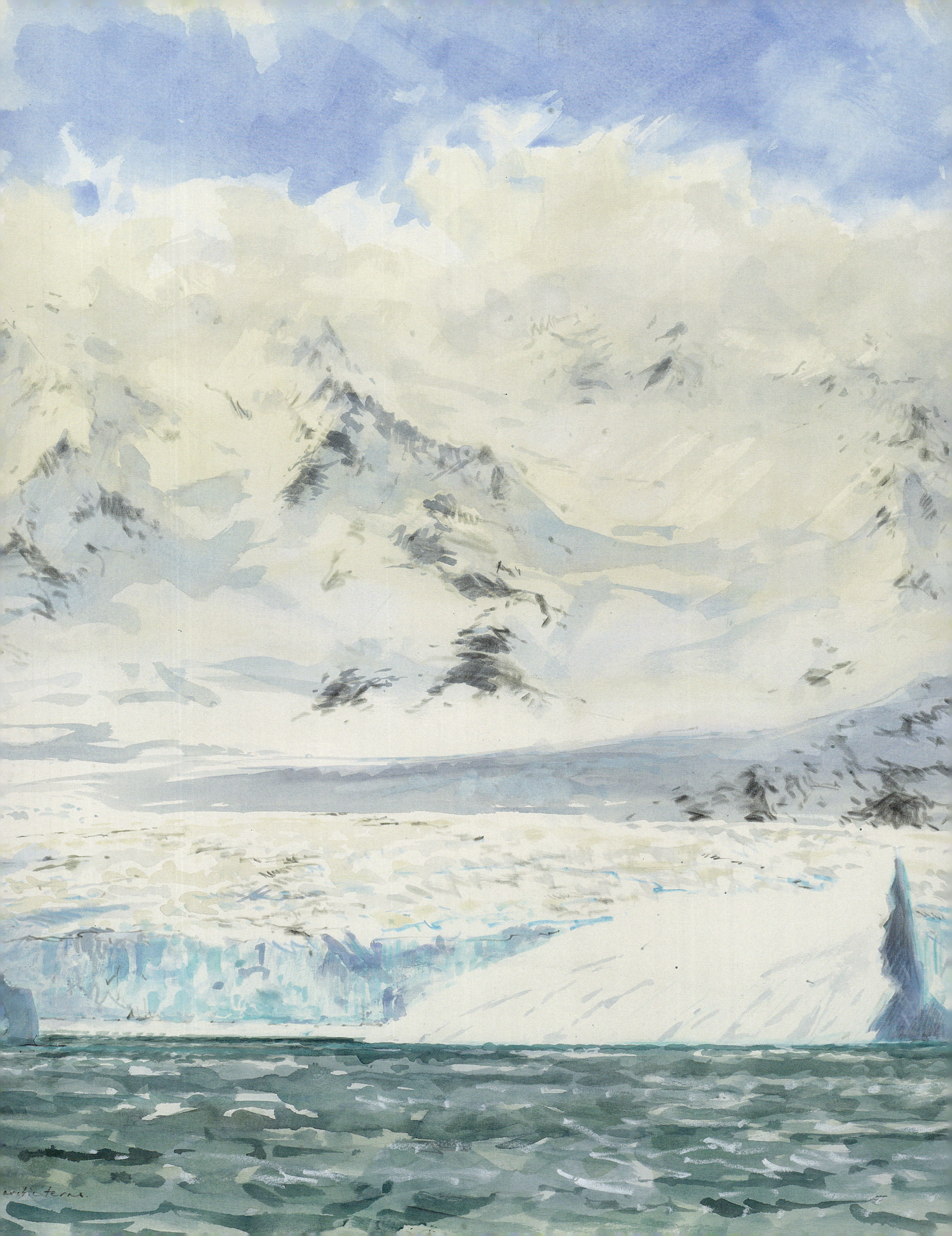

CHAPTER 2

First encounters

16 From the head of Cumberland East Bay across the Nordenskjöld glacier and beyond. South Georgia, October, 2009 (detail)

Early morning in late-November on Bird Island and the rain is sweeping in again, funnelling up Bird Sound on strong gusts of wind. The steep cliffs and snow-covered peaks of South Georgia on the other side of the Sound are just visible through the greyness. Further round to the south, great plumes of spray rise from waves crashing into fractured icebergs jammed against the toothy pinnacles of Jomfreune. Ahead of me on Wanderer Ridge tiers of wind-blown tussock grass with open patches of peaty bog rise gradually towards the scree slopes of La Roché peak, the highest point of the island shrouded by the scudding low cloud and rain.

A short distance ahead,crouched in a hollow formed on a pile of compacted grass and mud the size of a sawn-off dustbin, is a pile of soft wet down with velvety dark brown-black patches showing through. As I move a little closer, the head of a young wandering albatross swivels up to reveal a strikingly beautiful face. It is pure snow white framed by smudged black cheeks and a cap crowned by downy wisps. Its body is a bulging sack draped in a mosaic of downy patches and new dark feather tracts pushing through from beneath. As the young bird struggles and turns defensively towards me, its clatters its enormous pink bill and makes a guttural snapping sound. In a few moments it is almost standing, tilting back on its legs. It is a huge, almost the height of a table top.

It is time to go quickly through my preparations, With the ring held ready in my mouth, rucsack open with ringing pliers and notebook loose inside, ring number noted along with nest location and date, I drop my bag close-by. Holding on to the 'bodger' – a thick broom handle with a crook-shaped open wire loop at one end – I begin my approach. Ringing a wanderer chick is not a very graceful process, but after the 866 or so we will ring this season – the tenth so far for me this morning – it is a familiar and well-rehearsed procedure.

Now that the young albatross has raised itself up to full height, I position the crook behind its neck, and pull the bird gently forwards. At the same time my free hand reaches down quickly to seize and hold tight to its razor-sharp bill. If not caught cleanly, it could either mean painful cuts and bruises to exposed wrists, or pungent stomach contents spewed all over me – with the subsequent warm but uncomfortable oily drip down my sleeve or into my rubber boots. Standing, but hunched over and still holding the bird's bill, I pull its head between my legs and gently clamp its neck. With the mighty wingspan clumsily spread-eagled but safe from accidental damage and the chick secure, I feel for the pliers and pick the ring from my mouth. Pulling out the bird's left leg, and carefully placing the ring round the lower part and I close it tight with a firm squeeze of the pliers. With my kit back in the bag, I hold the bill again, pass the bird back through my legs and, checking whether it is safely stowed back on its nest, let go and step away.

It has taken perhaps less than a minute for this bird to become identifiable to science. From now on every encounter will add details to its life history. Reading the ring will be particularly unceremonious and inelegant events for the bird, but each re-capture will add significantly to the data that help us understand albatross biology and behaviour. How old would it be when it returns to the island for the first time to breed? How far will it wander in first few years of life at sea? How will the patterns of its plumage change with every moult, morphing from slaty-brown and blackish juvenile plumage to the almost pure white of old-age? How long will it live? Where will it die? On a longline?

How and why had I been granted the huge privilege of handling such a beautiful bird on this a miserably wet day on this remote island in the sub-Antarctic? When I was getting to know the BAS scientists and their work 'down south', one chap in particular seemed to share my enthusiasms, and we got on really well. Despite lacking a formal education in zoology or biology, Pete Prince's wildly enthusiastic approach to fieldwork, his deep knowledge of natural history and instinctive abilities as an ornithologist and field naturalist – and experience as a bird ringer – made him an enormous asset to the Bird Island programme. It also led him to set up his own spare-time research project looking at the feeding ecology of blue petrels and Antarctic prions. When we met he was back in Cambridge on a short-term contract writing-up the results of his fieldwork.

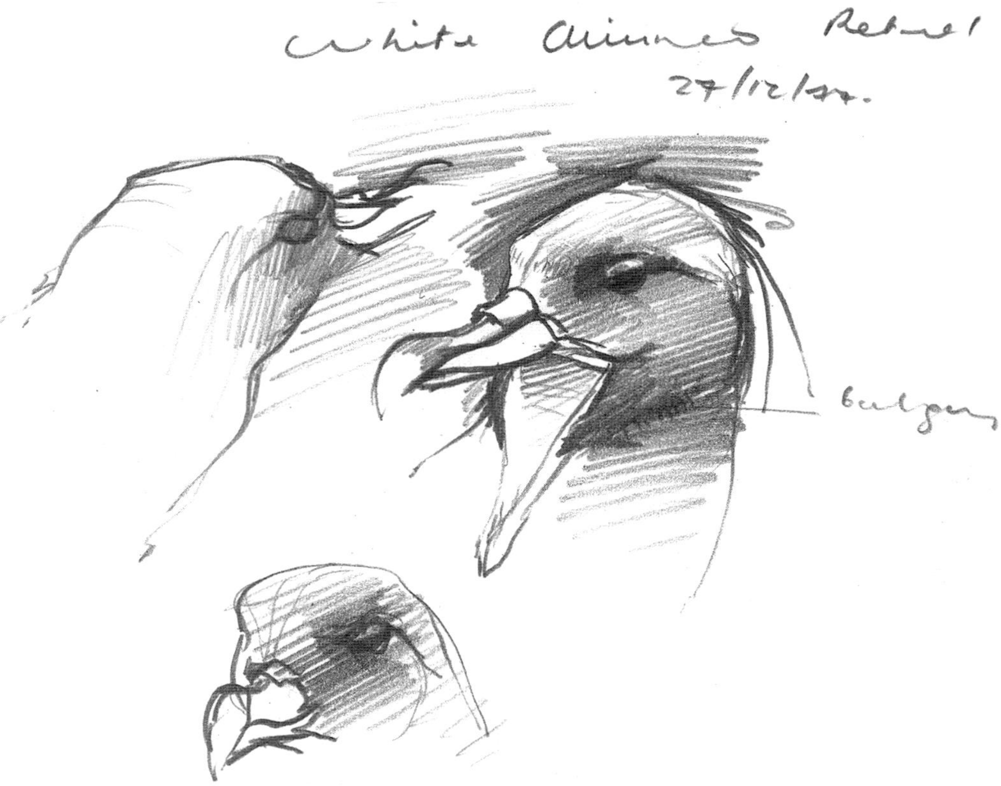

18 White chinned petrel calling outside the burrow, Bird Island, 1977
15 × 21 cm · pencil

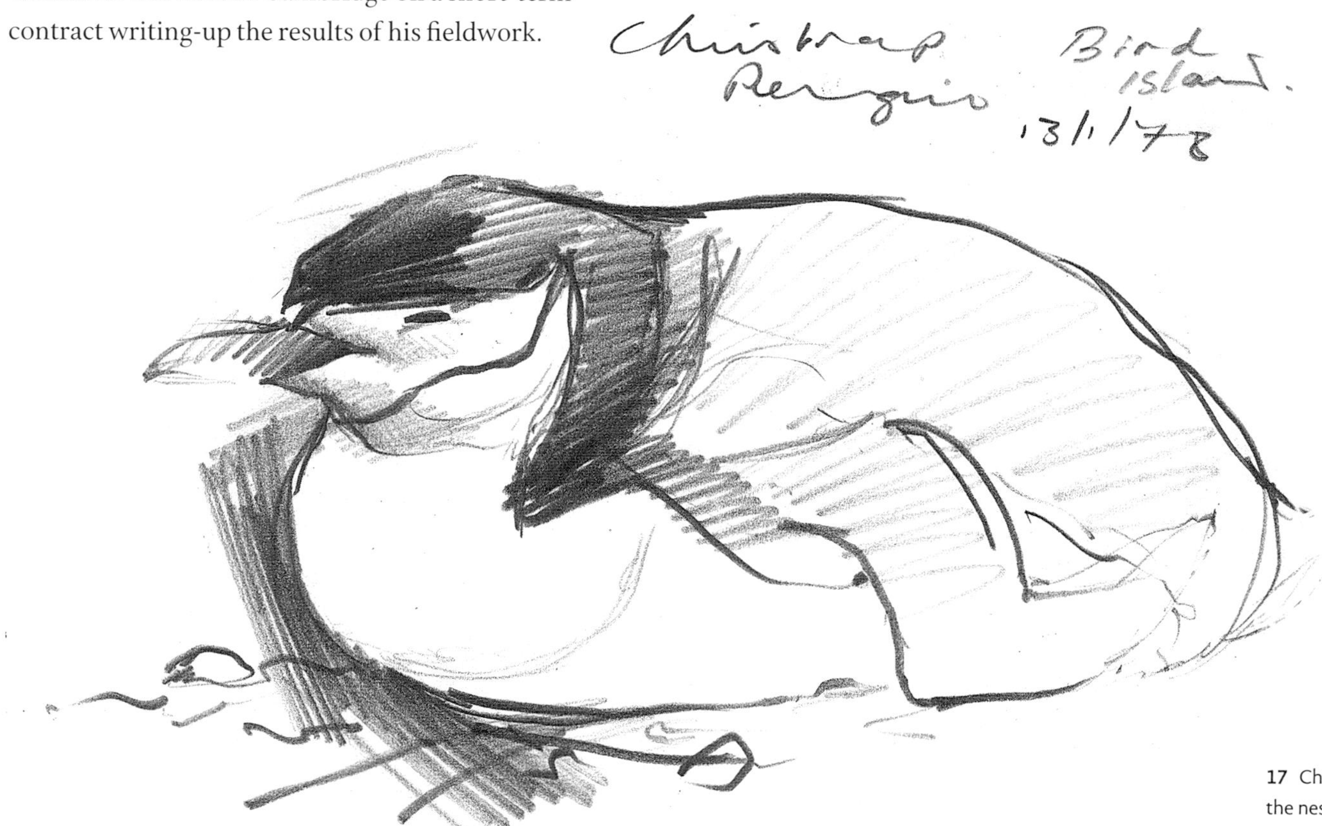

17 Chinstrap penguin on the nest, Bird Island, 1978
15 × 21 cm · pencil

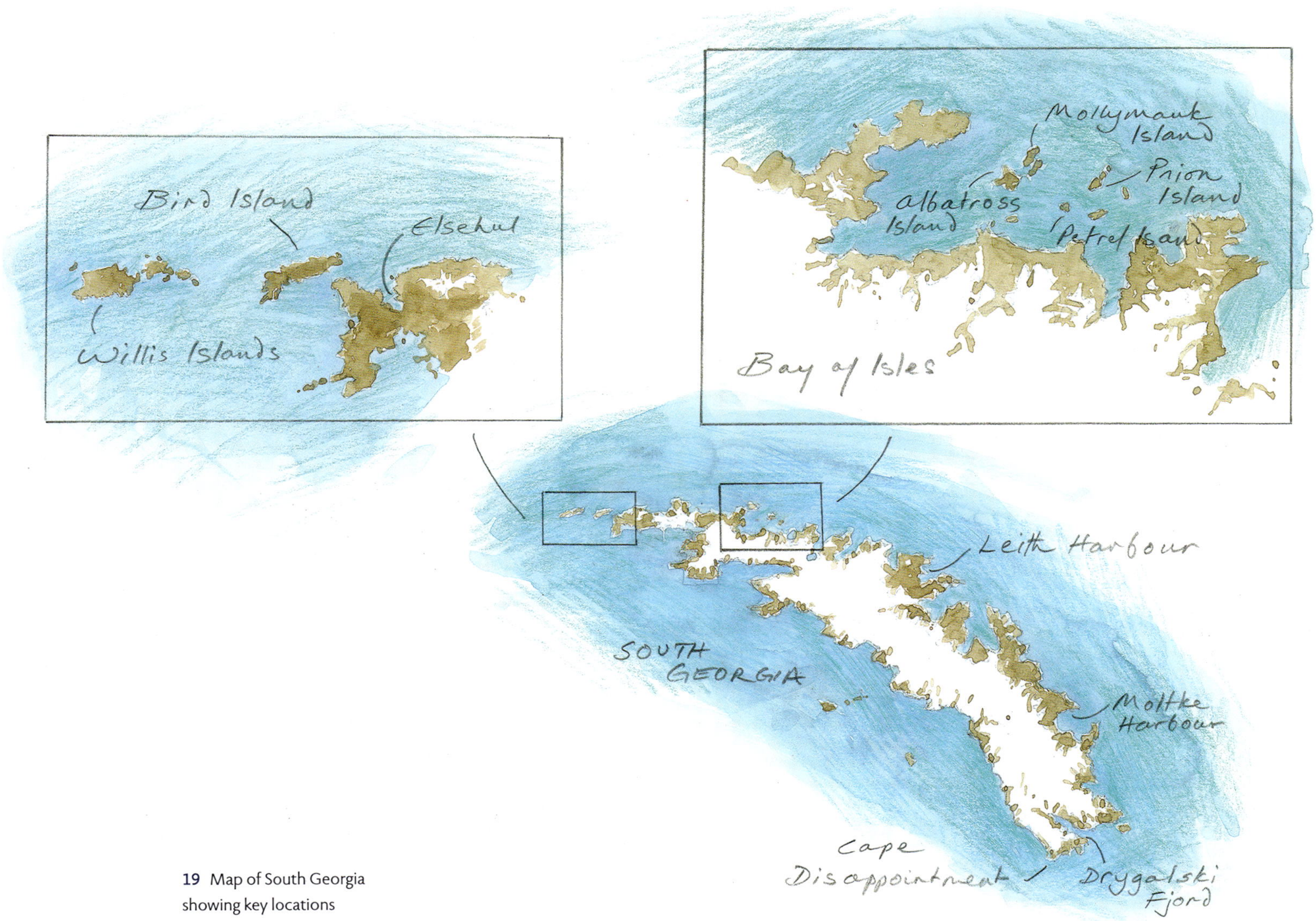

19 Map of South Georgia showing key locations

Pete was a very charismatic man, with a full circular sweep of thick, black close-trimmed beard, tousled hair that suited him well, and a bear-like build which he kept reasonably fit with savage bouts of five-a-side football. More than anything else, he loved to share his enthusiasms and passion for birds, football and life generally with anybody. Pint in hand and cigarette on the go, Pete often told me about his Bird Island experiences – about the petrels and prions, the albatrosses, the whales, seals and penguins. Needless to say, I was captivated by the extraordinary nature of the life on that remote sub-Antarctic island where a lucky few could live close to so many animals that had no fear of man.

It all sounded so dramatic, especially to a fine art graduate and keen naturalist. I was already excited by my potential career in natural history film-making with the RSPB, but I had always kept alive a passion for fine art and drawing. Any spare time was spent filling sketchbooks with landscapes and studies of birds. I was used to working through binoculars and telescope. Now I was being told on South Georgia that it was possible to get as close as humanly possible to some of the most fabulous birds set in landscapes that were simply breathtaking.

Like virtually all creatures of remote oceanic islands the birds and seals of Bird Island have learned to live without fear of large land predators. Few people have ever landed on Bird Island and very few have lived there for any length of time. Early sealers collected fur seals and whalers occasionally took eggs and birds, but the island had been largely ignored. On an Admiralty chart of 1909, it was marked simply as a tiny triangle with no names or features. Later there were infrequent landings by scientists, pioneering adventurers and government officials, but the first permanent building – a garden shed – was built only in 1958 by Nigel Bonner who was conducting seal research. In the same year, Lance Tickell arrived on South Georgia to study wandering albatrosses. When he managed to reach Bird Island, he stayed long enough to be convinced that he should remain with the albatrosses through the winter months. The United

SEABIRD DRAWINGS, SOUTHERN OCEAN

Jizz is a term used by birdwatchers to describe the indefinable and unique quality of a particular species' overall impression or appearance noted from features such as shape, posture and movement. The origin of the word is uncertain, but it is said to come from the corruption of the wartime: 'General Impression of Size and Shape' (GISS, or 'jizz') to help speedy recognition of aircraft or ships.

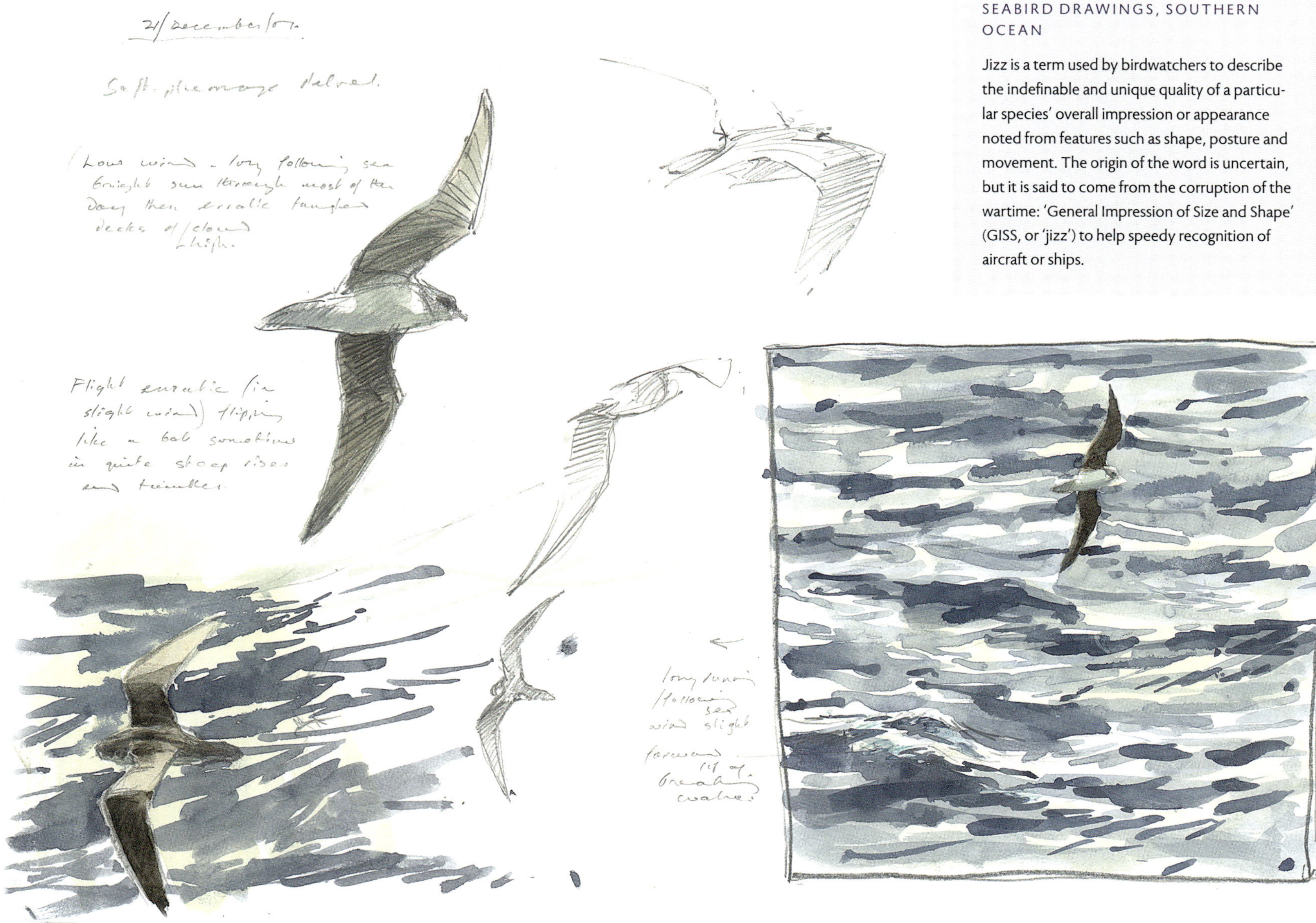

20 Soft-plumaged petrel, Southern Ocean, December, 2007
30 × 42 cm · watercolour and penci

States Antarctic Research Program (USARP) provided funds and he established two more robust huts. The main building, Lönnberg House, was named after the Swedish biologist Einar Lönnberg who had expressed great concern over sealing and whaling during a visit to South Georgia in 1906. After completing his fieldwork, Lance returned home to write it up, leaving Lönnberg House to be occupied by fur seals. Then, in 1971, the facilities were taken over by the British Antarctic Survey and occupied by a research team that included Pete Prince as a field assistant.

Within months of returning home in 1974, BAS decided that Pete was the ideal person to lead a small team back to Bird Island to resume research on fur seal and wandering albatross. Recognizing the opportunity of a lifetime, Pete put together a proposal for an additional study – comparing the feeding ecology in black-browed and grey-headed albatrosses, two species that were physically similar but known to have significant differences in breeding biology. With a research biologist appointed to undertake the seal work, he needed two field assistants for the albatross research. With no time to set up formal job interviews, one night in the pub Pete made me an offer I could not refuse!

Until that time I'd had little contact with research biologists, but it has always seemed to me that there are common elements between them and the artists who take the natural world as their theme. From what I was learning, we both shared the same excitement about getting close to the subject and observing every movement and detail and, of course – in a pre-electronic age – methodically recording everything on paper. For scientists and artists interpreting their raw data was invariably undertaken much later in the lab or studio, long after the field encounter. And on Bird

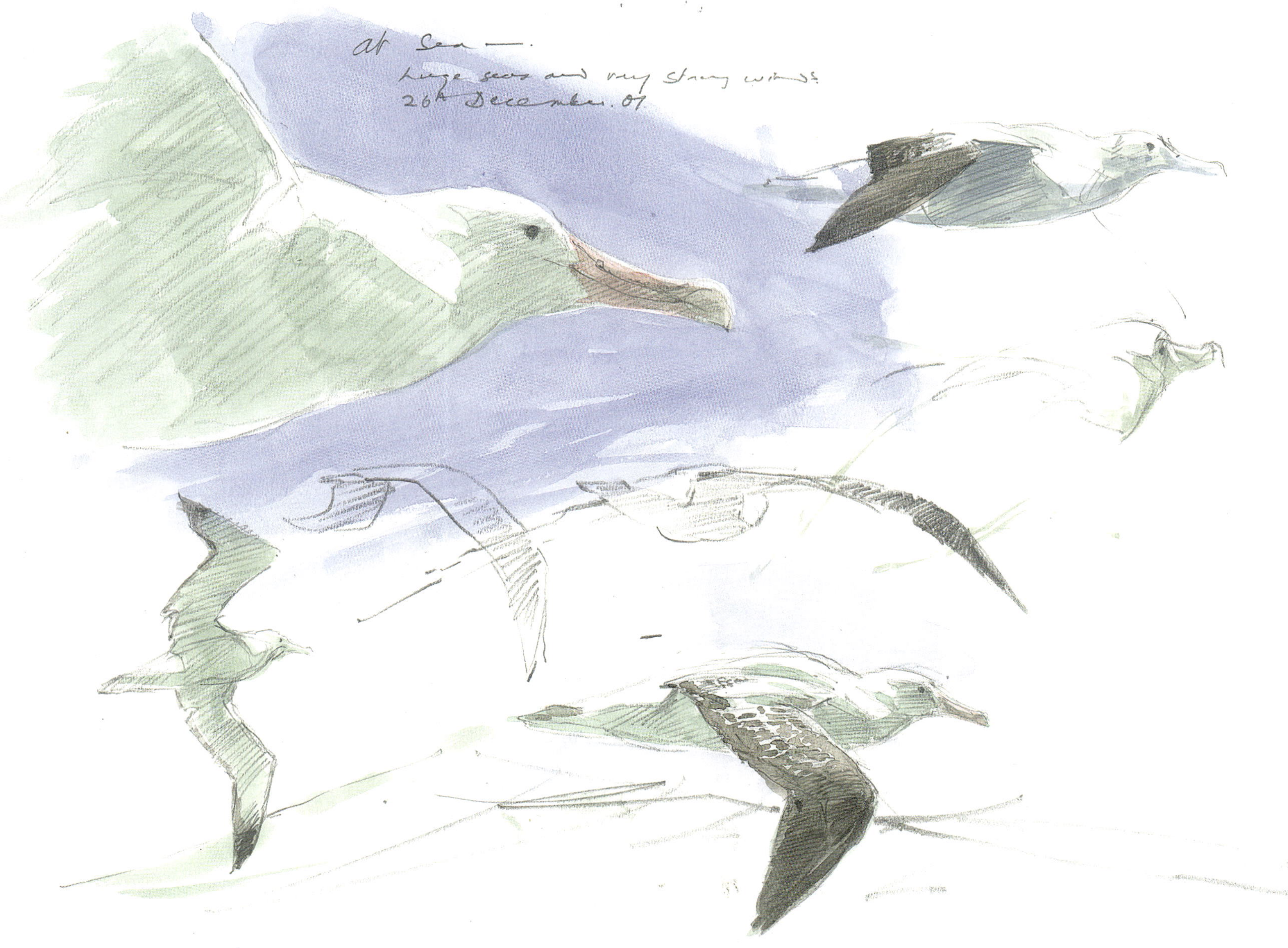

21 Wandering albatross at sea, Southern Ocean, December, 2007
30 × 42 cm · watercolour and pencil

Island, just as Pete had done, I could also have my own spare time project – I could paint and draw!

From the earliest days of my interest in art I believed that painting from life and exploring a subject first-hand was the best way to go. By looking at the colour, line, and form of a living creature or landscape and recording information that captures the detail, and also expresses what you feel about the subject, it is possible to create a more exciting and dynamic result. The keen birdwatcher in me wants to record a phase of juvenile plumage or the subtle differences between Indian and Atlantic yellow-nosed albatrosses, but the artist wants to express the patterns the same birds make as they fly over the enormity of the seascape. Working from photographs can help with the detail, but it cannot convey the thrill of an intimate encounter. A few lines and colour dabs in a field sketchbook, however crude they appear, are always more helpful in unravelling a three dimensional world and exploring the not-so-obvious in a subject. Recently, I read that an artist's job is to deepen the mystery, and not explain things like a journalist, and I found myself recalling Aristotle's deceptively simple observation that 'The aim of art is to represent not the outward appearance of things, but their inward significance'.

My focus invariably is on the dynamics of the subject, particularly living creatures where movement is the essential element I am keen to pin down – especially the flight of birds. I want to convey a feeling for the essence of the species and the space it inhabits; not create a static portrait. With observations of plants and vegetation it is the way that wind shape them or how they chase the light and grow within a habitat that interests me. With landscapes it is the movement of clouds in the sky and the changing light that shows or sometimes hides the

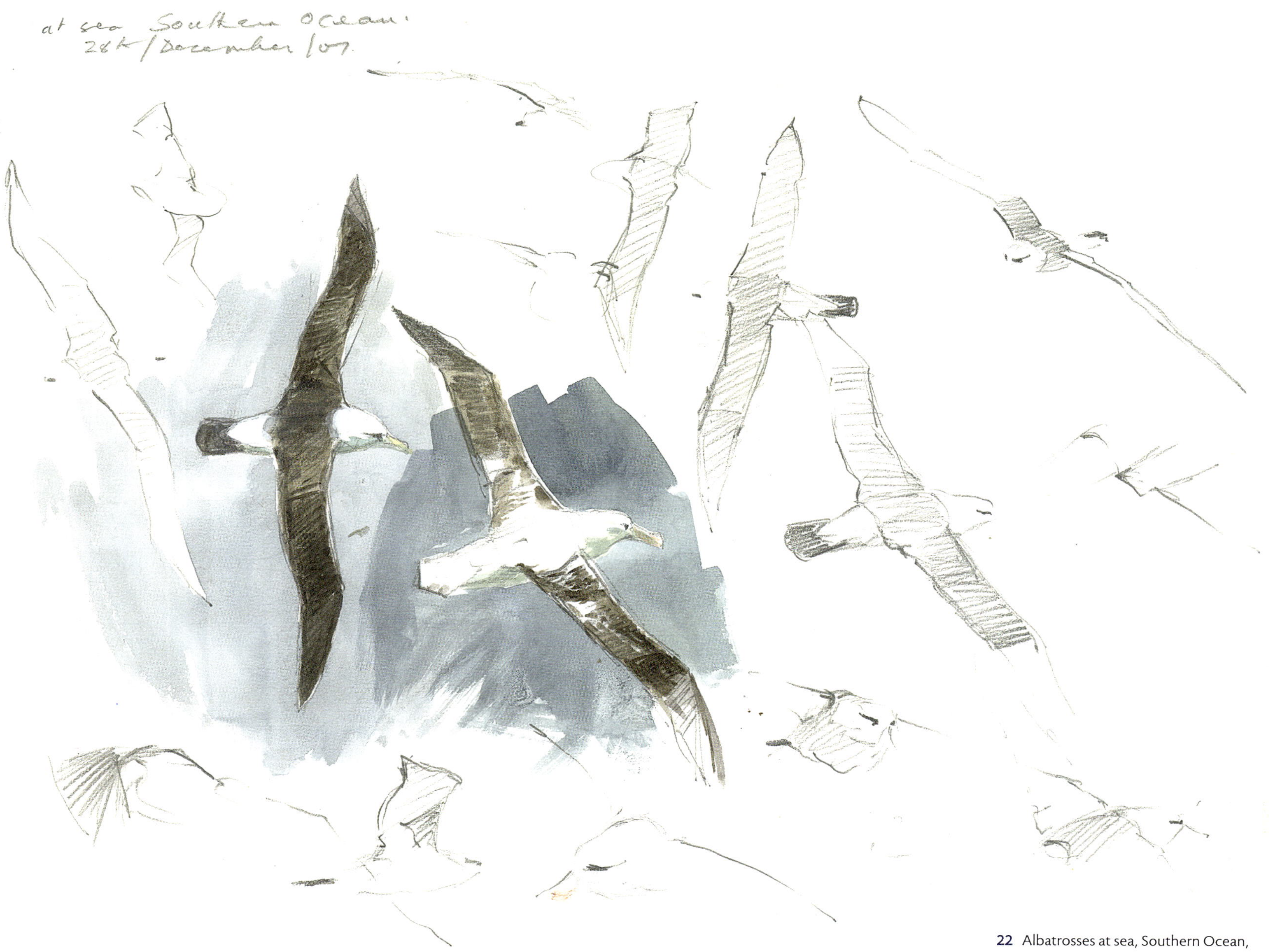

22 Albatrosses at sea, Southern Ocean, December, 2007
30 × 42 cm · watercolour and pencil

landforms from easy view. To my eye there is a restlessness in nature that makes it exciting.

To capture movement, in birds particularly, a fleeting glimpse is not enough. Repeated observations are needed to build up a more complete picture. With smaller birds, the problem is that they often fly away too soon. I might get a chance to draw no more than the shape of the head. With the next sighting I may add the bill, then the outline of the body or the pattern of the wings. In that way, I assemble images of whole birds that are more of an interpretation than a realistic snapshot.

Where action is repeated over and over again, it is possible to concentrate on key aspects. The head: how is it held in relation to the body and angle of flight; is it hunched in, or stretched forward? The wings: is each held exactly the same either side or is one angled more strongly than the other as the bird turns? When they flap are they stroking the wind or fanning it? Where does the shadow fall in strong light; what are the subtle tones that reveal the form when the light is dull? There are so many details to observe and set down on paper. Each pass of the subject is different, and it doesn't pose for a second. But the snatched fragments that spread across the sketchbook pages combine into a fluid interpretation that captures the so-called 'jizz' of a bird, and the unique sense of space that surrounds it at that moment in time.

Because I work in the field for long periods and sometimes in difficult conditions, I have developed

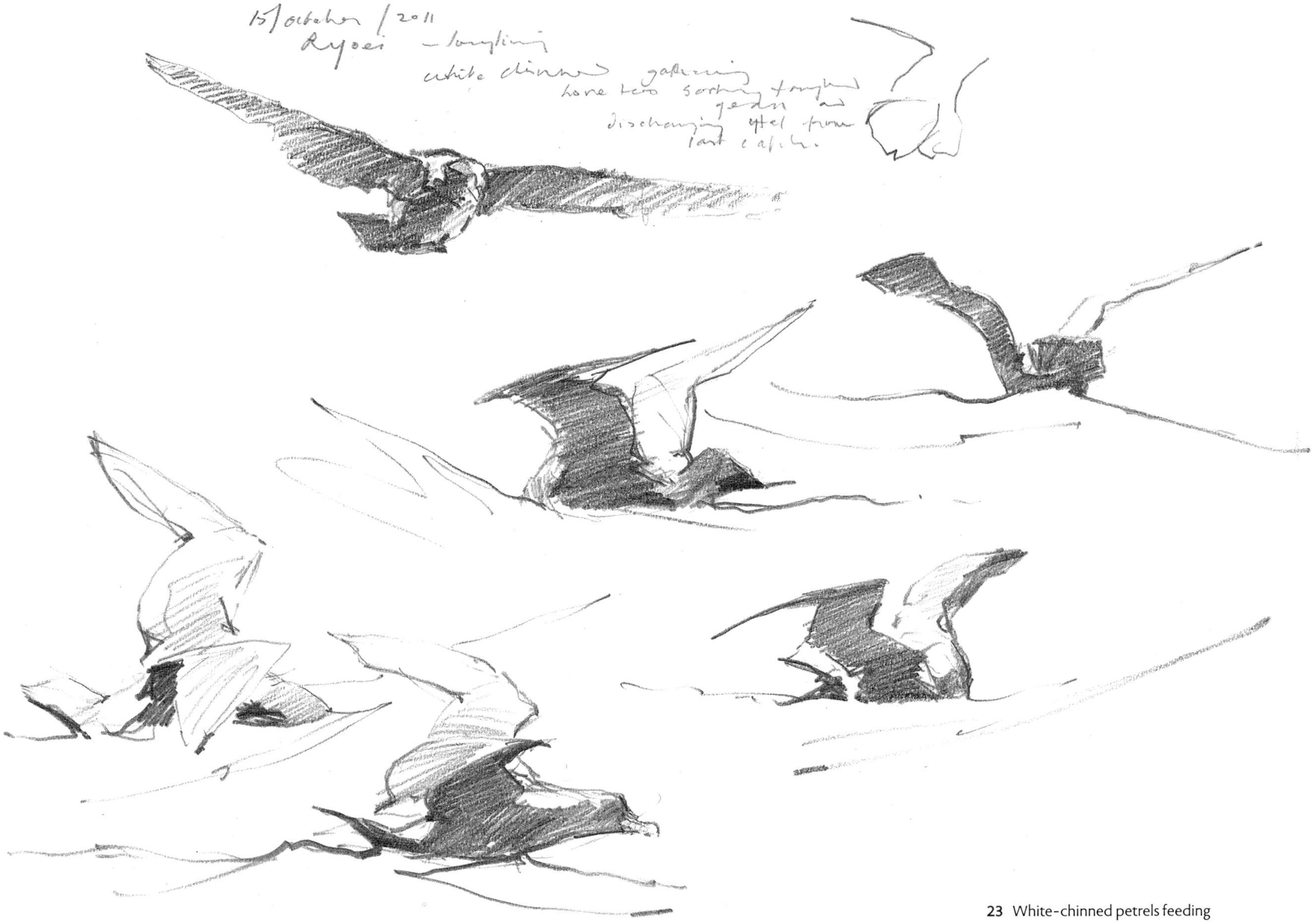

23 White-chinned petrels feeding around the ship. *Ryoei*, October, 2011
30 × 42 cm · pencil

various items of painting equipment to make it easier to paint and draw outdoors in wild places. I made sketchpad holders with flaps that can be flipped to cover a page when it rains. I carry a small piece of canvas the size of a tea towel to lay on the ground as a 'table', so that pencils and brushes thrown down carelessly do not land out of reach in deep vegetation, and a larger plastic sheet to throw over everything when the heavens open – a sheet that doubles as a sunshade. Water pots can be jammed into holding rings attached to the canvas square so they neither blow over or away altogether over the side of a ship!

This system had worked well at home so I was hoping that all the same principles and bits of kit would work on Bird Island, although the weather would be much worse. With no chance of resupply during our stay on our remote sub-Antarctic island, the priority was to make sure I had enough paper. I decided it would be better to take reams of cheaper cartridge paper rather than a few precious sheets of expensive watercolour paper.

With all my art materials packed and a crate of sketchpads ready for shipping, I was ready for Bird Island and the adventure 'down south'.

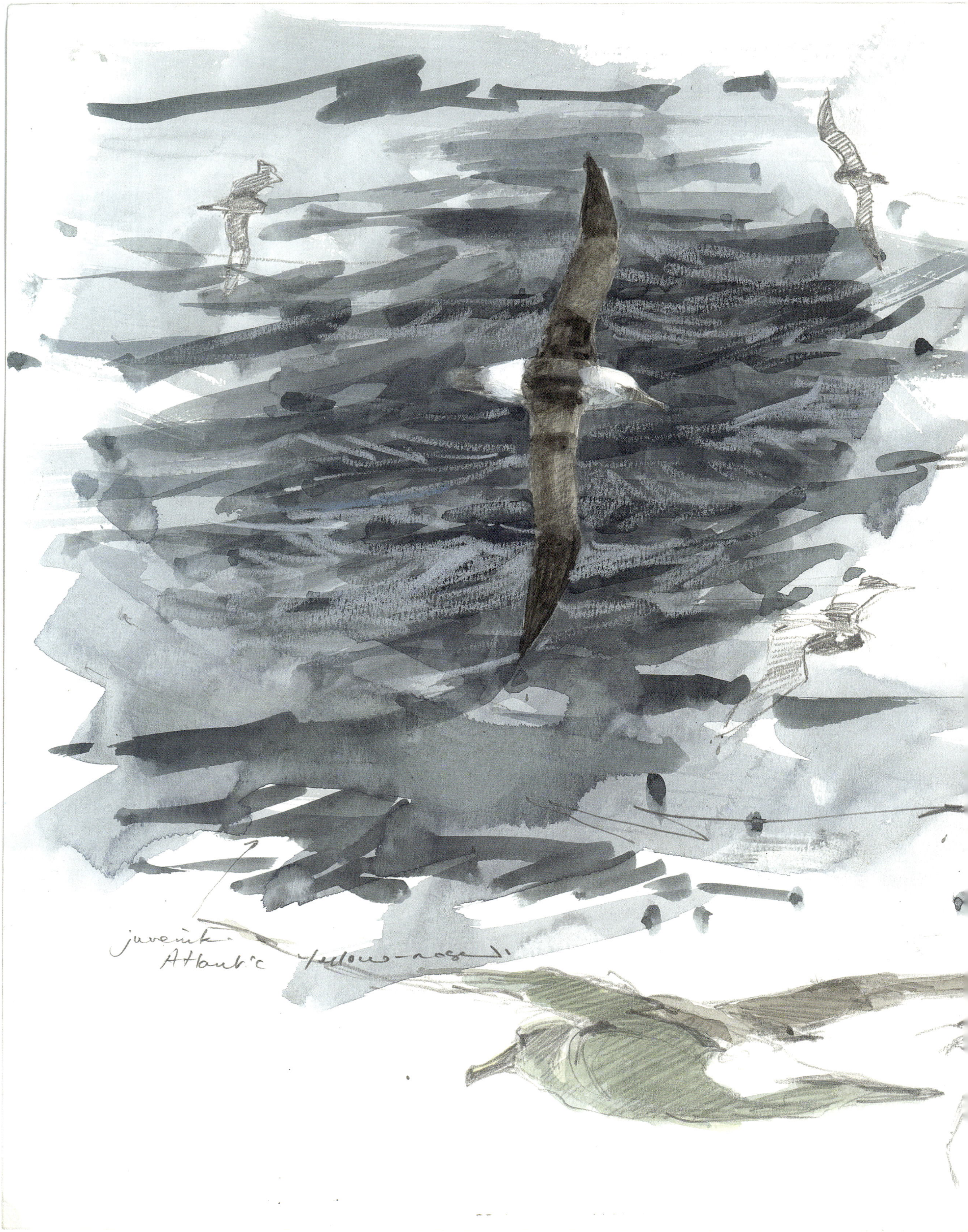
juvenile
Atlantic
yellow-nosed

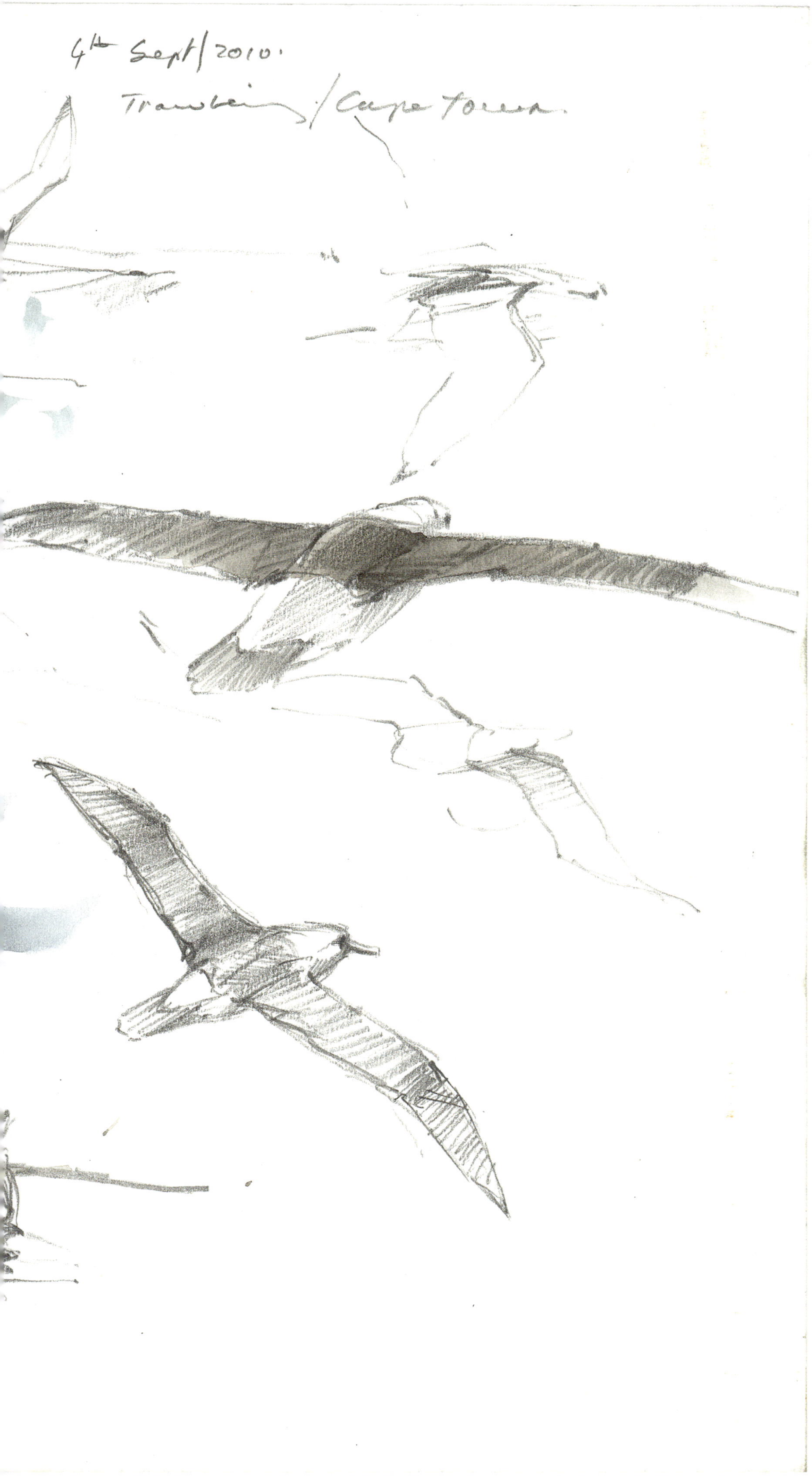

24 Mollymauks off South Africa, September, 2010
30 × 42 cm · watercolour and pencil

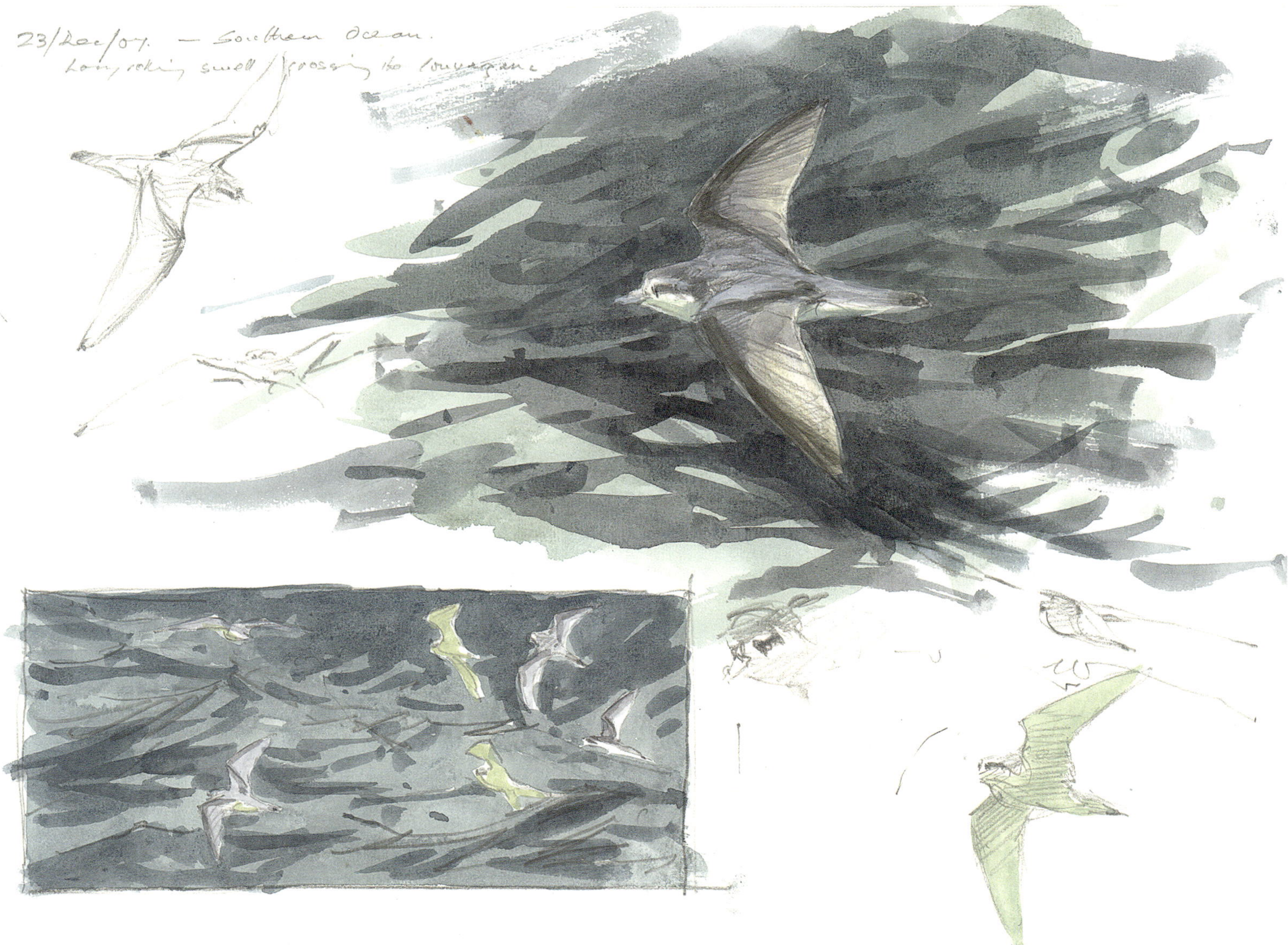

25 Antarctic prions at sea, Southern Ocean, December, 2007
30 × 42 cm · watercolour and pencil

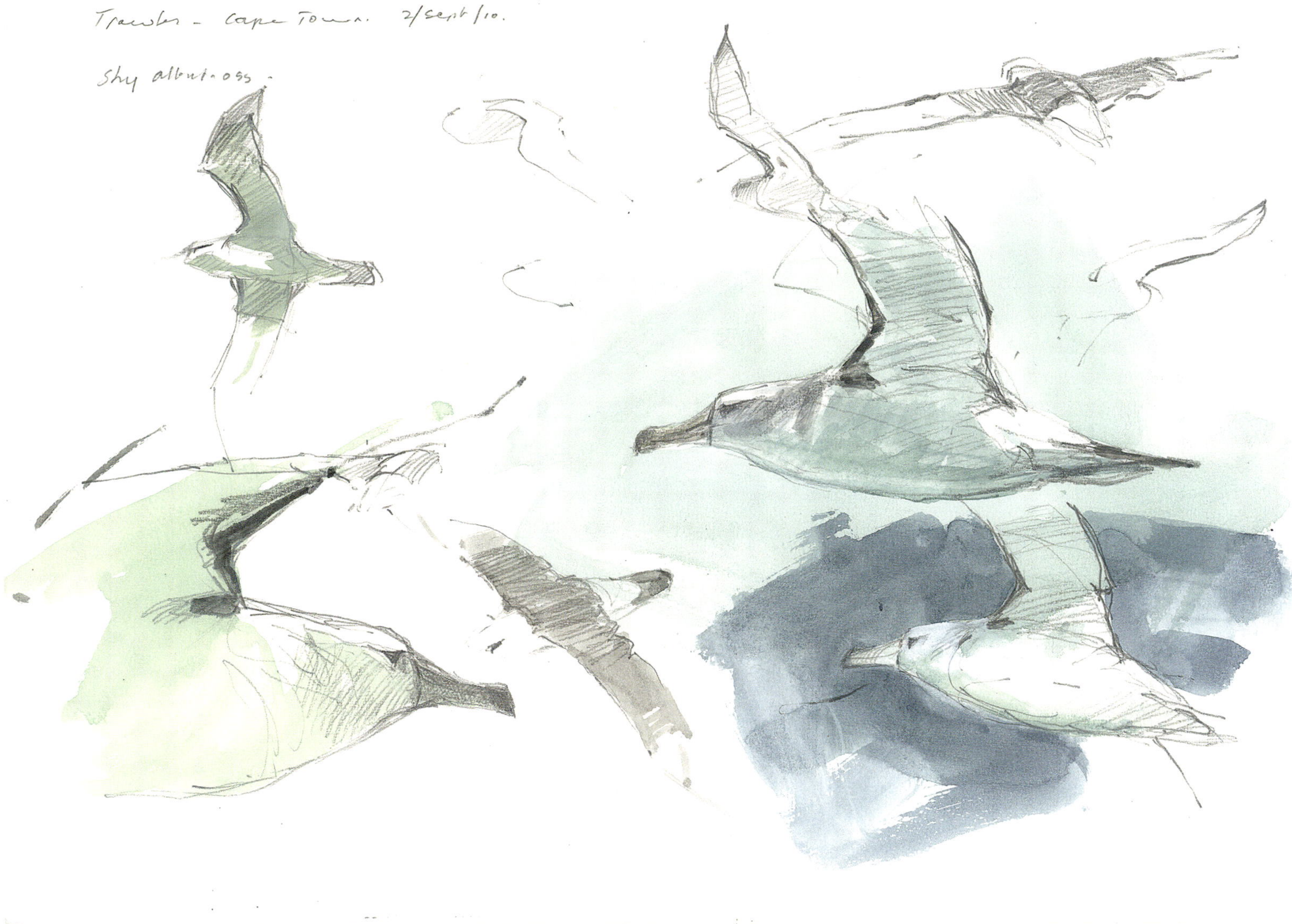

26 Shy albatross, South Africa, September, 2010
30 × 42 cm · watercolour and pencil

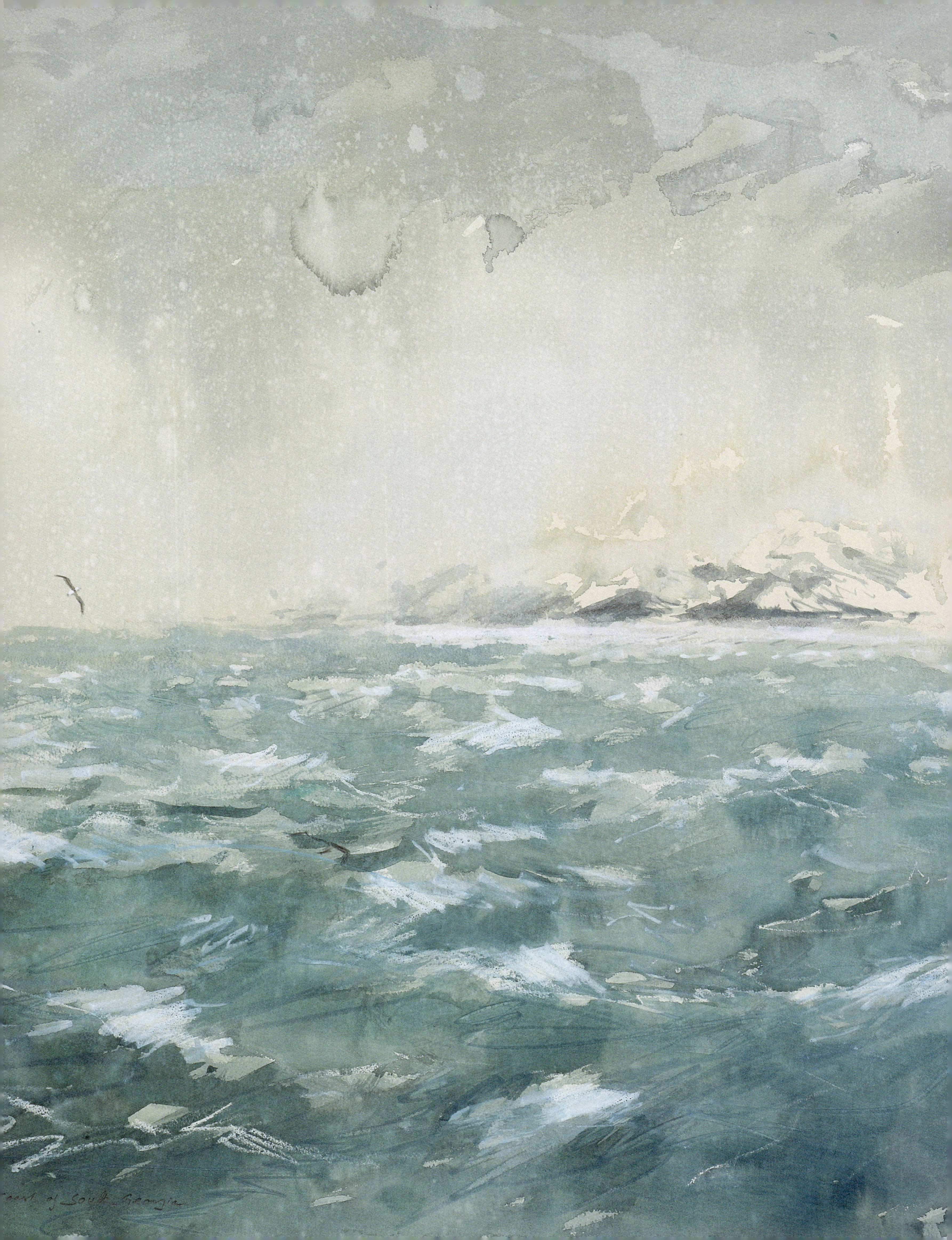
of South Georgia

CHAPTER 3

Heading south

27 Albatross and storm at sea off South Georgia, 2008 (detail).

The Southern Ocean isolates the Antarctic continent with some of the world's windiest and roughest sea conditions. It was officially defined in 1961 as those parts of the Atlantic, Indian, and Pacific Oceans between 60°s latitude and the Antarctic landmass, but it has a much more significant biological boundary called the Polar Front. There the cold, dense surface waters of the circumpolar ocean flowing north meet the warmer water flowing south to create a spectacular upwelling of nutrient rich sea. Although it is crossed at about 50 degrees south, its path is strongly steered by sub-marine topographic features, and the exact boundary meanders over a wide latitudinal range. Indeed, there are really no 'strict borders' to the World's five great oceans. Rather than lines across degrees of longitude and latitude, they are defined by fluid edges where temperatures change and mixing currents swirl around continents and over seamounts rising from the ocean floor. As a result, they are in effect one continuous inter-connected body of salt water.

The ecological realm that lies outside the shallower coastal waters and continental shelf is the pelagic zone, named from the Greek term *pelagikos* meaning 'open sea'. Most ocean organisms live in the upper sunlit zones where phytoplankton feeds a myriad of grazing and foraging fish, crustaceans and other species; which in turn attracts larger predatory fish; which in turn are the food of top predators. So the upper zones of the open ocean are the space where schools of yellowfin and bluefin tuna chase massed shoals of fast-moving baitfish like mackerel, saury and anchovy; where great whales sieve millions of tonnes of swarming krill; where dolphins lunge at giant 'bait balls' of sardines; where squid swarm up from deeper waters as darkness falls; and where sharks prowl and turtles cruise. It is also the realm of pelagic seabirds where albatrosses, shearwaters and petrels effortlessly ride the wind and skim the waves in search of food, some species spending years at sea and others circumnavigating the globe. The most highly pelagic of all seabirds are the Procellariiformes, or tubenoses – among them petrels, shearwaters, fulmars, prions, but first and foremost, the magnificent albatrosses.

The journey south towards the Southern Ocean and my summer home on Bird Island seemed to be defined by lines of a different kind – from Samuel Taylor Coleridge's 1798 narrative poem *The Rime Of The Ancient Mariner*. We sailed on his 'painted ocean' crossing the tropics into the South Atlantic where the swell was long and the breeze warm accompanied by sooty and greater shearwaters. Now and then Leach's storm petrels appeared and passed quickly over the wake where Wilson's storm petrels lingered far longer. And in the stronger winds and heavier seas south of the Tropic of Capricorn soft-plumaged and grey petrels swept past in company with Atlantic petrels, while the huge forms of giant petrels followed the ship for hours, and good numbers of white-chinned petrels '... chased us south along'.

Although Coleridge's famous lines catch the mood and feel of the ocean, he never sailed further south

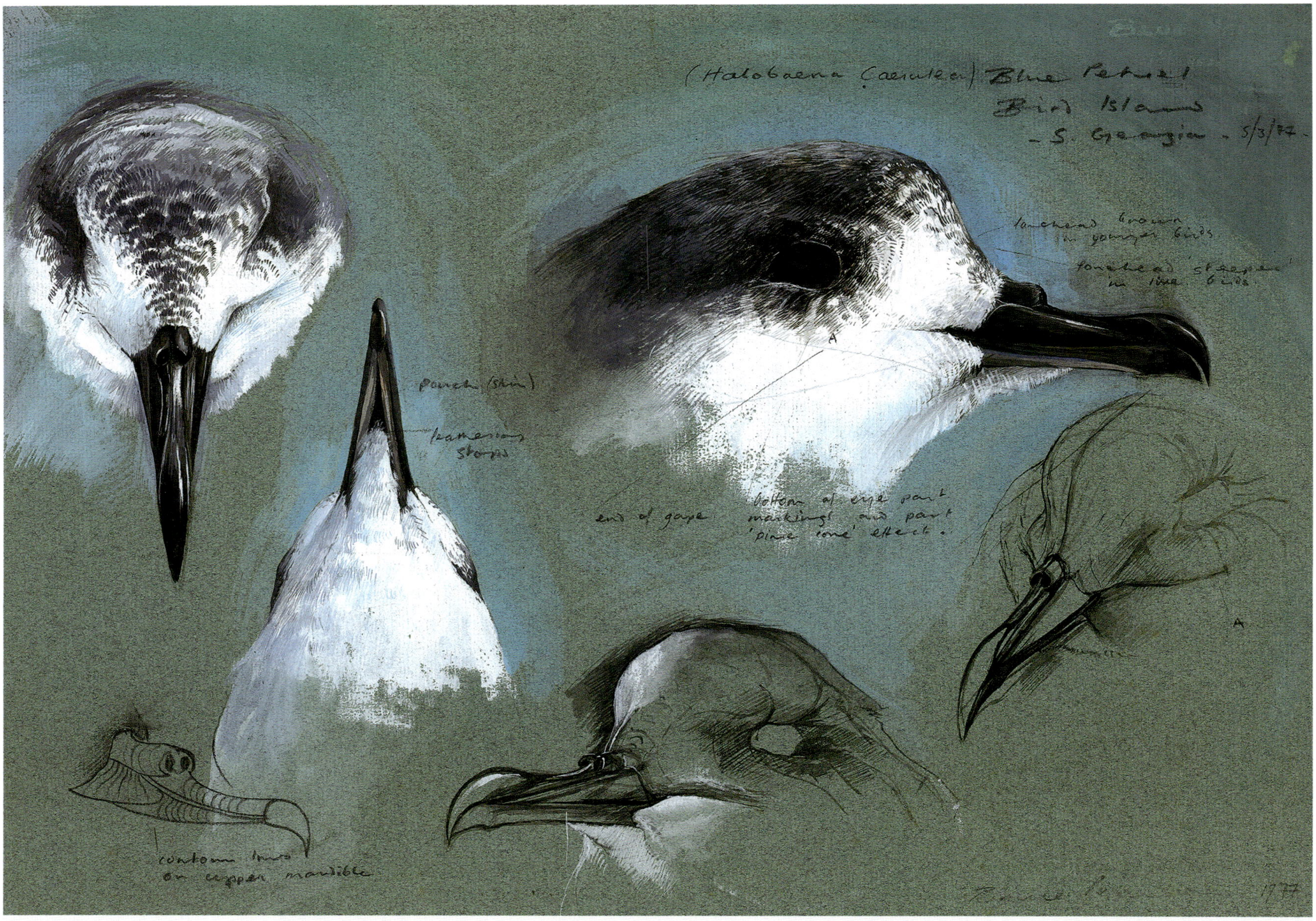

PROCELLARIIFORMES

A unifying characteristic of this group of birds is the pronounced external tubular nostrils that run from the base of their bill towards a hooked tip. Their 'tube noses' are associated with a marked development of the olfactory part of the brain giving them an incredible sense of smell that rivals that of any animal on earth.

The glands secrete a concentrated salt solution out of the bird's blood which trickles out through the nostrils.

28 Specimen study, blue petrel (*Halobaena caerulea*), Bird Island, 1977
30 × 42 cm · watercolour and ink

than the Mediterranean. For a few years from 1781, however, he was a pupil at Christ's Hospital, a London boarding school where the Master at the time was the astronomer, William Wales. Wales had accompanied Captain Cook on his great voyage of discovery, and perhaps his tales of adventure and exploration among the icy wastes of the Southern Ocean inspired young Coleridge's imagination.

'At length did cross an Albatross'. I was writing notes in my cabin one morning when a non-birding shipmate suddenly put his head round the door; 'There's a bloomin' great chicken outside'! I rushed up and climbed quickly to the monkey-island above the bridge to make sure I got a view, and there it was – my first wandering albatross, the largest flying bird in the world effortlessly riding the wind in long sweeps and rising arcs. It was a breath-taking moment, with the great bird and the whole ocean around it searing an image and excitement for the restless rhythm of the natural world that has lasted me every one of the 35 years since that sighting.

We continued south, 'And a good south wind sprung up behind; The Albatross did follow'. Now there were many smaller mollymauk albatrosses, mostly black-browed with fewer grey-headed albatrosses sailing majestically with them. They were all as fabulous as anything I had heard described back in Cambridge; their flight so liquid, a free flowing series of sweeps and arcs with barely ever a flap of the wings. One moment they were sliding diagonally down a rolling wave front as if surfing a cushion of air along its crest, then rising high into the wind to hang poised at the top of the arc, before they caught the wind and swept back down towards the following wave.

Identifying species was difficult, without the wealth of information available in many field-guides used today. Big charismatic species like the great albatrosses could be wanderers, or southern or northern royals. Some of the smaller petrels were black-bellied and Wilson's storm-petrels for sure, but vanishing swiftly between waves could be grey-backed storm-petrels or larger and faster flying Kerguelen Petrel. There were white-chinned petrels in good numbers, but easy sight of the spectacled petrel's variable facial pattern was more difficult. By

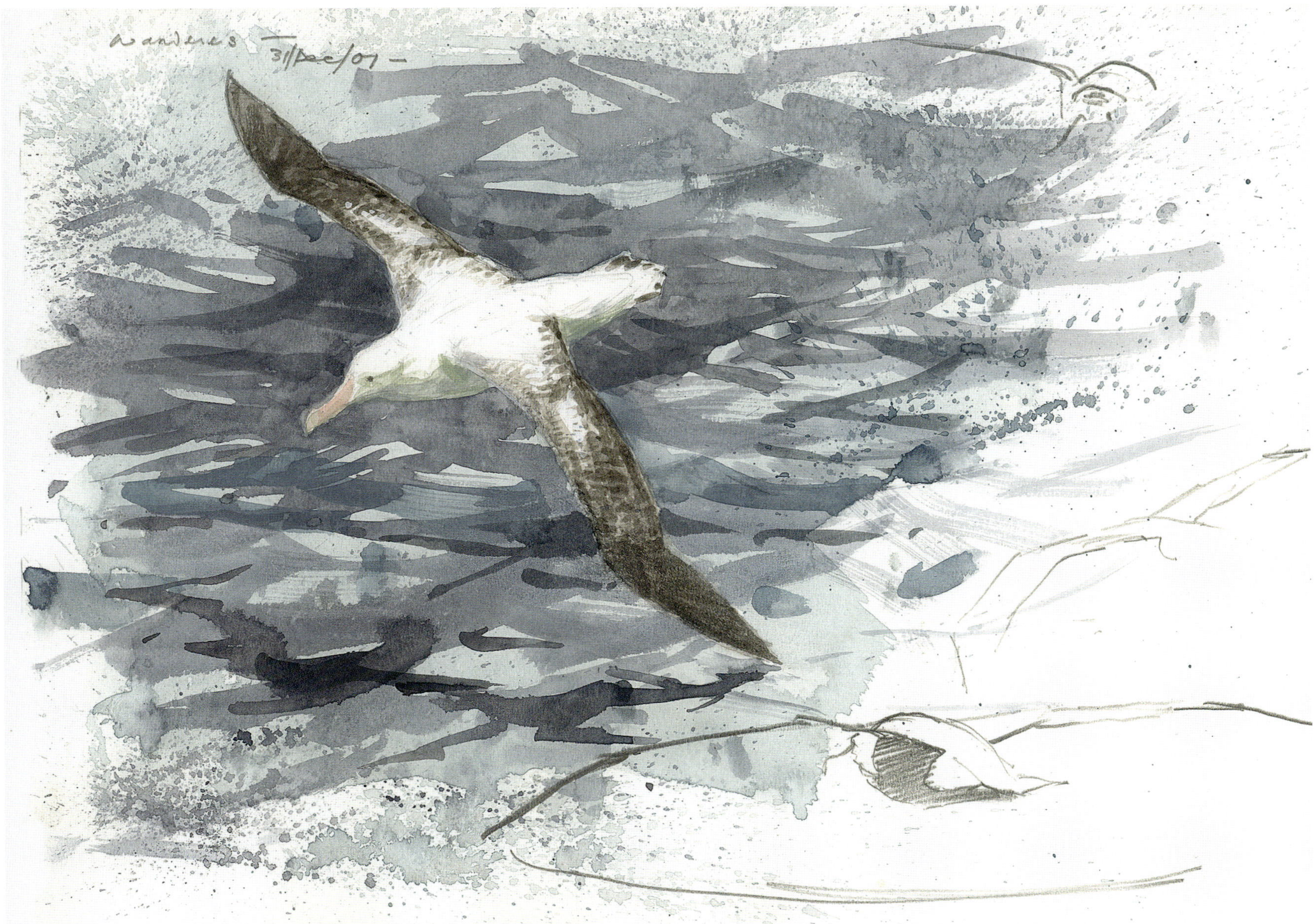

29 Wandering albatross, December 2007
30 × 42 cm · watercolour and pencil

FLIGHT OF SEABIRDS – DYNAMIC SOARING

Despite the apparently effortless way that pelagic seabirds – albatrosses especially – travel over the oceans, their flight is a complicated dynamic activity. A quick glance assumes the wings are fixed motionless in an outstretched position, but tiny adjustments of wing configuration and attitude that respond to the changing conditions of the wind and sea are happening all the time.

Studies have shown that long-winged seabirds use two distinct flight techniques; dynamic soaring and slope soaring. Even after watching for hours on end, the boundaries between these techniques are not always obvious. What I am seeing are birds minimizing their effort by gliding across wave fronts to gain energy from the vertical wind gradient – which moves faster higher up away from the drag of the surface waves – and then turning into the wind again, gaining height, and gliding back down to sea level.

Wandering albatrosses have been shown to cover up to 10,000 km in 10–20 days, and one grey-headed albatross was recorded as circumnavigating Antarctica in just 46 days.

far the easiest to identify were the abundant chequered black and white cape petrels, one the best known seabirds of the southern hemisphere, and mentioned in the account of practically every voyage since the earliest days of exploration.

Not readily to hand on board, unfortunately, was Robert Cushman Murphy's splendid 1936 study *Oceanic Birds of South America*, Excitedly, I had read it cover to cover before leaving. Not only because Murphy was one of the 20th century's great ornithologists, but because he was best known for studies of the natural history and biogeography of marine birds, an interest inspired by his 1912–13 journey on board the last of the open-boat 'Moby Dick' whaling ships to South Georgia. One of the paintings in the book captured my imagination and was titled, '*Wandering Albatross and Wilson's Petrels, and a double circular rainbow sketched by the author in the South Atlantic*'.

Every day the light and mood of the sea was different. Some days a long rolling swell sparkled beneath mackerel skies, while on other days howling winds and passing storms piled up the waves to create an impenetrable haze of salt spray and rain. 'And now the storm-blast came, and he was tyrannous and strong'; Coleridge's lines and Murphy's painting were starting to come to life.

With the ocean's moods changing rapidly and the constant companionship of seabirds, there were creative opportunities galore. I was entranced by the antics of the mollymauks arcing flight all around the ship – sweeping across the stern so close that I could clearly see the deep brown eye and sometimes a wing tip just slicing the surface. With a headwind they cruised slowly just above the decks passing over the superstructure as if in slow motion. Then I could see the constant adjustments of slender, quivering planes along the wings and down the tail as they trimmed their flight – occasionally hanging and looking down with head slightly cocked, as if interested in the affairs on deck. Usually, it was impossible to tell whether the same birds followed us day after day, but sometimes an individual with a clear identifying mark

30 Black-bellied storm petrels, *Ryoei*, October, 2011
30 × 42 cm · watercolour and pencil

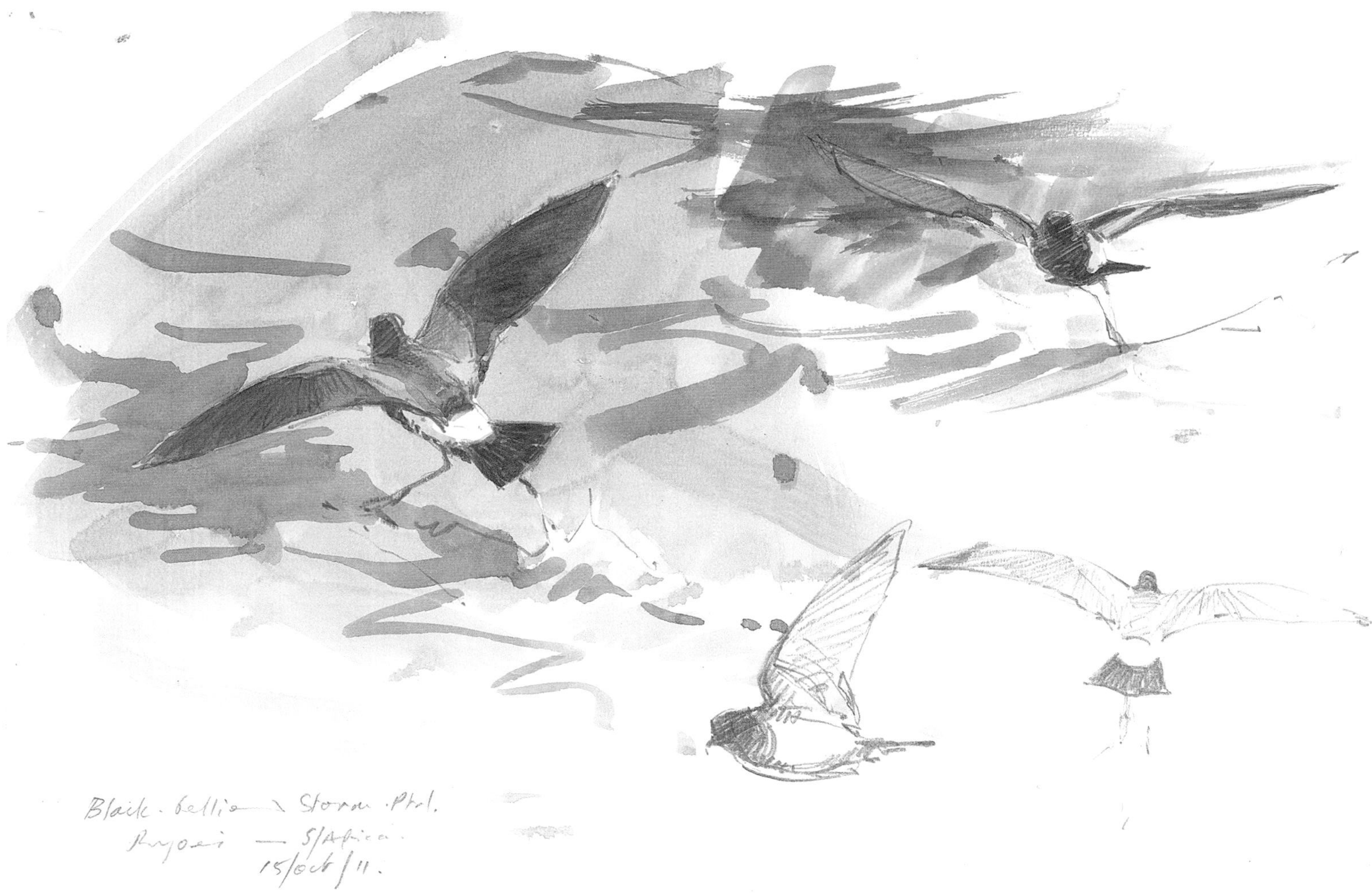

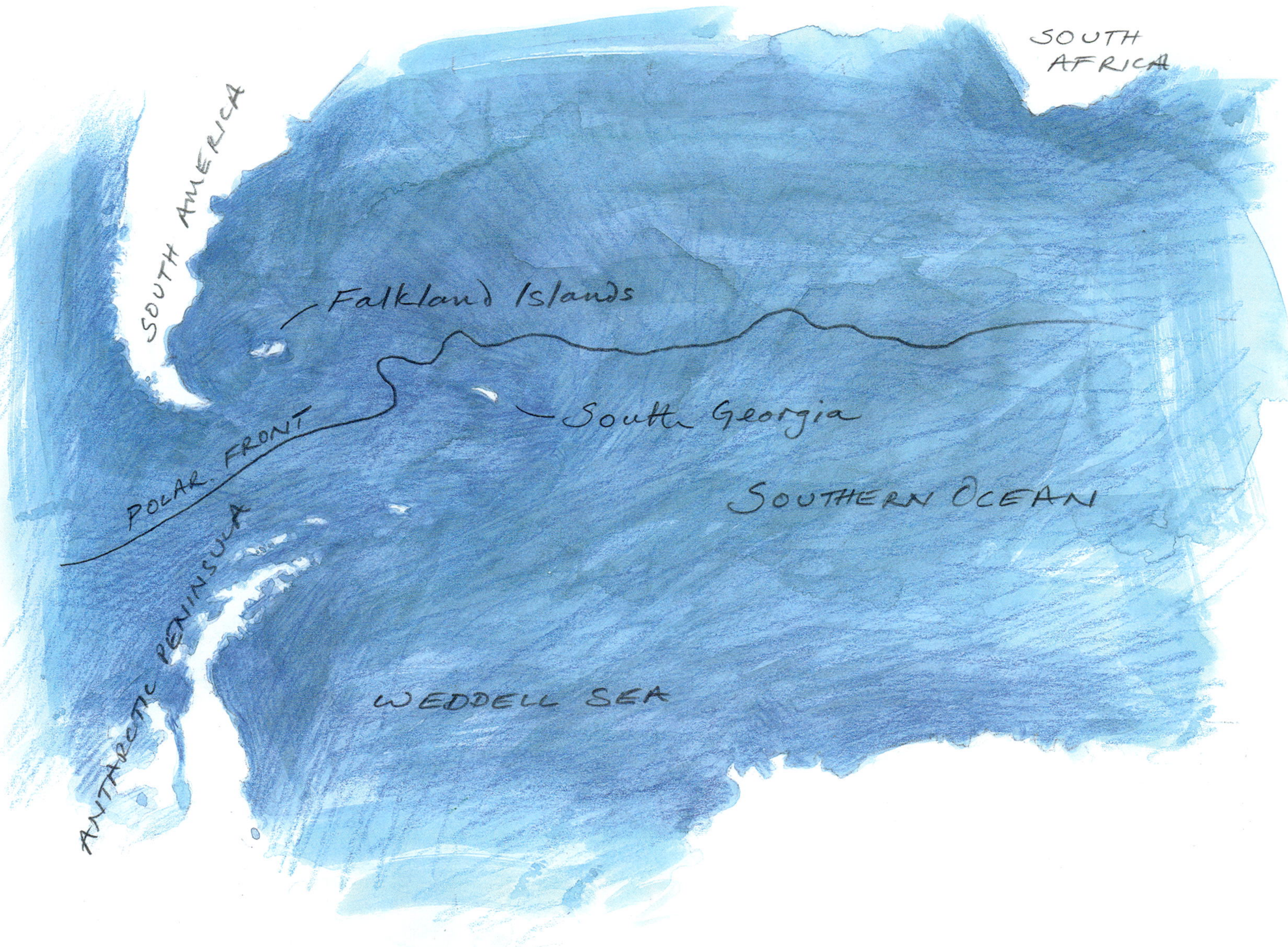

31 Map of Southern Ocean, South Georgia and Polar Front

like a missing or broken feather could be seen for more than a few days. So perhaps some do follow ships for prolonged periods. But why were these birds following us? Was it anticipation of good feeding opportunities when galley waste went overboard, or was it turbulence created by the forward motion of the ship that created air currents to facilitate less energetic flying?

When waste was thrown overboard, the competition for food between the birds was keen. The mollymauks suddenly spread their webbed feet like huge paddles, and with wings drawn back and tails up, they spilled wind and dropped chaotically onto the water. Wings ajar, they glided forwards against the wind, paddling with their feet, quarrelling and chasing in the surf, and grabbing the offal tumbling in our wake. White-chinned and cape petrels darted in and out of the confusion and behind them Wilson's storm-petrels skipped around picking at the scraps.

We worked our way south, ploughing through all kinds of seas and encountering a wonderful range of South Atlantic seabirds with every degree and minute of increasing latitude. Into the Roaring Forties a gale with spitting sleet and driving rain came up from the south-west, tearing the surface of the sea into piles of surging foam. And still mollymauks and petrels followed us seemingly oblivious to the conditions. The only difference that I was noting was their banking turns seeming to have slightly more tension as they pushed harder round against the wind.

The ocean wanderings of tubenoses are far from aimless. They are efficient foraging trips over immense areas of ocean in search of abundant but scattered food – squid, shoaling fish and crustaceans swarming at the surface, and carrion as well as waste from ships. Flying over a vast, featureless ocean their survival depends on finding the proverbial needle in a haystack. So, with their well-developed sense of smell, the birds follow invisible scent contours that act like signposts in an olfactory landscape superimposed on the ocean surface.

Tubenoses can detect minute amounts of compounds over huge distances. The smells of both decomposition and excretion reveal where phytoplankton is plentiful around upwellings, seamounts, shelf breaks, and convergences, or where carrion is floating. Feeding on the phytoplankton there will be shrimps, krill, jellyfish and a host of diverse zooplankton. And feeding on the zooplankton will be fish that are the food of bigger predatory fish and other marine life in turn, right the way up through the food chain to the seabirds and other large predators. As the focus of their foraging expeditions narrows, pelagic birds will also use visual clues to pinpoint prey, including the activity of other birds, marine mammals, and, of course, fishing vessels.

When the storm had run its course the ocean was still riotous but without a veil of spindrift, the spray plumes of spouting whales were easier to detect. If fast-moving seabirds were proving hard to identify, trying to confirm the identity of passing whales and dolphins was even trickier. Some distance to starboard, two plumes arose suddenly only moments apart as two long rolling curves of shiny grey-black appeared close together beneath the vanishing spouts. Their dorsal fins briefly lifted before they rolled beneath the waves. They were rorqual whales for sure, but which species? Relative size is difficult to judge in a featureless seascape, but from the sickle-shaped fin and feeling for the size of the beasts – they were most likely fin whales.

When shafts of sunlight broke through, the sea turned into a vast patterned plane of bright liquid silver scattered with patches of deep indigo. The whole oceanic

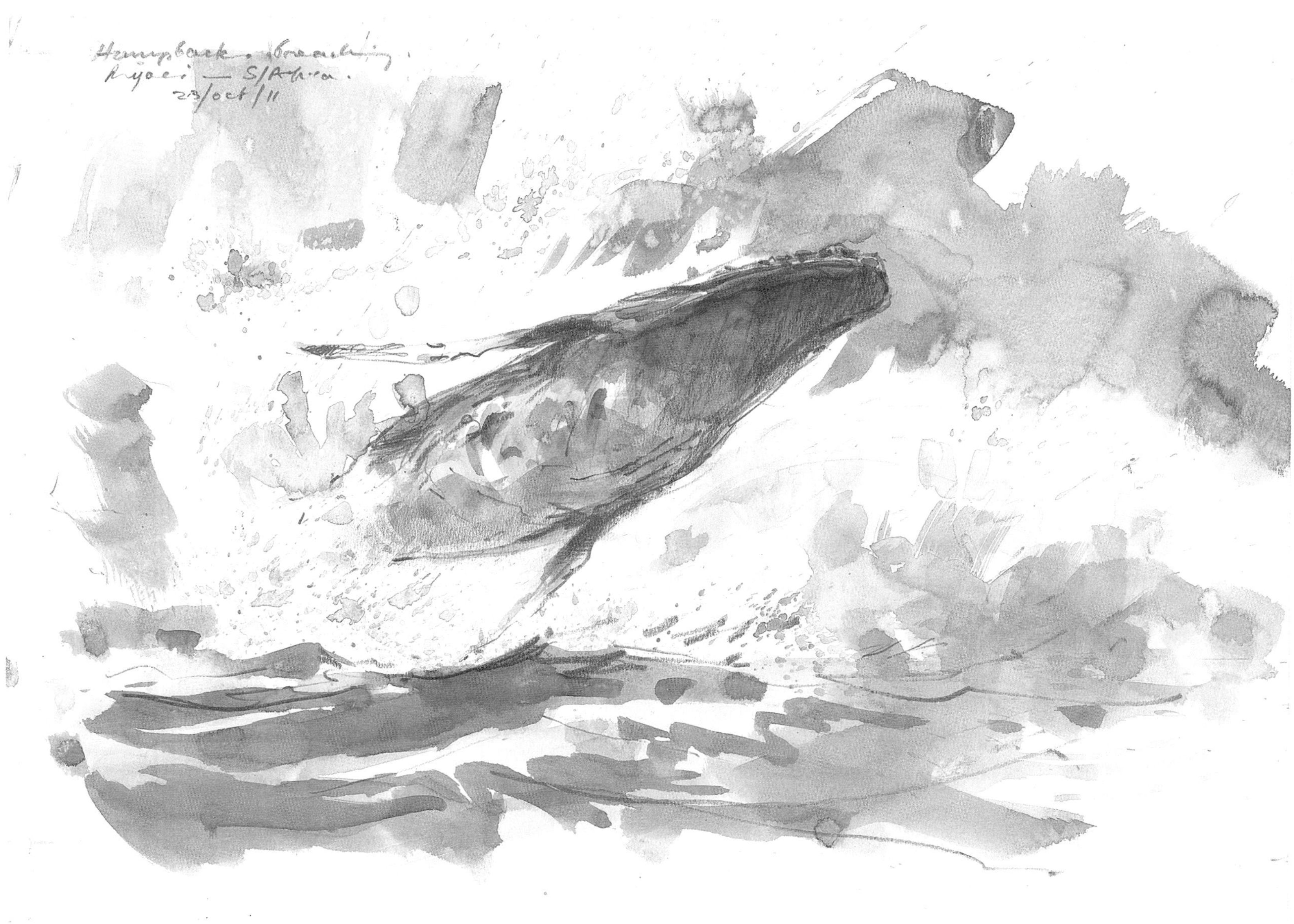

32 Humpback whale breaching, *Ryoei*, October, 2011
30 × 42 cm · watercolour and pencil

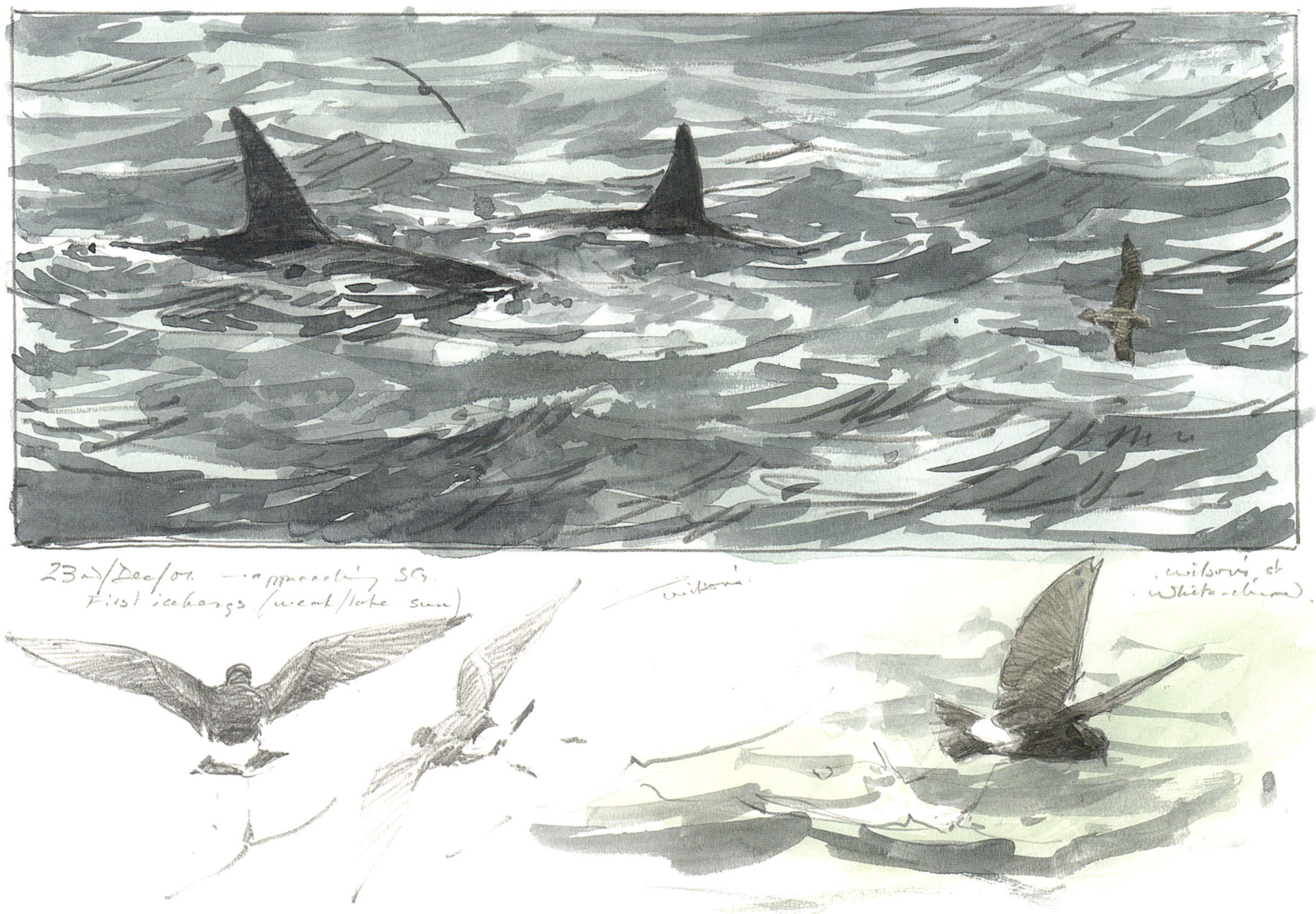

33 Sothern Ocean, killer whales and Wilson's storm-petrels.
30 × 42 cm · watercolour and pencil

vista covered in scything shapes of seabirds: southern fulmars, blue petrels, a mix of prions, and the warm grey-brown tones of Atlantic petrels bright against the cold steely blue-greys of the surrounding sea. For a first-time seaman like me the dramatic light and profusion of birds created an unbelievable spectacle, but I soon discovered that trying to distil its essence and convey the excitement in my sketches was difficult in these shipboard conditions. Capturing the spirit of Coleridge's 'painted ocean' would need more practice and adjustments to the field painting kit I had developed for home use.

Even though well into the areas of ocean known as the Roaring Forties and Furious Fifties there were times when the wind died and cold wet air settled the surface of the ocean to a glassy rolling swell. But not for long; soon it would pick up again bringing squalls, and driving the birds up into their familiar patterns of flight. With the sighting of a beautiful light-mantled albatross, its sharp dark features contrasting with a sprinkling of powdery blue prions, there was a change in the air. The temperature dropped and there seemed to be an increase in the number of now familiar seabirds riding the wind all around us. The change marked our crossing of the Antarctic Convergence or Polar Front. Although we had not yet seen the ice, we began to feel its breath.

The convergence of the less salty and cooler Antarctic waters and the warmer more saline waters to the north forms a significant biological boundary that effectively forms a closed ecosystem – one of the largest marine ecosystems in the world. At its edge, surface temperatures drop by 2–3°C and in the upwelling water nutrients are dissolved, fertilizing the microscopic plankton and making the cold sea surprisingly productive. The Southern Ocean is a world where very few venture to face the extremes of weather and endurance, but where, with the fertility of its waters and the nature of its winds and weather, albatrosses and other pelagic birds thrive.

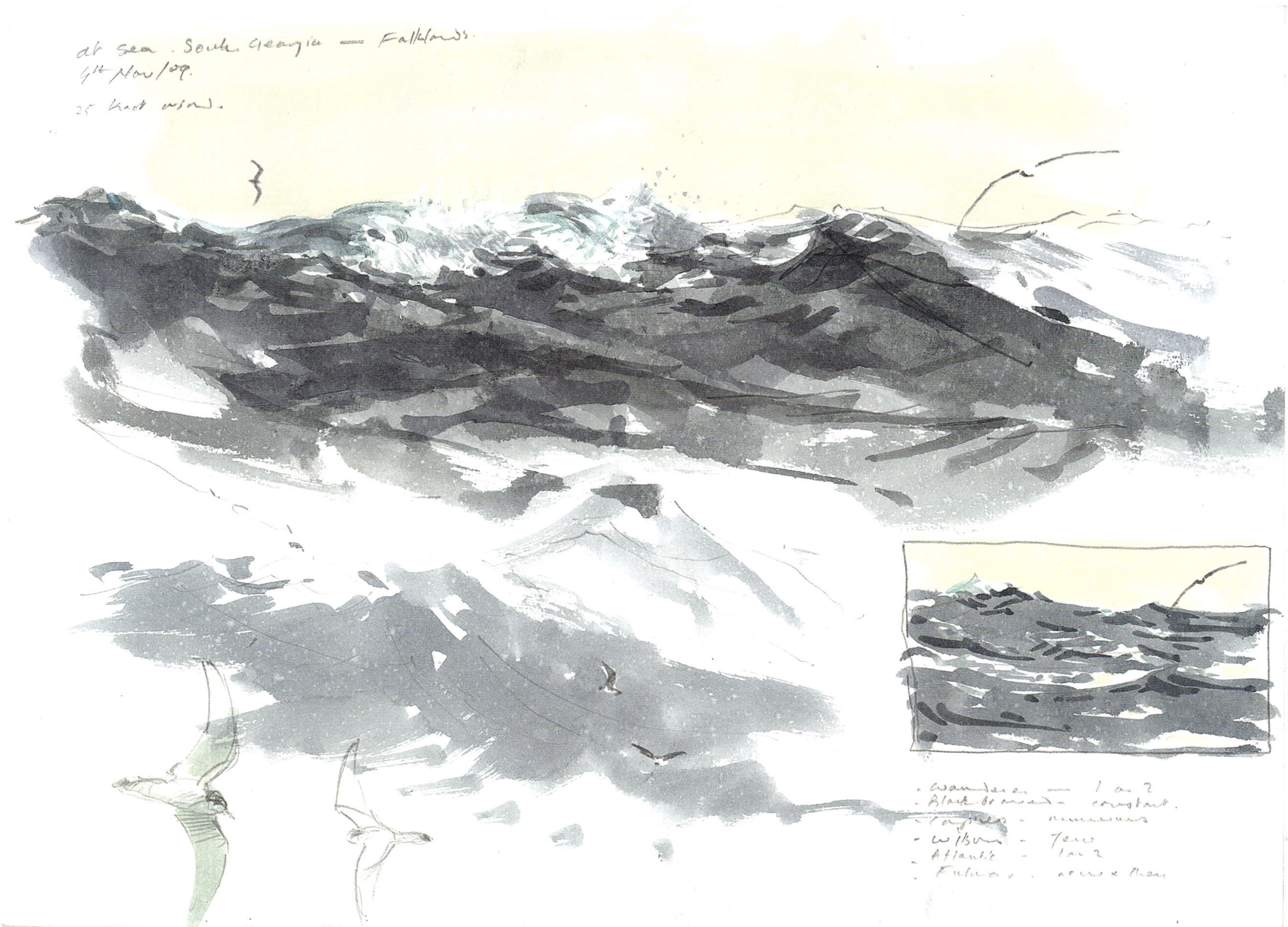

34 The Southern Ocean, November, 2009
30 × 42 cm · watercolour and pencil

Between latitudes 30°s and 65°s the broad band of strong westerly winds are referred to as the Roaring Forties, Furious Fifties, and Screaming Sixties. These latitudes are known for wild and unpredictable weather, and the anarchy of these seas is notorious. In this part of the world, weather systems and water circle the globe unobstructed by landmasses. They gather momentum as the blasts of stormy fury squeeze through the Drake Passage between the tip of Tierra del Fuego and the Antarctic Peninsula, and head for South Georgia.

Only a 100 nautical miles or so from Bird Island and South Georgia, there was now a significantly different feel and look to the seascape. In a patch of sunlight opening along the southern horizon, a vast tabular iceberg lay like a distant landmass, its shattered emerald cliffs and columns rising to a glistening white plateau. Around its edges the sea crashed into deep fissures and crevices in the ice throwing up jets of spray that swept downwind in a haze. All around were birds – hordes of cape petrels; a floating carpet of prions rolling with the rise and fall of passing waves; many black-browed and some grey-headed albatrosses drifting in long rising curves against the horizon and sweeping low into wave troughs where black-bellied storm-petrels dipped, danced and fluttered lightly up the waves. Now the tubenoses were joined by penguins. Flocks of gentoo penguins porpoised and gathered on the surface with only their sleek heads and upright tails showing above the water. Tiny diving-petrels erupted from the waves in hordes, fluttering across the surface and crashing in and out of the waves before

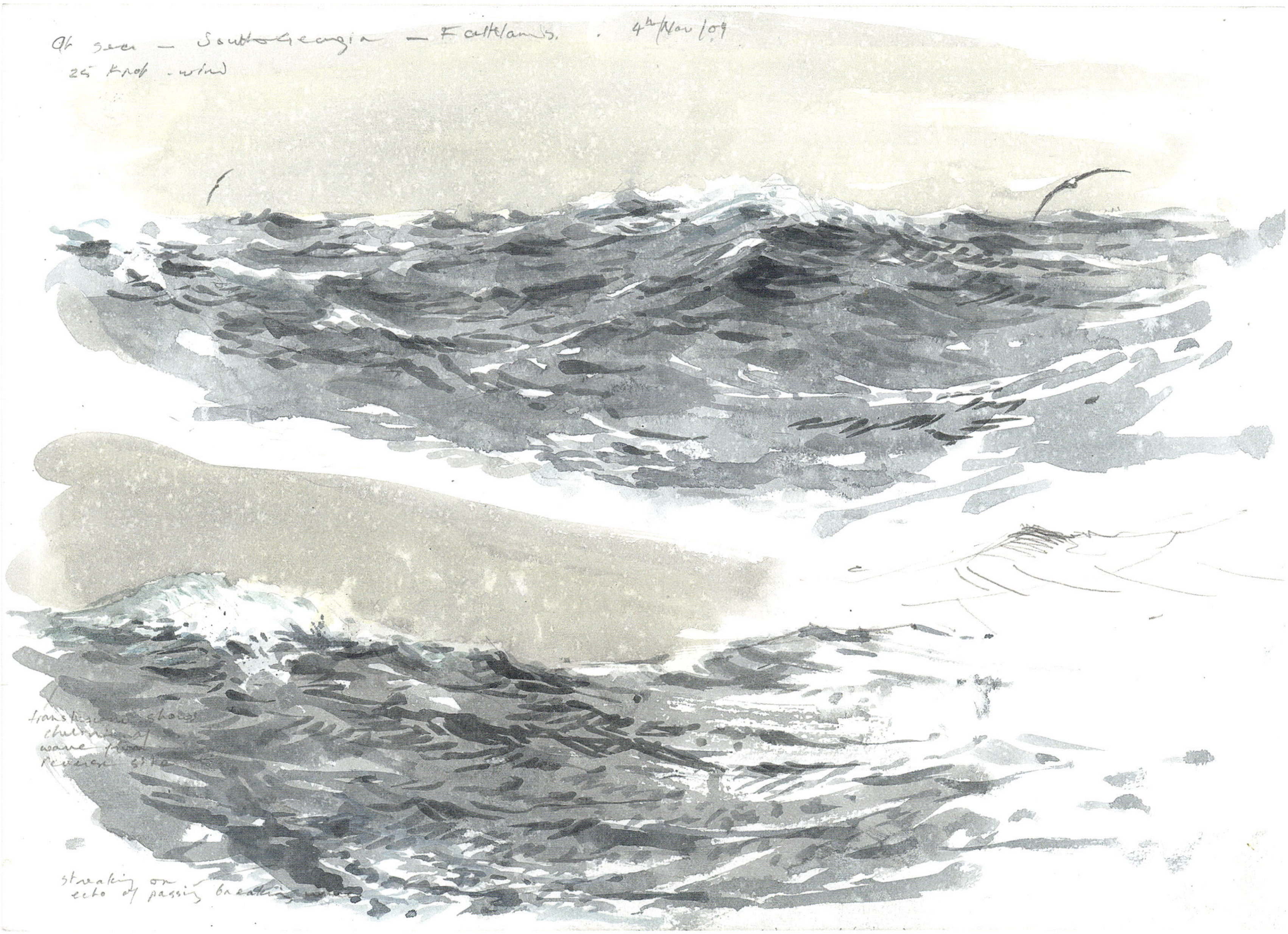

diving out of sight again. And there were blue, giant, and white-chinned petrels, as well as Wilson's storm-petrels among the abundance of birds. And lastly, the occasional massive form of a wandering albatross cut through them all, riding the wind like a huge white cross drifting through the sea spray and rain.

If there was excitement in witnessing the magnificence of the birdlife and seascape surrounding us, there was also a tremendous sense of excitement about the adventure ahead and the tasks we had to complete over the coming months on Bird Island. The feeding ecology and other studies that Pete was about to embark on were ambitious. Completing them would certainly be great fun and a tremendous adventure, but the significance of the outcomes would not be realised for a good few years.

35 At sea between South Georgia and Falkland Islands, November, 2009
30 × 42 cm · watercolour and pencil

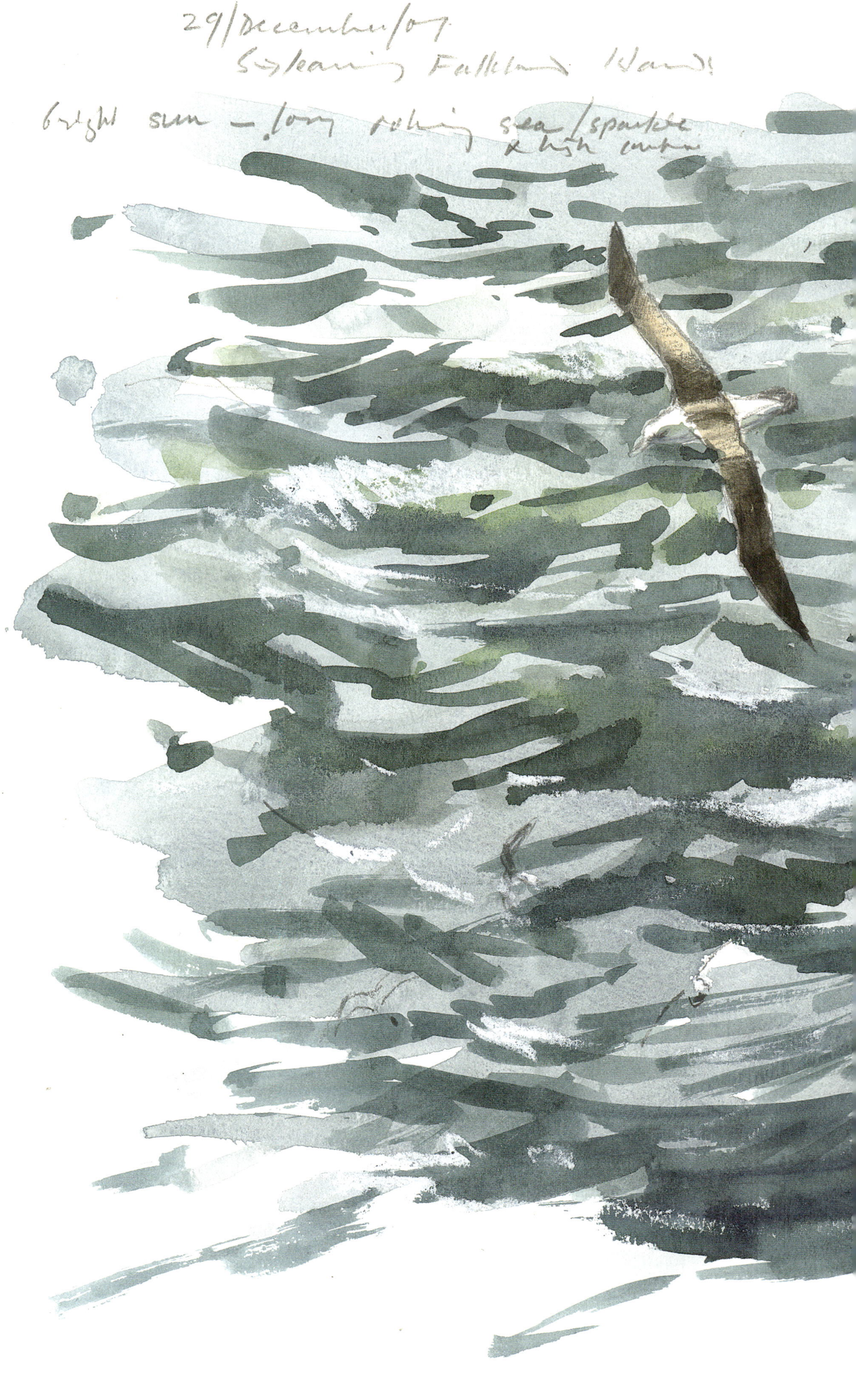

36 Black-browed albatross at sea, the Southern Ocean, December, 2007
30 × 42 cm · watercolour and pencil

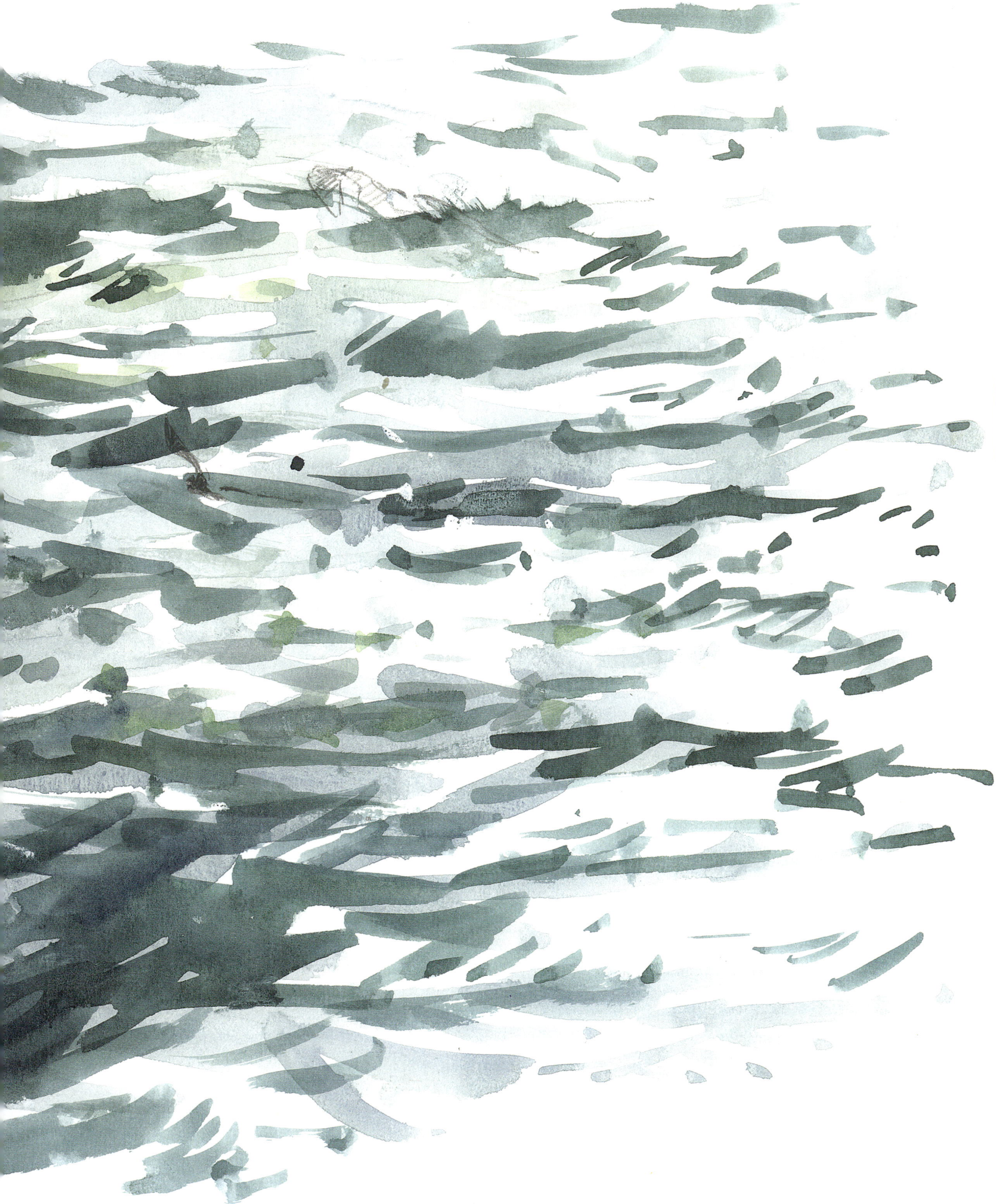

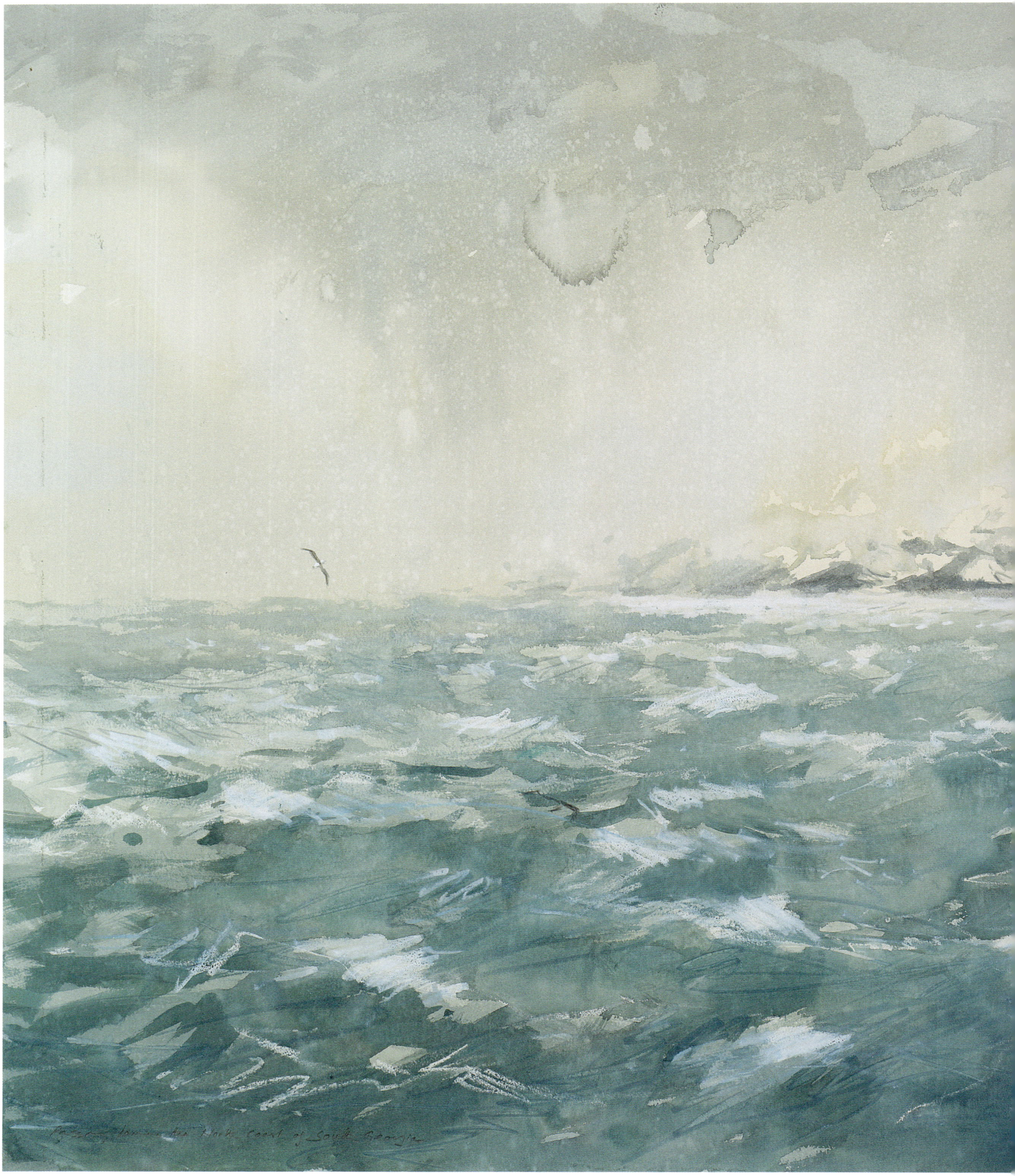

37 At sea off South Georgia, December 2008
86 × 152 cm · watercolour / mixed media

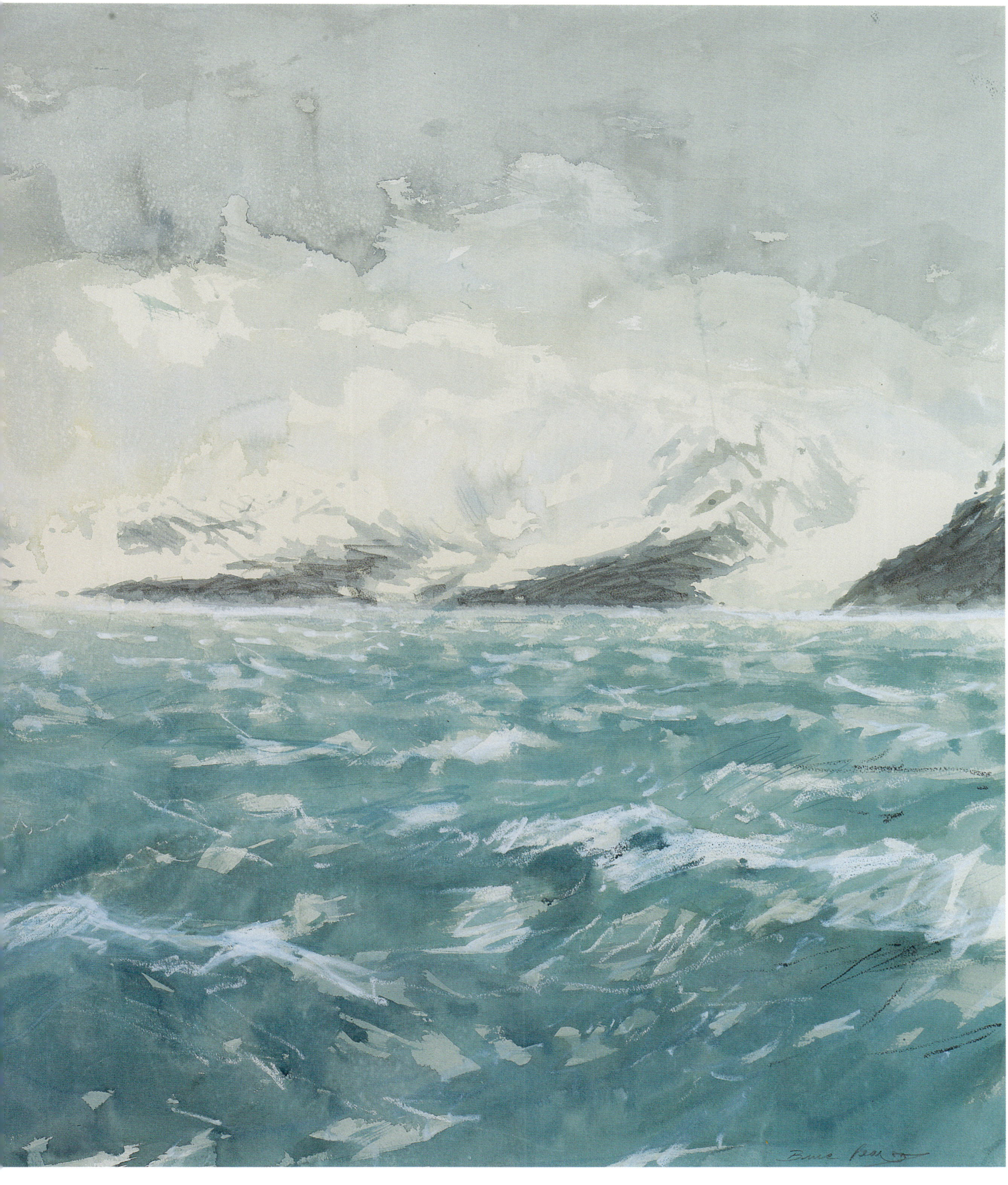

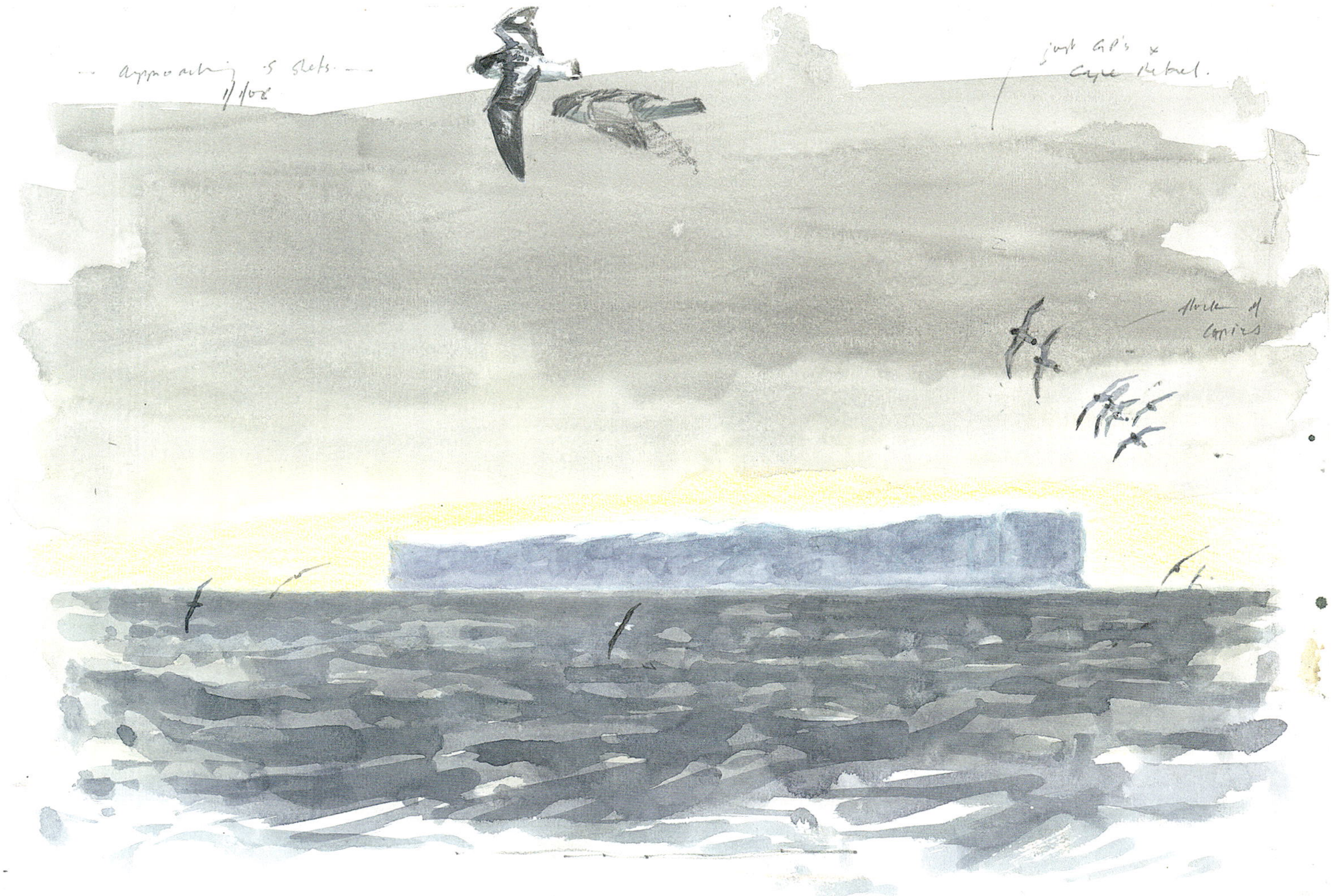

38 Tabular iceberg and cape pigeons, Southern Ocean, January, 2008
30 × 42 cm · watercolour and pencil

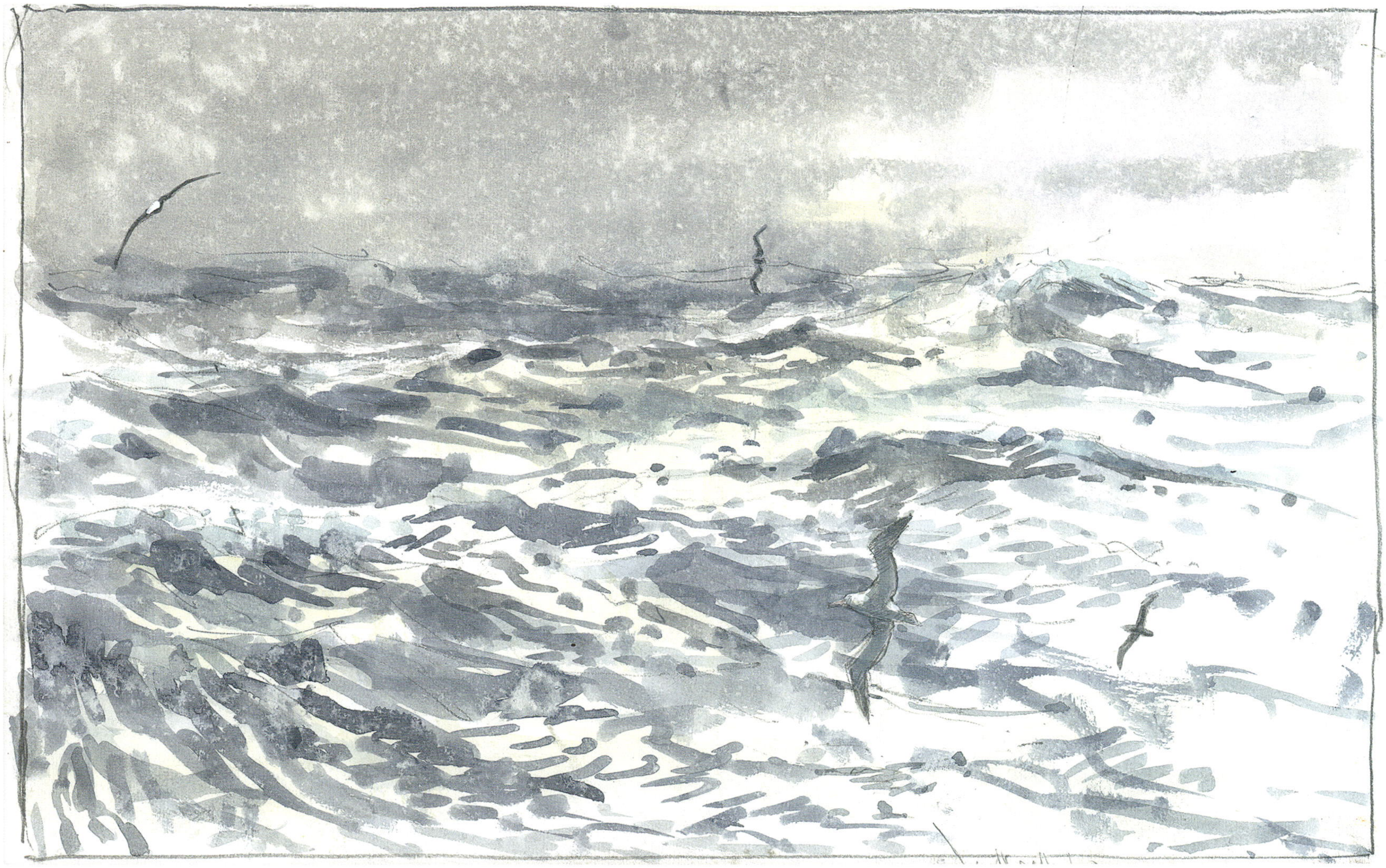

39 The Southern Ocean north of South Georgia, 22nd September, 2007
30 × 42 cm · watercolour and pencil

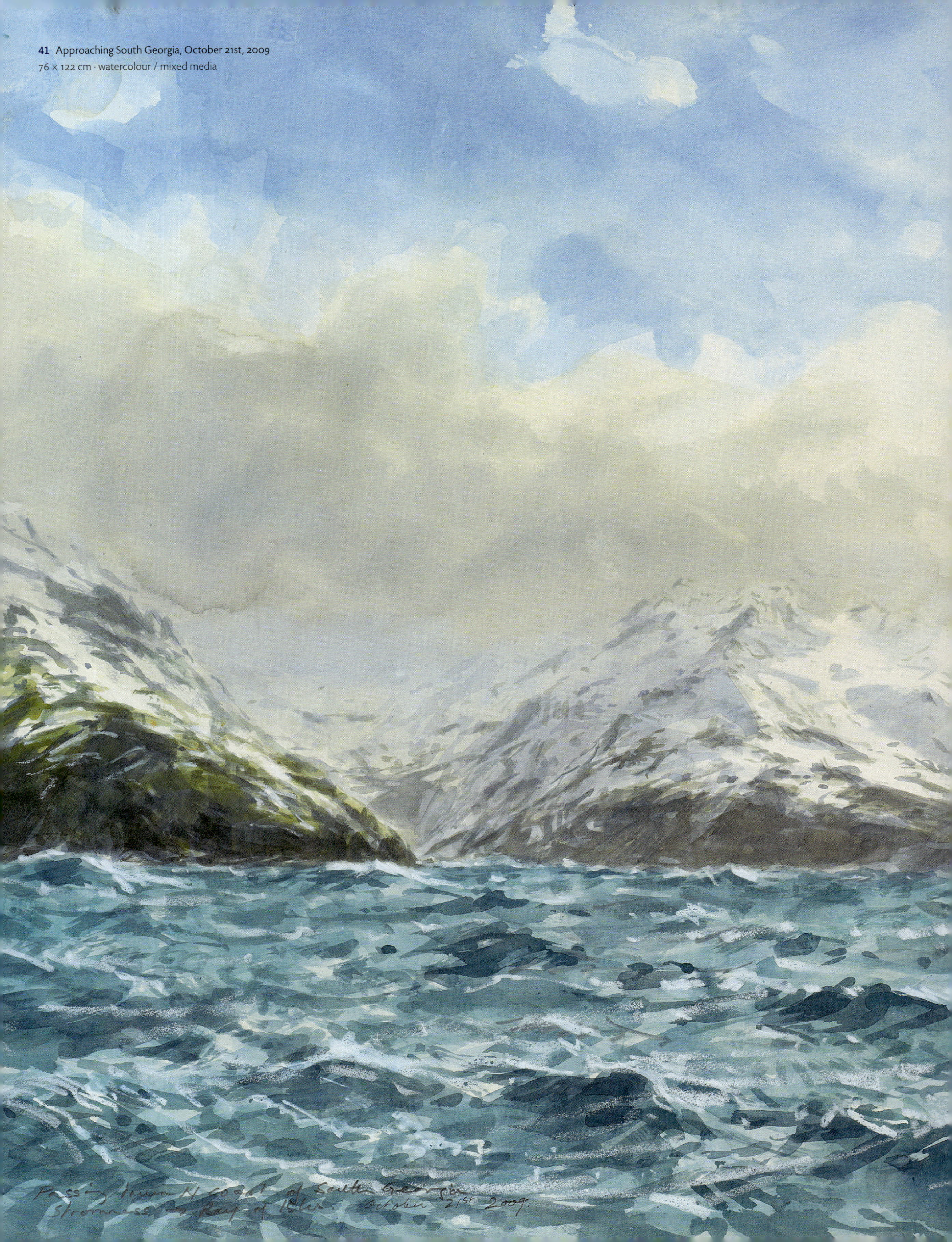

41 Approaching South Georgia, October 21st, 2009
76 × 122 cm · watercolour / mixed media

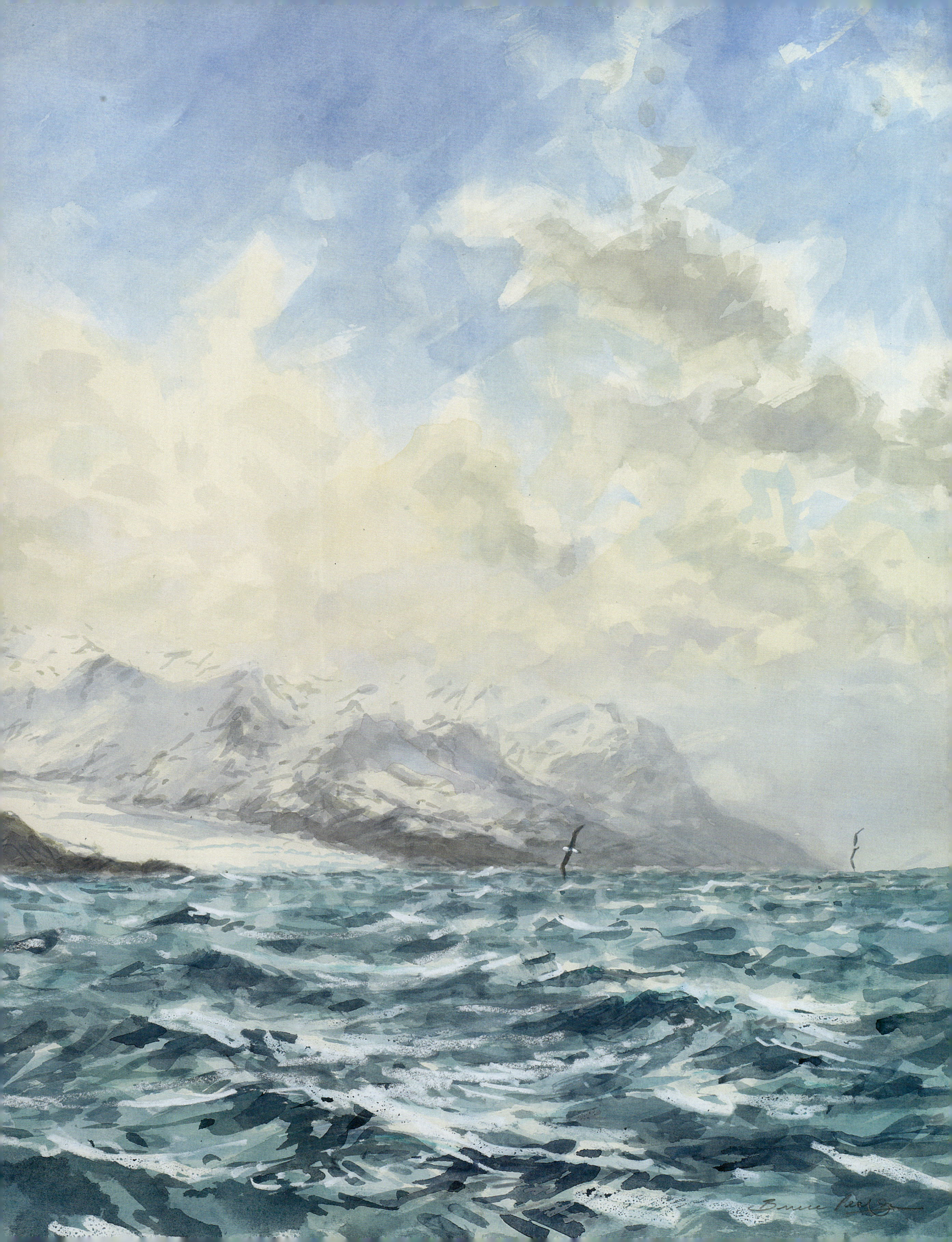

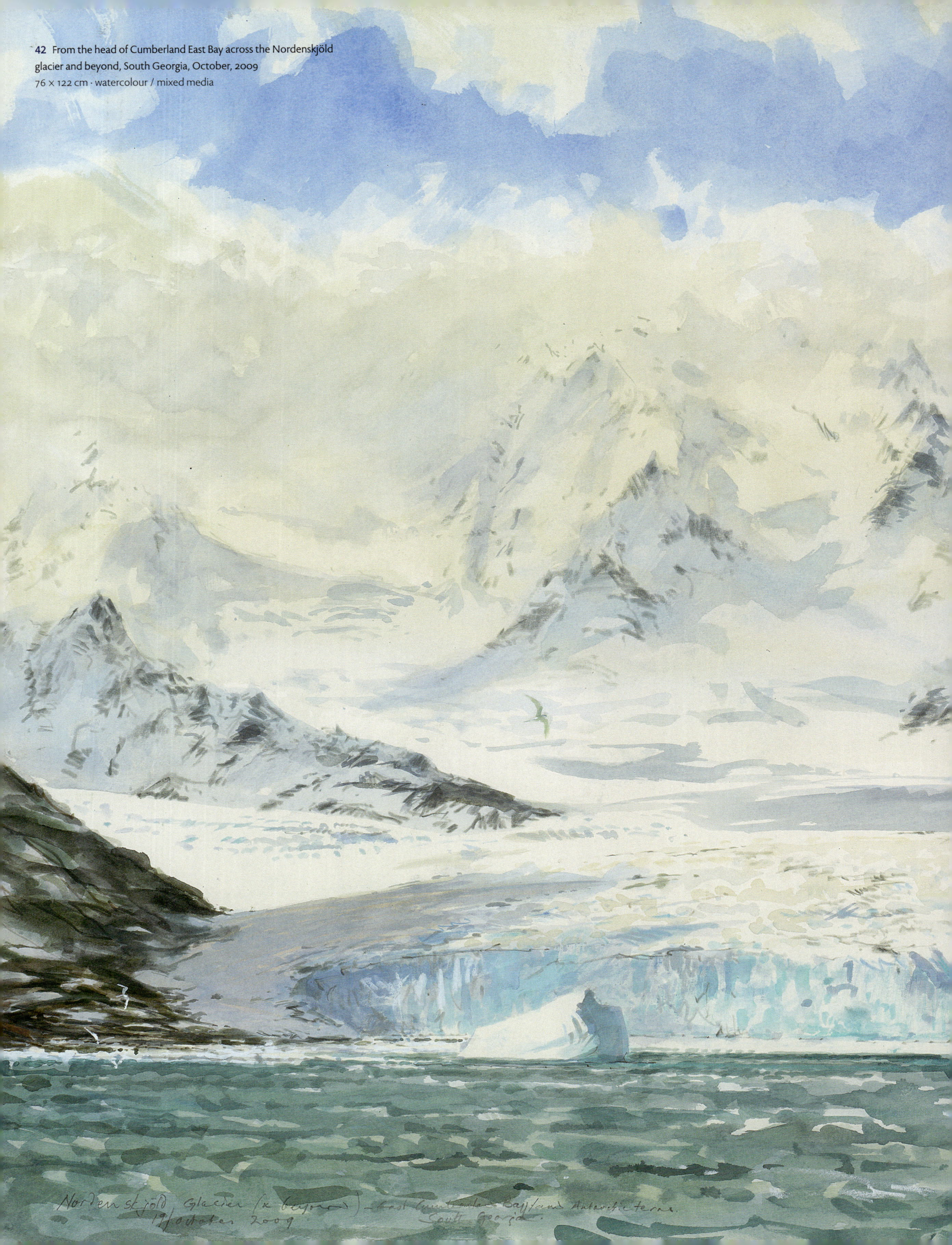

42 From the head of Cumberland East Bay across the Nordenskjöld glacier and beyond, South Georgia, October, 2009
76 × 122 cm · watercolour / mixed media

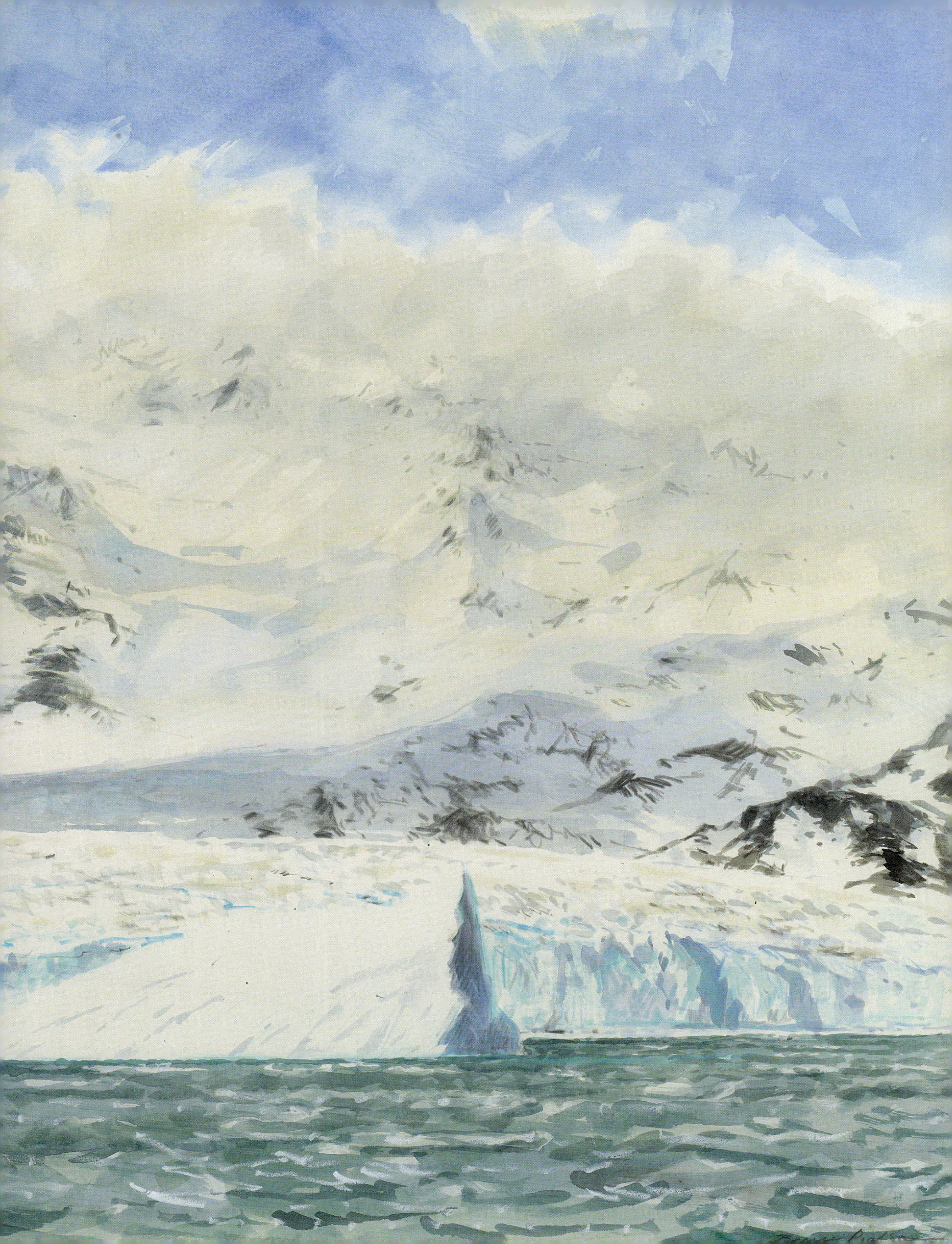

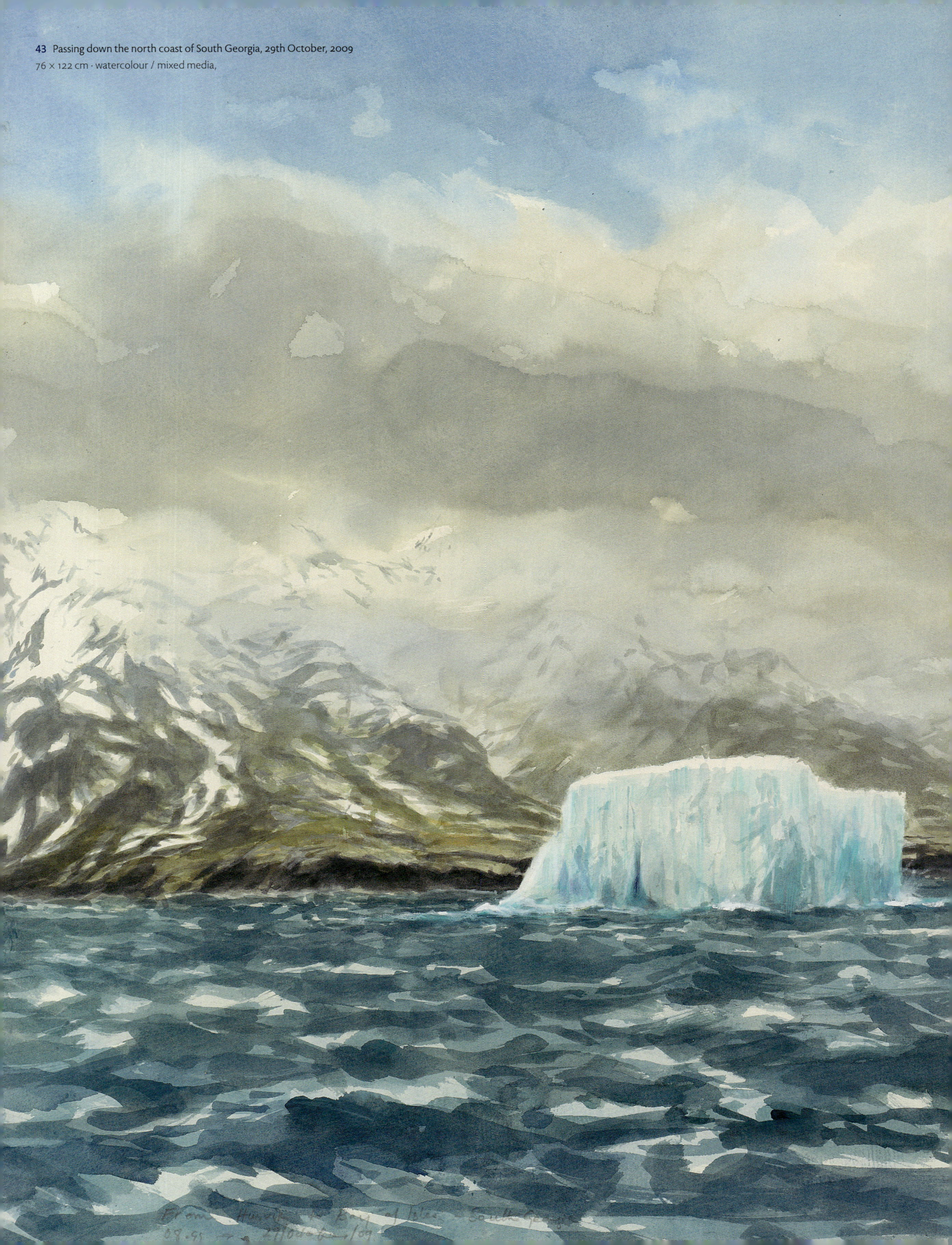

43 Passing down the north coast of South Georgia, 29th October, 2009
76 × 122 cm · watercolour / mixed media,

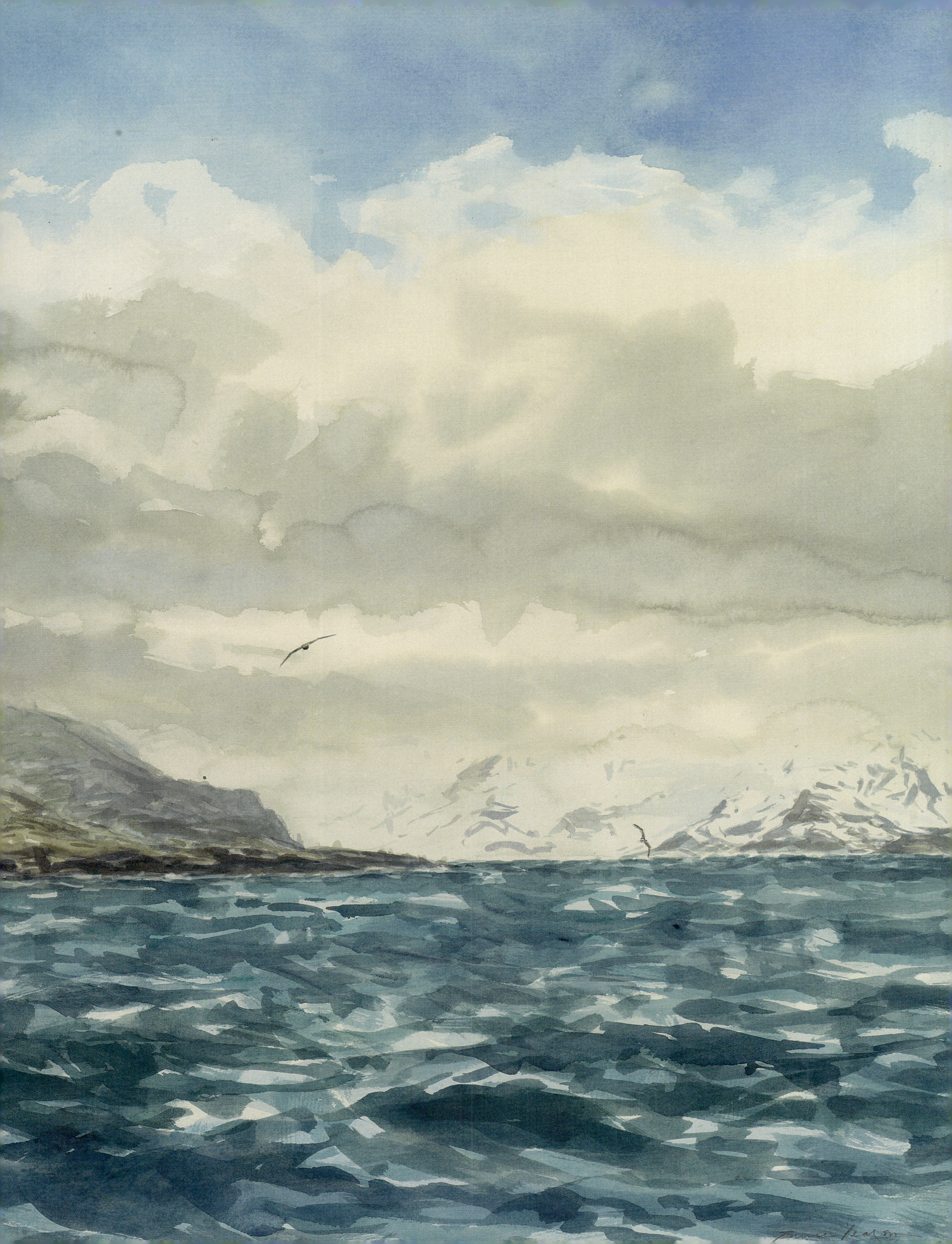

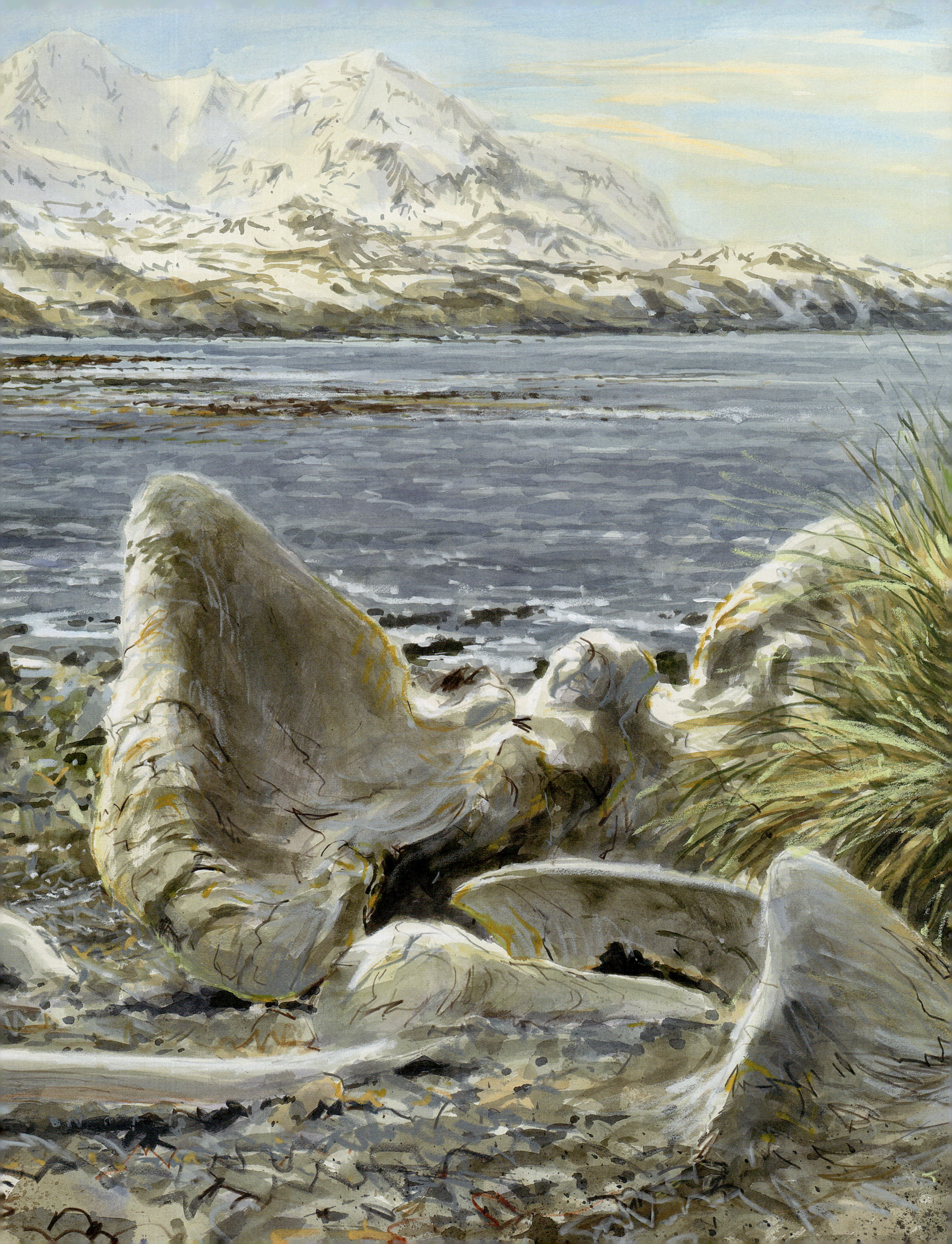

CHAPTER 4

Bird island summers

44 Whale bones, South Georgia, 2011 (detail)

On the morning of 14th January 1775 midshipman Thomas Willis on board HMS *Resolution* sighted what he thought was a large iceberg. The ship, commanded by Captain James Cook, was in waters close to where we are now, and on a voyage in search of Terra Australis Incognita, the southern continent long-imagined to lie at these latitudes, or far beyond.

It turned out that Cook and his crew were not approaching an iceberg but land. Passing on its northern side Cook named it for his midshipman, Willis's Island. Just beyond lay another smaller island and 'On account of the vast numbers that were upon it', Cook called it Bird Island. Then, across a narrow stretch of water, they found a much larger landmass with icy peaks and glaciers stretching over the horizon down to the south east. Sailing its northern shore, Cook landed two days later to claim the land for the British Crown, naming it Isle of South Georgia. He pushed on, mapping the coast, and rounding a cape at the southern end, realised that it was only a large island and not the hoped for Terra Australis Incognita; he named the point Cape Disappointment. Cook's Antarctic voyage remains one of the greatest voyages of exploration and discovery – and it put Bird Island on the map.

South Georgia is a crescent-shaped island about 170km long and 2–40 km wide and lies on the Scotia Arc, a mountainous ridge beneath the Southern Ocean that links South America with the Antarctic Peninsula. Half the island's area is a spine of ice-covered mountains and permanent snow surrounded by ice-fields. Huge glaciers spill into fjords and push their snouts into the sea; others terminate on land with plains of debris fanning from their ice fronts. At the south-eastern end the ice-sheet and jagged peaks and pinnacles drop almost vertically to the sea. The northern coast is a mosaic of deep fjords, bays, pools and lakes, and flatter ground creating a less forbidding landscape dominated by tussock grass.

After the weeks at sea my eyes were becoming well tuned to the subtlety of colours the ocean throws up and the dramatic light and ever-changing patterns the winds create on the water. And I was now familiar with the different characteristics and 'jizz' of the many species we had encountered. Then I became aware of something else – a faint fishy and slightly acidic tang carried on the wind. It was, I learned, the smell of seabirds, penguins and seal beaches. Dead ahead into wind were the Willis Islands, with Bird Island beyond, and farther on the icy peaks of South Georgia were showing between the clouds of an early November morning.

Bird Island loomed close ahead and we hove-to at the mouth of Bird Sound, a narrow stretch of water separating us from South Georgia. Directly in front spectacular rock platforms rose above the beach. Above them, green tussock meadows and mounds were layered below the scree and steep rocky slopes of the hills. From a distance it looked as if every square metre of ground was filled with life – seals, penguins, and albatrosses. The slopes and cliffs were dusted thickly with mollymauk albatross colonies, the upper meadows flecked with the white of wanderers, and the beaches below covered with fur

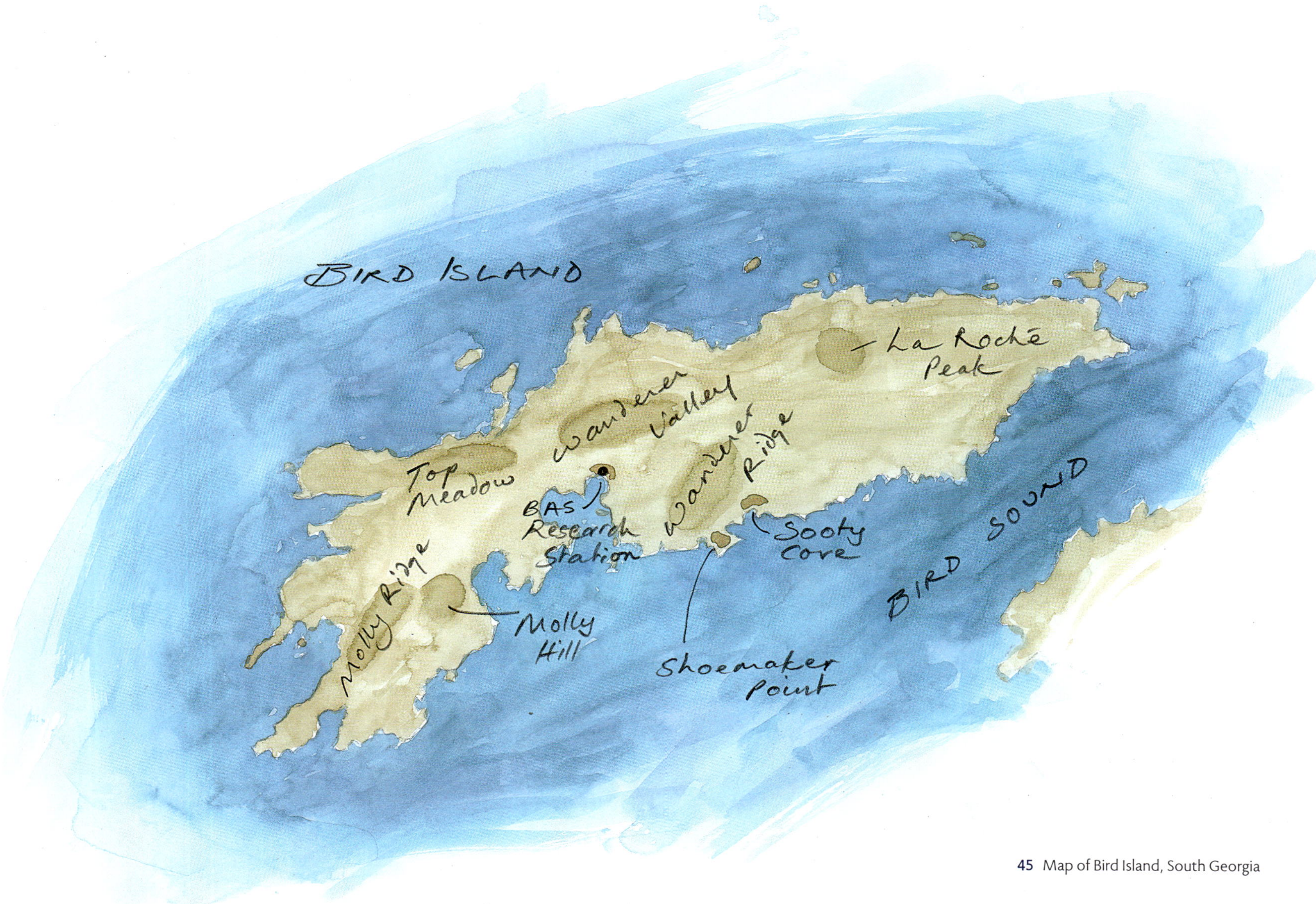

45 Map of Bird Island, South Georgia

seals interspersed with a few pods of elephant seals. And above it all swept skuas and giant petrels, and it took quite a while to absorb what was an awesome sight. We had arrived at one of the world's greatest wildlife spectacles, and knowing this would be our home for the austral summer months for the next three years, it was a tremendously exciting prospect.

Within hours, and with the help of the crew of the RRS *John Biscoe*, we had all the crates, boxes, bundled hardware and fuel drums carried ashore and manhandled up the beach. The garden shed where Nigel Bonner lived in the mid-1950s took care of long-term storage and emergency food supplies. Along a slatted walkway towards the back of the beach, there was a small generator shed and workshop and the fuel drums were stacked alongside.

The main hut, Lönnberg House, took just about everything else. Oil-skins, 'bodgers', boots and jackets in an outer porch; crates of tinned foods, boxes of dried goods, drums of flour, rice and milk powder, bottles and jars of preserves and sauces. All were stacked inside the entrance and walled in by columns of cigarette cartons, tins of pipe tobacco, and crates of beer, whisky, gin and rum. They were issued because the supply of a remote all-male outpost was based on Royal Navy principles and the notion of daily tobacco and rum rations still lingered. Further in, work benches were crammed with research kit, notebooks, ringing equipment, files and the general clutter of a laboratory enclosed by cabinets, shelves, racks and drawers

Half-way down the hut a Rayburn stove was the centrepiece of the kitchen area and the reason for unloading over 200 sacks of anthracite. The tap at the sink was connected to a hosepipe that followed a stream up the hill to a large funnel in a pool behind a small dam. Beyond the kitchen area were bookshelves forming a wall to frame the sleeping quarters; bunks top and bottom and either side, with a dining table made of old packing crates in between.

The windows on one side looked out towards the rising tussock and scree slopes of La Roché peak. The other side faced south with views across Jordan Cove and the seal beaches towards Round How and beyond. Lönnberg House had the look and feel of a large bedsit bolted to a turn-of-the-century expedition hut and inhabited by a small crew of wild adventurers. But we kept it clean with a robust weekly 'scrub-out' and piling tins and other rubbish into empty fuel drums to go out on the ship. It was extremely comfortable and warm and we had almost everything we needed – a fortunate situation given our ship would not be back for five months, when it was time to go home.

There is a daily rhythm to the lives of the birds and seals throughout the short sub-Antarctic summer months and our own routines and rhythms quickly slipped into a pattern that had to synchronise with theirs. No point in setting up an hourly weighing routine in an albatross colony and then requesting everyone assemble at 6pm for dinner!

Once we had settled in, our first task was to ring all the wandering albatross chicks within the first couple of weeks because we had to catch them before they fledged and left the island. Wanderers have one of the longest breeding cycles of any bird. Eggs are laid over a period of five weeks during December and January and most eggs hatch in March. At the end of their first summer – as the first heavy snows of winter settle on the island – chicks are left for the next five months or so sitting in solitary splendour on their icy thrones, sometimes partially buried by drifting snow. Every few days one of their parents will return to feed its offspring. They are away at sea on trips of thousands of kilometres to catch food for themselves and their young, reaching the seas off Uruguay and southern Brazil.

Protected by a dense coat of pale grey down and a thick layer of fat the chick grows well through the winter gaining about 500gms each week. By the time we arrived in November, at the end of the southern winter, the young birds, almost a year old, would be a third heavier than their parents and just about ready to fly. First they have to slim down to become airborne. So there is a short period from mid-November to mid-December when

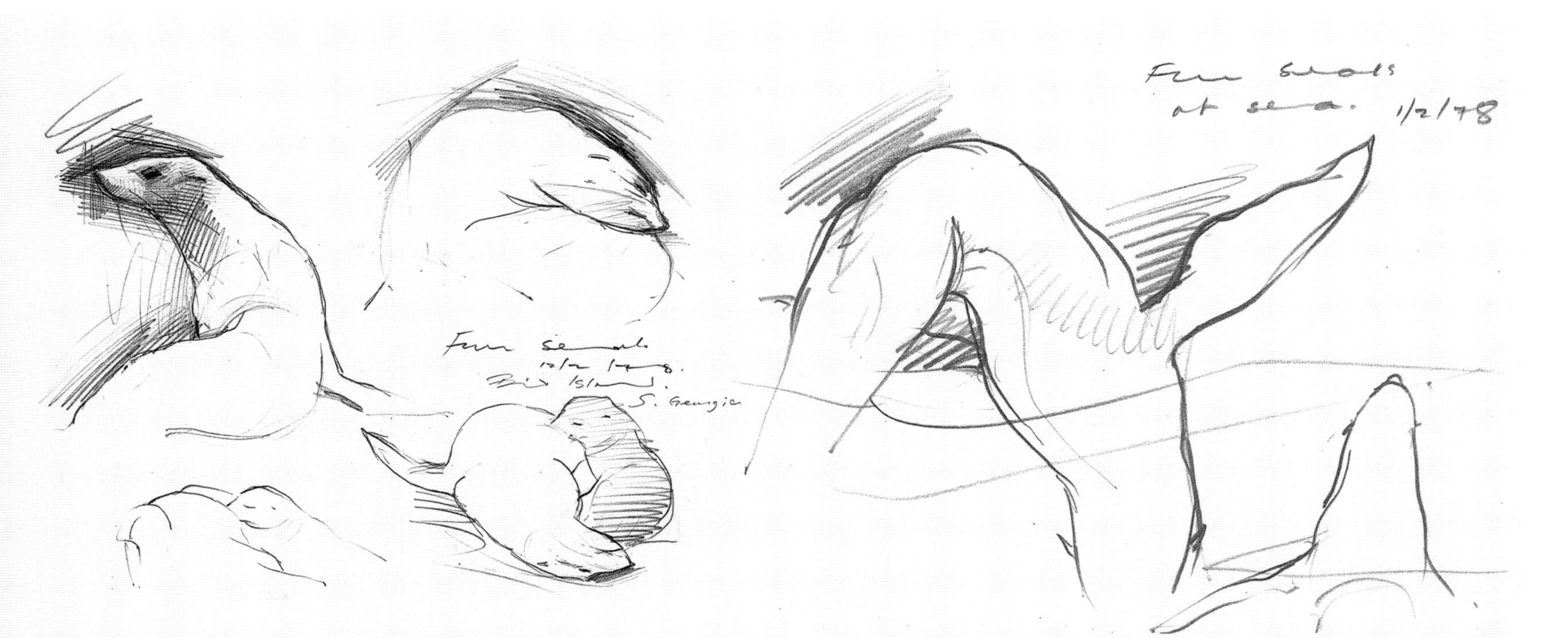

FUR SEALS

In 1786, a little over a decade after Captain James Cook published his finding of abundant fur seals on South Georgia the first sealers arrived to hunt them. In less than 50 years an estimated 1.2 million fur seal pelts had been taken and the species was commercially, and very nearly biologically, extinct. Only a few animals survived on outlying islands, including Bird Island, but this was enough to begin natural re-colonization when hunting pressure was lifted.

Fur seals feed mainly on krill, but also eat fish and occasionally kill and eat penguins. Their numbers have recovered dramatically in the late 20th century, due partly it is believed, to the removal of competition from the krill-eating whales. The Antarctic fur seal has gone from being one of the rarest large wild mammals to one of the most abundant on the planet.

46 Fur seals, Bird Island, 1978
30 × 42 cm · pencil

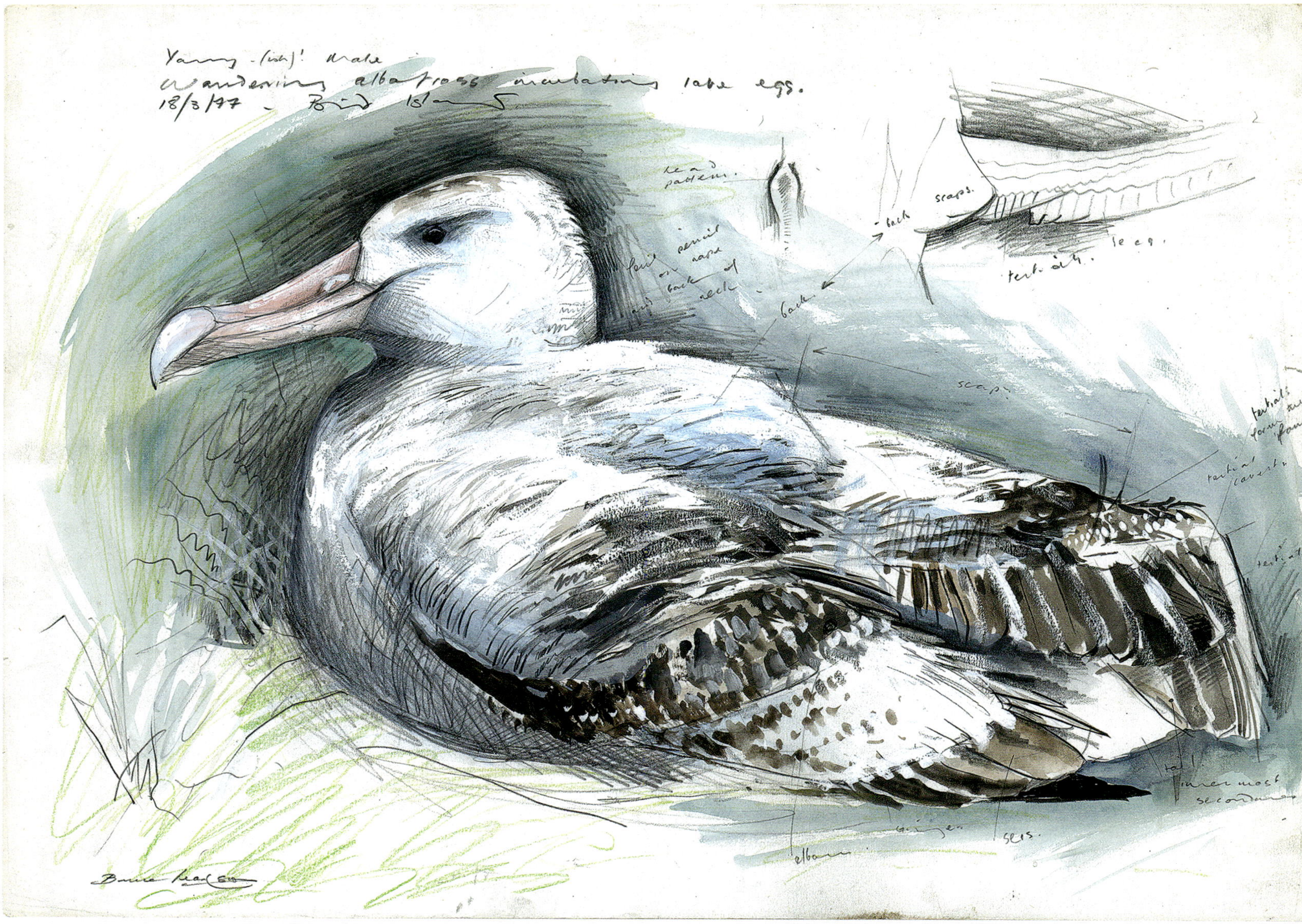

WANDERING ALBATROSS ON THE NEST

Both sexes help build the shallow conical nest of compacted vegetation and soil. The male typically gathers the nest material and the female does most of the building. After mating, the female goes to sea for a few weeks to feed before returning to lay a single egg between late December and early January. Having been incubated by both parents, the large egg hatches in early March or April – around 78 days after it was laid. The chick is brooded in turn by both adults for the first month or so, with each parent staying with it for 3–4 days while the other heads out to sea to feed.

47 Wandering albatross, adult incubating, Bird Island, 1977
42 × 60 cm · watercolour and mixed media

young wanderers are waiting to leave the island. They like to remain close to their own nests, a factor which makes them much easier to locate and ring.

Each day we would head for a different part of the island; up Wanderer Valley round the flanks of La Roché onto Wanderer Ridge and out towards the north-eastern end; or a trek up North Valley onto Top Meadow; then across Molly Meadow down towards the peninsulas at the south-western end of the island. With each of us equipped with a bag of ringing kit we spread out like a ground force of troops, sweeping between the tussocks and around the open areas of ground to make sure we accounted for every chick.

But it was not just young wanderers on the island during the first few weeks of early summer, there were plenty of adults too. Sometimes a parent still sat with its chick, perhaps having presented a last meal and simply unable to tear itself away from the site or young bird. Some might have been failed breeders that could have lost an egg, chick, or breeding partner at some stage but still returned to the nest. And there were a range of non-breeders; young birds not yet mated, possibly returning for the first time after their early years learning to survive at sea; and also gatherings of older birds about to start their long breeding cycle.

Like all albatrosses, wanderers form long-term bonds and remain faithful to both their mate and nest site throughout their adult life. Having invested an average of 350 days from egg-laying to fledging, parent wanderers do not have enough time to replenish their food reserves and breed again immediately, and only nest in alternate years if they are successful. As a result, adults at the end of their breeding, with chicks about to fledge, mingle in the colonies with newly-arrived birds that are about to start mating and laying eggs.

Established pairs arrive on the island from the end of November. The first are mostly older males that spend most of their time close to their nest, and they are followed by increasing numbers of females locating their mates. Paired birds only occasionally perform the full courtship display, reaffirming the pair bond through stylized rituals that are both intimate and serene. Unpaired and inexperienced birds solicit the company of others and gather on the higher flatter ground where the tussock gives way to lawns, mossy banks and shallow pools; perhaps just two or three individuals but sometimes up to six or eight birds. There the young wanderers perform elaborate courtship displays which involve a series of visual and vocal moves that they know by instinct, but must learn how to perform in the right sequence. Lasting anything up to 15 minutes, the display has been well studied and every behavioural element analysed and named:

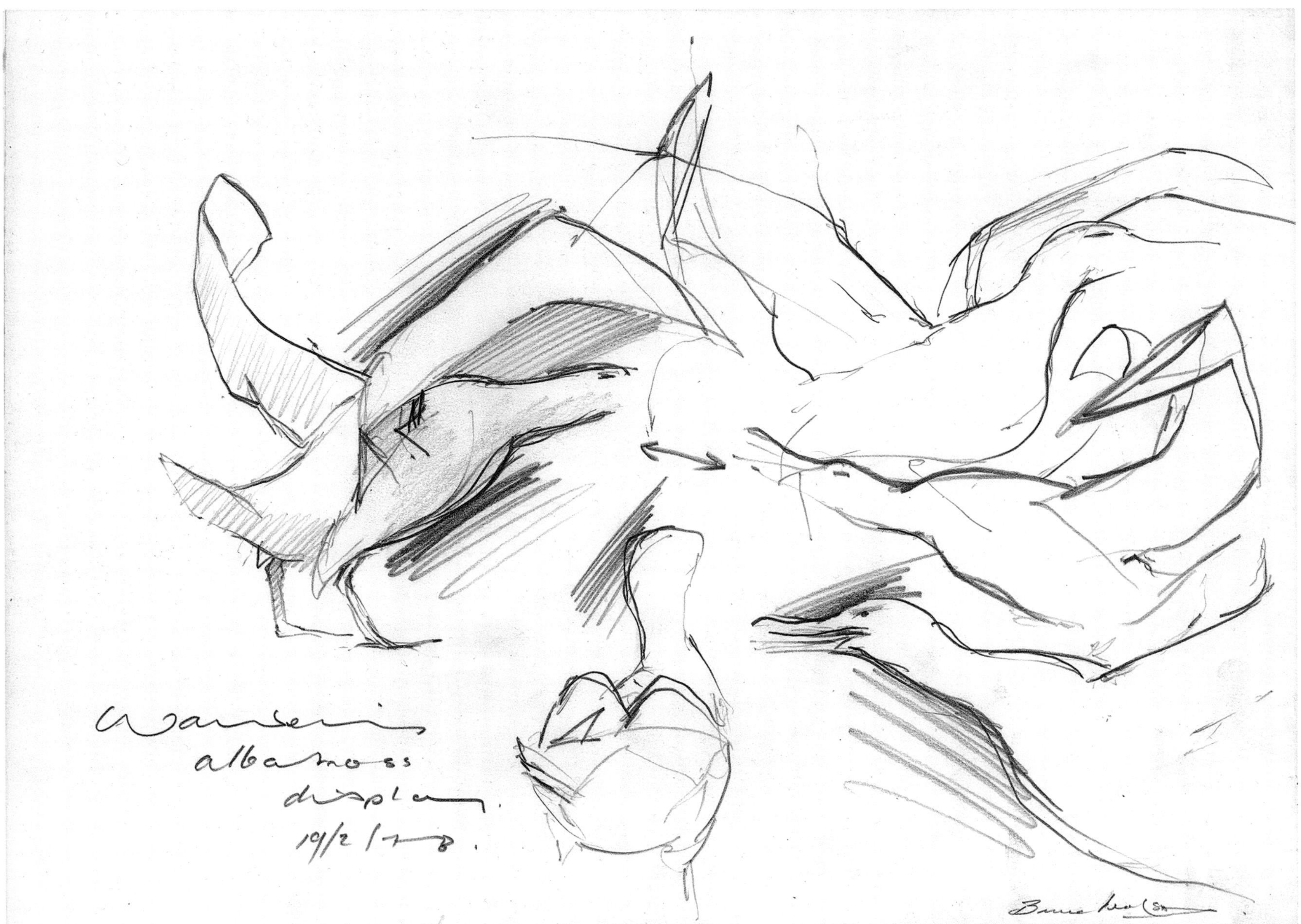

48 Wandering albatross display, Bird Island, 1978
30 × 42 cm · pencil,

allo-preening, head-rolling, bowing, sky-pointing, flagging, yammering, rattling, side-preening, flagging, and snapping. Whatever the scientific definitions, however, reaffirmation of the bond between wandering albatrosses, is one of the most beautiful and elaborate of all behavioural repertoires among birds. Coming upon a group in the throes of display always meant an opportunity to take a break and marvel.

A female walks forward, head down, and with slapping footfalls approaches her mate near the nest. She reaches forward, her head and neck quite rigid and the male responds similarly and adds a cork-popping, snapping sound before plunging his bill into the feathers on one side of the breast. They stand facing each other, bodies taut and heads held high, peering from side to side. Then the female reaches forward again, opens her wings, and snaps her bill towards the male. She swings her head down towards her feet briefly touching her lower breast then comes upright again before advancing towards him. Nearby, another younger female squats down, her head scanning the display ground. Beyond her, a male walks between tussocks at the edge of the arena, head down and nape hunched, his gait a slow head weaving plod.

Back at the centre of activities the male faces the female and rolls his head back, bill pointing skyward and with wings outstretched, squeals loudly. Still with wings spread, he reaches forward and down again, snapping his bill rapidly like the sound of sticks snapping. With wings closed but held taut, she moves forward with an exaggerated swaying walk, pushing him back. He pirouettes to keep facing her; with head back he points to the sky again and with a preliminary guttural croak arches his neck and shrieks. In the light of early evening, with shadows cast by their magnificent wing spans arching across the sculpted forms of their barrel-chested bodies – all set against a backdrop of rippling tussock and icebergs out to sea – there is a wonderfully theatrical touch to these performances.

The majority of display bouts end when the female walks away. That can happen at any time, in its full throes or as the rate of display decreases. Sometimes she follows the male back to his nest site; other times males walk back to their nest site after a display bout and begin yapping – a kind of gruff rasping sound with bill slightly open. If a female follows him, she might sit by the side of the nest watching and sometimes join in with the yapping. Bonded pairs might sit together, frequently stopping to preen each other, inclining their heads now and then and closing their eyes to facilitate the partner's gentle nibbling of lower cheek and throat.

I sat at the edge of a display making sketches. In a while there were birds close in and all around me. I could not move away easily since packing my kit would have disturbed the performance. So I kept still, gradually sliding down alongside my tussock stool to get out of the way. Wings reached over me and birds brushed past my sketchbook. For a brief moment it was like sitting awkwardly on-stage as the leading dancers and supporting chorus brought a dramatic play to a climax. Applause was fully deserved but, staying still and silent all I could hear was the blurry sound of distant seals barking and penguins braying, and the hiss of wind whipping through the tussock. And then there was a low-key encore from a yapping male wanderer on his nest 10 metres backstage.

Pete soon had the research programme established, and for black-browed and grey-headed albatrosses especially, he needed data on how frequently chicks were being fed, on how much food the parent birds were delivering each feed, and what was the food made up of? What was the rate of increase in body mass and wing length over the hours and days? To obtain information of that kind we had to set up a tented camp just below the colony so that birds could be handled and monitored frequently.

The tent was pitched on a level area below the colony's lower terraces and it gave us a front-door view of the natural world that was as magnificent as it was unique. Sitting on an upturned box at the entrance meant about 60 nests were in sight; the nearest about 5 metres away, the furthest along the skyline 20 metres above.

In the early days, regular weighing and measuring the birds and undertaking other tasks around the colony were usually lengthy two-man operations. As we visited each nest to weigh the chick, it would turn to face us, leaning back defensively, chopping noisily and threatening to spew up stomach oil. We would grab the bird clasping its wings against its body before lifting it onto the pan scales. Putting the chick back in the nest after weighing was simpler: reaching up and behind again and taking hold of the pan so the chick could be tipped back into the nest hollow sliding out of the pan like sugar off a spoon.

Later generations of Bird Islanders had it easy. The team at BAS developed ever-more sophisticated devices that weighed the birds automatically every few minutes

BLACK-BROWED ALBATROSSES

The black-browed albatross breeds annually in colonies on steep cliffs and slopes. The nest is a cone about size of an upturned bucket with a shallow depression in the top.

Black-brows feed mainly on krill, with some fish and squid. The exact diet depends on locality and time of year and reveals a unique bimodal foraging strategy. Incubating birds stay close to the colony and forage over the shallow shelf areas around South Georgia, but change to making trips up to 3,000km when feeding the chick later in the breeding season.

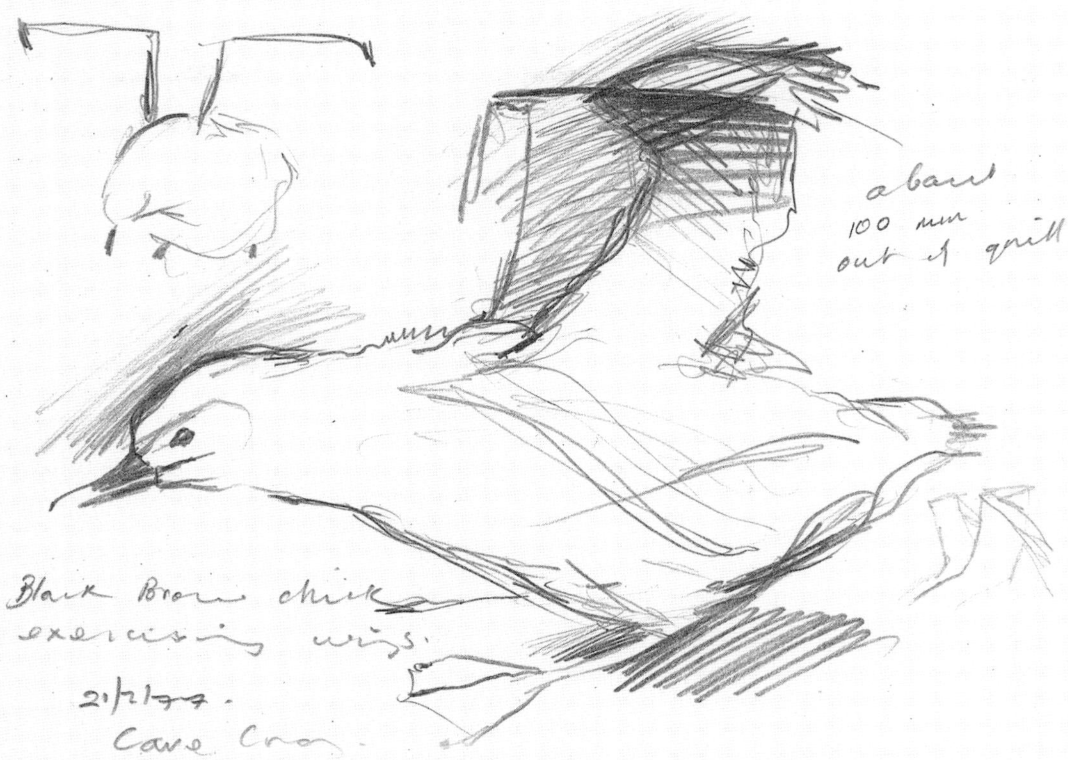

49 Black-browed albatross chick exercising, Bird Island, 1977
15 × 21 cm · pencil

over an entire breeding season. The researchers were now 'machine minders' who visited the colony every few days to collect and replace the 'black boxes' containing all the data.

Catching the weight of a feed was much more difficult and needed a race up the slippery slopes between wet tussock mounds and nests. The aim was to weigh the chick just before a feed and again immediately afterwards. Returning adults land, and with obvious intent, plod their way towards their nests, pausing occasionally with their heads down. On recognizing its parent, a chick starts to call with a grunting mew that grows more intense as the adult gets closer. Immediately the chick starts nibbling and tapping its parent's bill. The begging culminates in the adult lowering its head and extending its throat, and pausing briefly between three or four convulsions, spilling a feed into the begging gape of the chick.

We also needed to know the constituents of a feed – fish, krill, squid, or an oily soup? Such information could only come from catching returning adults just before they delivered the meal and getting them to regurgitate it into a polythene bag. We waited a few metres from the nest, watching while the adult was solicited noisily by the chick. As the feed was about to begin we reached behind the adult's neck with the 'bodger' and, pulling it forward, quickly threw an arm over it and hugged it to secure the wings. Leaning forward and holding the head over the gaping funnel with the sample bag clipped to the downpipe, the bird's natural defence when threatened is to regurgitate and meant a warm, brownish-pink, lumpy broth with a skim of deep orange oil was quickly in the bag. The smell wasn't pungent, more a waxy, oddly sweet mustiness, like an overwhelming scent of massed wild flowers. It tainted every nest, burrow chamber, egg, chick, and adult, and perfumed every fibre of our clothing, while spillages seemed to cover every piece of equipment – including our notepads and sketchbooks.

To someone looking on from the outside, aspects of the daily handling of the birds and collecting samples might have seemed a little rough at times. We always treated the albatrosses as gently as possible and firm action to immobilize a bird was invariably safer than letting it struggle and flap. For the scientific objectives, handling was essential to ensure the data could contribute to a better understanding of the birds' ecology. This would be crucial when the threats to seabirds increased significantly in later years. For me, it was simply a privilege and unrivalled opportunity beyond anything I could ever have imagined.

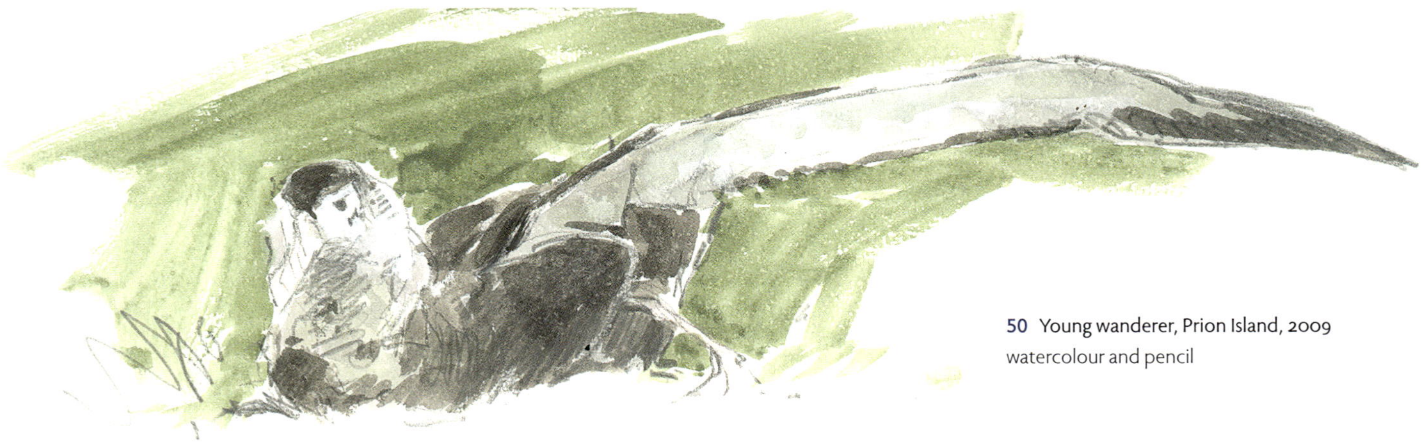

50 Young wanderer, Prion Island, 2009
watercolour and pencil

Being able to look into the eye of an albatross, feel the extraordinarily softness of the feathering around the head and belly, to fold in the 3.4 metre wingspan of a wanderer, catch the oily-scented mustiness and note their every move: these were extraordinarily exciting experiences. It was that intimacy and close-up witness of the character of the wildlife that I was desperate to convey in my paintings and drawings. I became determined that just portraying the surface detail of the subject would never be enough; there was an emotional attachment and excitement about the natural world that had to be included as well.

Albatrosses are the epitome of elegance on the wing, so a good place to sit and draw the mechanics of bird flight was the cliff-edge of a mollymauk colony. I would find a place out of the wind, but where a strong cross-light perfectly illuminated the movement of flight feathers and body plumage as crowds of birds loafed around in the up-draughts. The birds would sweep by, before coming round again, to slow down and hang on the wind – even drifting back up the breeze; while twisting and turning in the turbulence with their wings and tail held at exaggerated angles.

When we went out at night, the air was filled with a constant chorus of multitudes of small seabirds calling from burrows under the tussock, under boulders on the hillside, and in peaty chambers on the seaward slopes. The soft dove-like purring of Antarctic prions came up from beneath our feet and was punctuated by chattering blue petrels and Wilson's storm-petrels. The harsher tones of South Georgia diving-petrels came from long burrows dug into fine scree on higher slopes; and white-chinned petrels at their burrow entrances gave the repeated rattling squeak – like an old-fashioned sewing machine – that earned them the name 'shoemaker'.

Every day of those three summer seasons on Bird Island was special. But some of the most dramatic and memorable days were in late December when the open areas of tussock and mossy breaks were busy with young wanderers trying to get airborne for the first time. Fat but shedding weight fast, the young birds will have been all but abandoned by their parents. They spend the time preening and sleeping. To strengthen their wings, they stand up, wobbling and flapping vigorously, and then slump down again, simply too heavy to break the bond with the home turf. Then, when the wind gatheres strength, they would flap hard and leap valiantly into the air, sometimes collapsing in a heap a few yards from the nest, sometimes making it down the runway to stand at the end staring out to sea, before turning to plod back up the slope to the familiar surrounds of their nest. Eventually the day comes when the wind catches their wings and they lift off and disappear out to sea.

But not all young wanderers make it successfully to lift-off and a life at sea. Some starve to death if the parents fail to feed them properly; some are abandoned when parent birds fail to return. Some injure themselves by crash-landing during practice flights. It was absolutely heart-breaking to see perhaps three or four young birds a year starved to a gaunt frame draped in wet matted down, or loosely trailing a twisted, broken and sometimes bloodied wing.

But most make it, and on one memorable occasion, I saw wanderer number 508–0292 take to the skies for the first time. The day began with low cloud dragging freezing squalls across the island, but by early afternoon it started to clear and the wind strengthened. On Top Meadow I watched as the young wanderer stood facing the wind. It held its wings out stiffly, turning slowly left and right as if gauging the wind. Leaning forward it began to beat hard and in a moment was aloft, wavering erratically a few metres above ground before a gust of

GREY-HEADED ALBATROSSES

The grey-headed albatross breeds only every two years in colonies on steep coastal slopes. If a pair manages to raise a chick successfully they will not breed in the following year, taking time off and covering huge distances, perhaps even circumnavigating the globe several times.

Birds return to the colonies between late September and early October and a single egg is laid soon after in a nest very similar to black-browed albatross. Incubation lasts for 72 days and chicks hatch by December, fledging from April to May. Once a chick heads out to sea for the first time it will not return to the colony for 6–7 years.

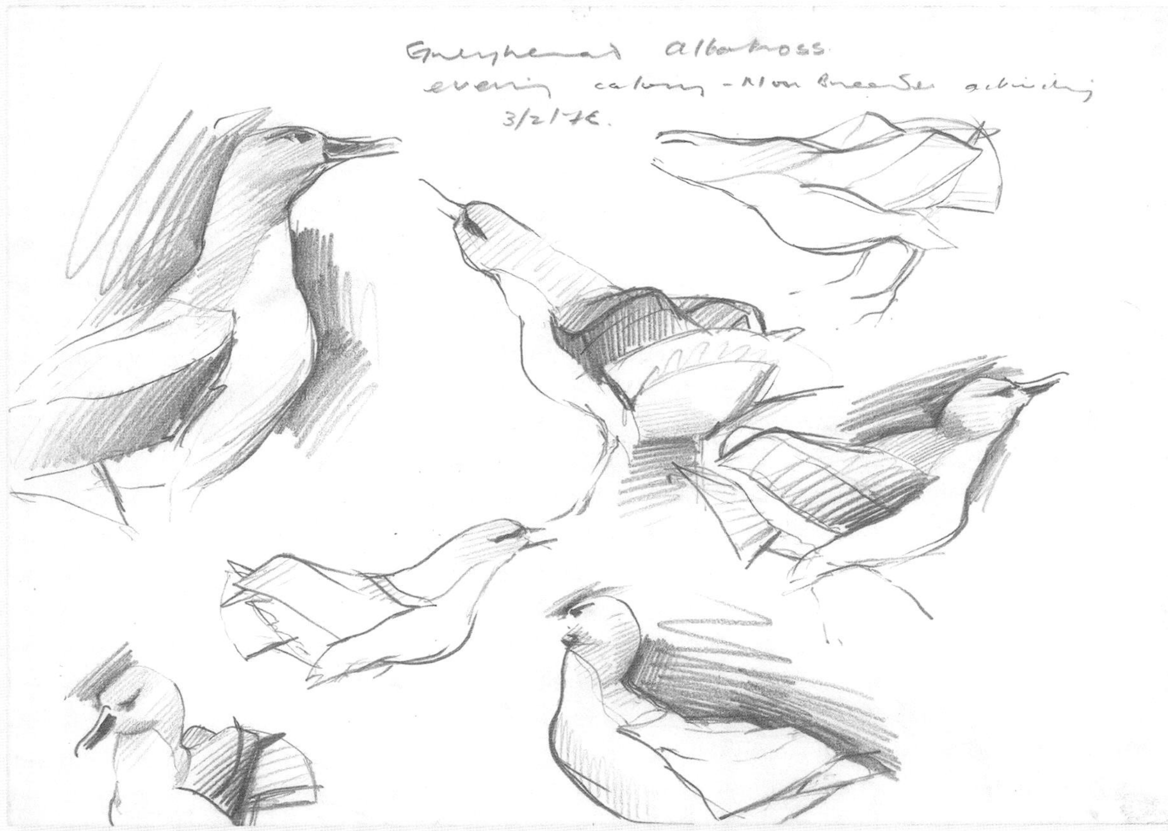

51 Grey-headed albatross, colony activity, Bird Island, 1978
34 × 48 cm · pencil

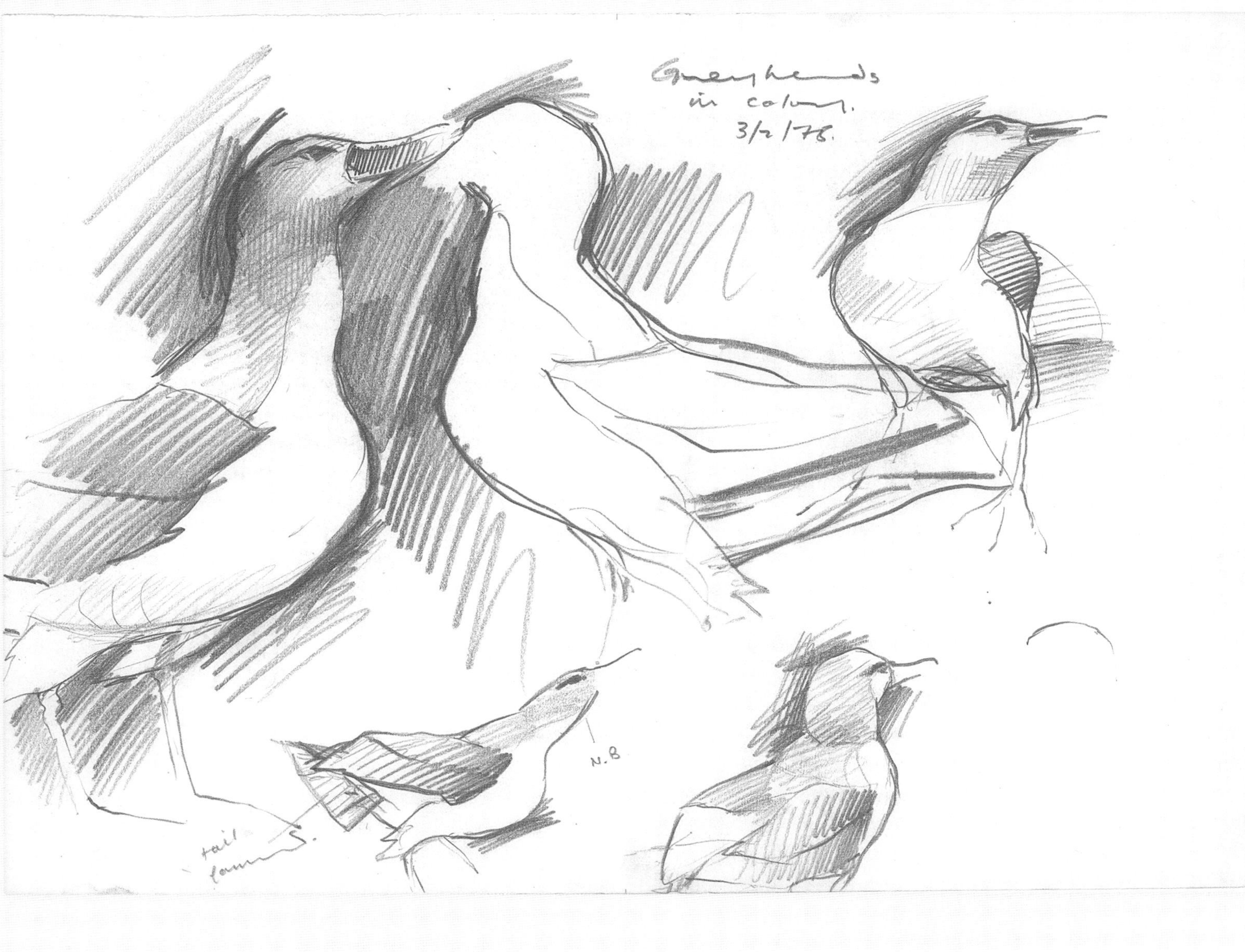

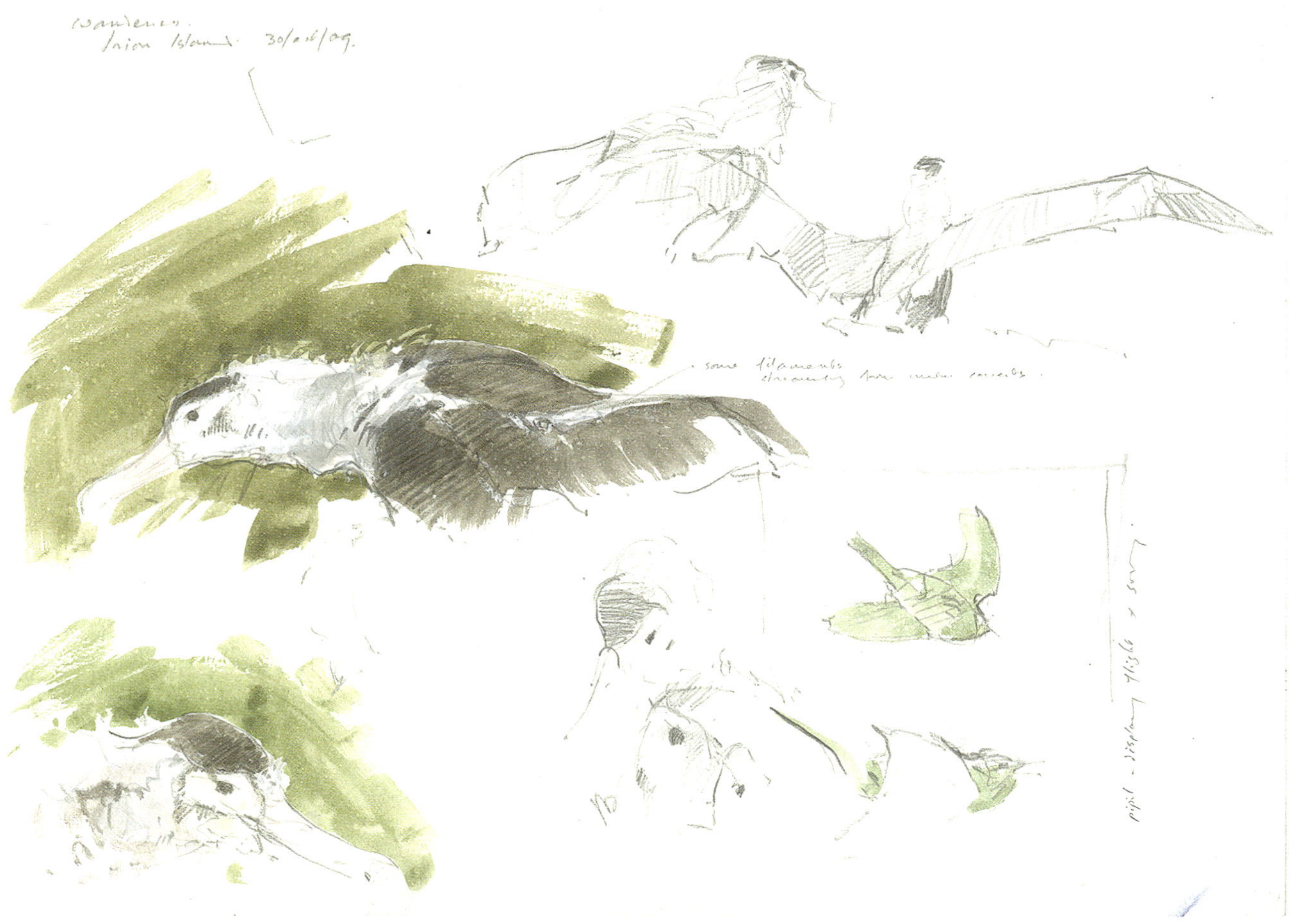

52 Young wanderer, Prion Island, 2009
30 × 42 cm · watercolour and pencil

wind caught it and it tumbled back to earth. In a while, another few bouts of flapping and stumbling glides brought it closer to the cliff edge.

I waited while it rested; and then it stood up again: its body tense and wings taut, its head swinging once more. Buffeted this way and that by the wind rippling the tussock along the cliff edge, it spread its vast span of wings, poised heraldically for a few moments, and then began to pump the air vigorously. In a moment it was airborne and moving forward, skimming the tussock and flapping hard. It seemed to hang crazily for a moment before the wind lifted it higher and higher and carried it down the slope. The bird disappeared out of sight below the cliff edge and I waited, breathless. A few seconds later it appeared again but now low down, moving fast out to sea alternately gliding and flapping erratically. Soon it was lost among the melée of birds quartering the sea. Was that the wind in my eyes making them water? More likely a fleck of wind-blown tussock, as I remember.

Wandering albatrosses are almost as long-lived as humans. Like us, they are slow to reach sexual maturity and take a long time to raise their offspring. The chicks are slow to grow-up. They have to learn how to forage, and must survive for nearly a decade or more before being recruited into the breeding population.

The maths are simple: there must be enough birds surviving into adulthood and then producing enough chicks to sustain the population. But over the past decade, the maths have not been working. The wandering albatross population on Bird Island has declined by 4–5% per year and even this seemingly modest annual decline over a long period can have alarming consequences. In the 35 years since I watched 508–0292 leave Bird Island, the wandering albatross population has almost halved. I am told that this season (2012) there are 1325 breeding pairs; the count my last summer (1977) was 2524 breeding pairs.

Black-browed and grey-headed albatrosses have suffered similar declines. All three albatrosses are now classed as globally threatened. Despite still appearing numerous, they face a high risk of extinction if current trends continue. The reasons why this catastrophic situation has arisen are all too apparent from recent discoveries made on Bird Island. Half of diet samples taken from wanderer chicks revealed that they had ingested fish hooks. The hooks, usually with bits of line attached, would have been lodged in discarded bait and offal picked up by parent birds when feeding around long-line fishing vessels and fed to chicks.

For the past three decades the work by the British Antarctic Survey on Bird Island has been at the forefront of research into seabird ecology and population studies, and has led the global efforts to reverse the downward trend towards extinction. But, very sadly, Pete Prince didn't live to see the enormous difference his work would make. He died suddenly in 1998 when his contribution was already internationally recognised but when he still had research ambitions and ideas galore. A recent paper published in the journal British Birds reviewing the Important Bird Area status of South Georgia carried the dedication, *'To the memory of Peter Prince (1948–1998), who worked at South Georgia from 1971. His enthusiasm and commitment to the development of Antarctic ornithology was unbounded and left an indelible impression on all who were lucky enough to know and work with him'*.

LIGHT-MANTLED ALBATROSS
TANDEM DISPLAY

The most elegant and beautiful of all albatrosses – in flight and plumage – is the charismatic light-mantled albatross.

It breeds along much of the coast of South Georgia, nesting singly or in small groups on steep tussock slopes, sometimes far inland. Displaying birds stand on cliff ledges with head and neck extended vertically, calling to passing birds. The call is a mournful, two-syllable and muted trumpet-like sound that on a still day carries far. Hearing it is one of the most evocative of sub-Antarctic experiences.

During the breeding season pairs of birds perform tandem aerial displays by gliding along the nesting cliffs and sweeping round out to sea in close formation and perfect synchrony. It is as astonishing as it is exquisite.

53 Light-mantled albatross display flight, South Georgia, October 2009.
Watercolour and pencil, 30 × 42 cm

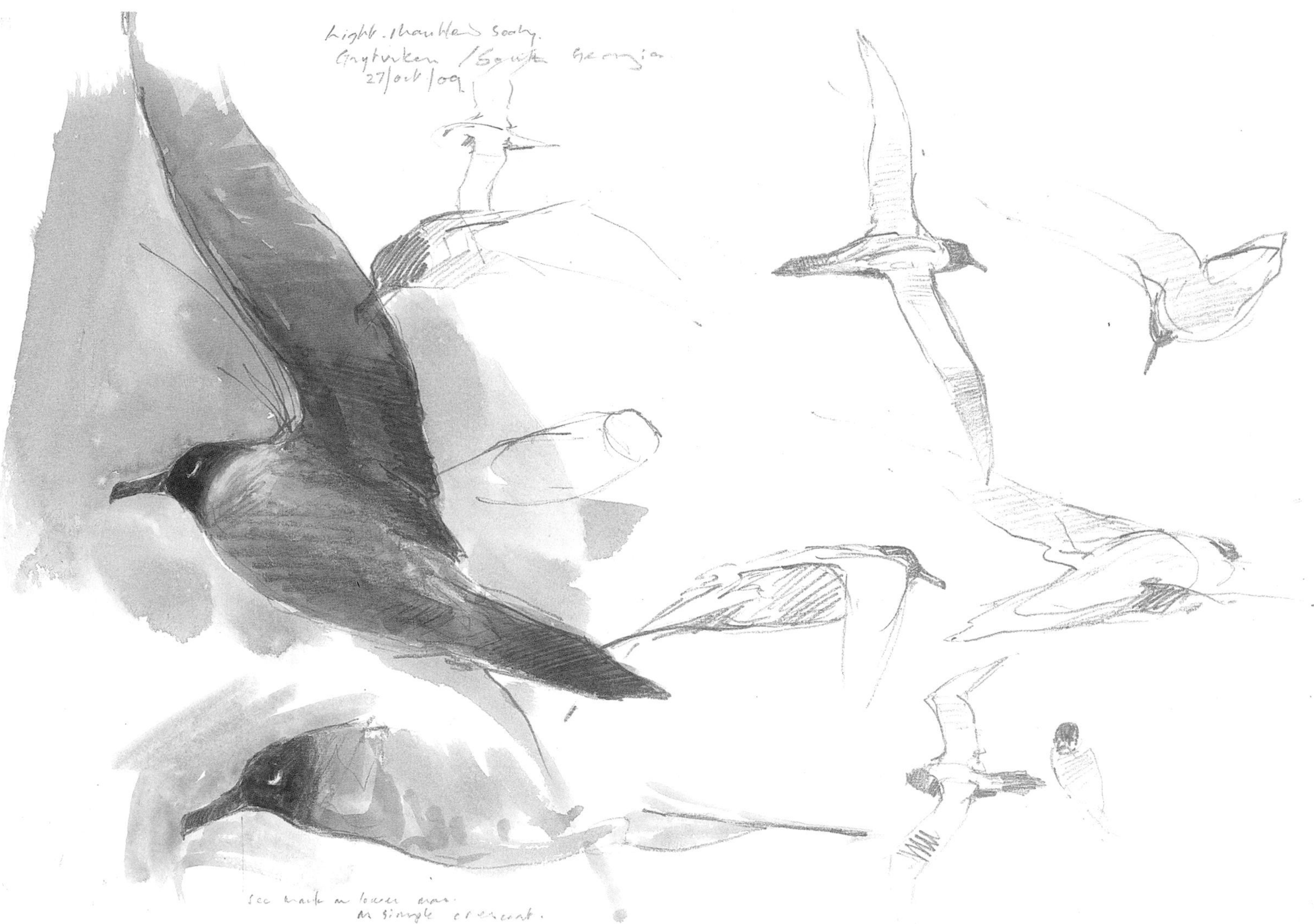

So how should the life-story of the wanderer chick I watched leaving Bird Island unfold? Ahead of 508–0292 as it flew out to sea that December day long ago was the vast expanse of a Southern Ocean that would support it for the next 40 or 50 years. Perhaps it might live to an even greater age – one great albatross is thought to have reached 61 years of age. For the first five years and more it would roam the ocean learning how to forage and survive. During this time at sea a pattern of moult would gradually transform its dark slaty-brown juvenile plumage through patchy paler phases towards a whiter adult plumage. Then, after perhaps six or eight years – and with the beautiful mottled and vermiculated plumage characteristic of an immature wanderer – it would return to Bird Island.

During the next few short summer seasons it would join the other courting adolescents and non-breeding adults on the display grounds and become increasingly familiar with their rituals and routines. It would learn to recognise other wanderers as individuals and build a relationship with one bird in particular. Both would then start coming ashore earlier each summer, until, after perhaps another five years, they would arrive at about the same time as the older established breeding adults. Aged 11 or 12 years 508–0292 and its partner would possibly attempt to breed, maybe failing the first few attempts. Females, on average, are slightly younger than males when they start breeding; however, there is considerable variation, with some breeding as early as the age of seven, and others not until 16 years. Eventually they would successfully raise a chick to fledging. This could be perhaps 15 years after 508–0292 took wing for the first time.

Is that the life-story of the young wanderer that has the potential to outlive me? And where is it now?

54 Tandem Display, 2012
Etching, 20 × 26 cm

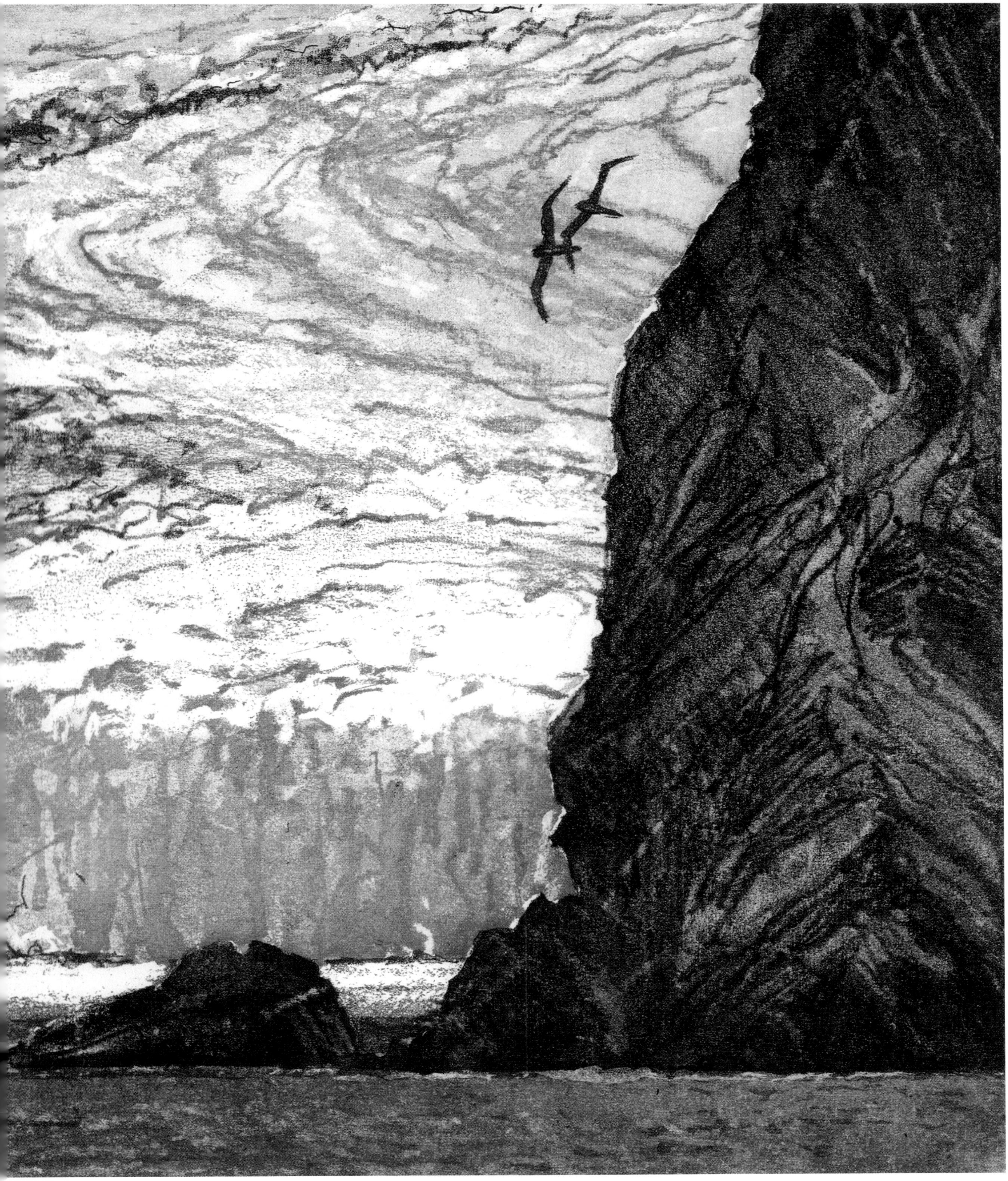

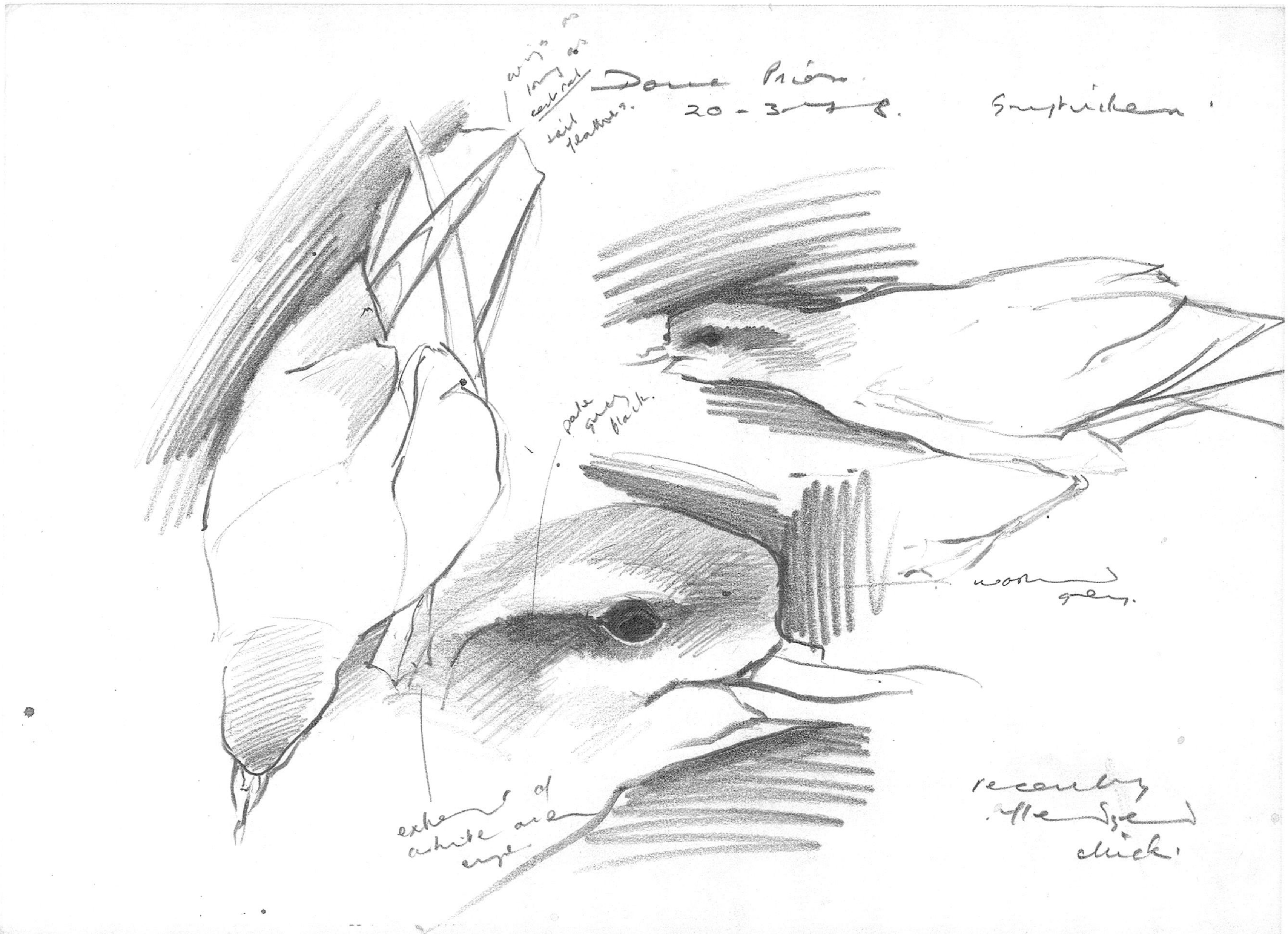

55 Antarctic prion, South Georgia, 1978
30 × 42 cm · pencil

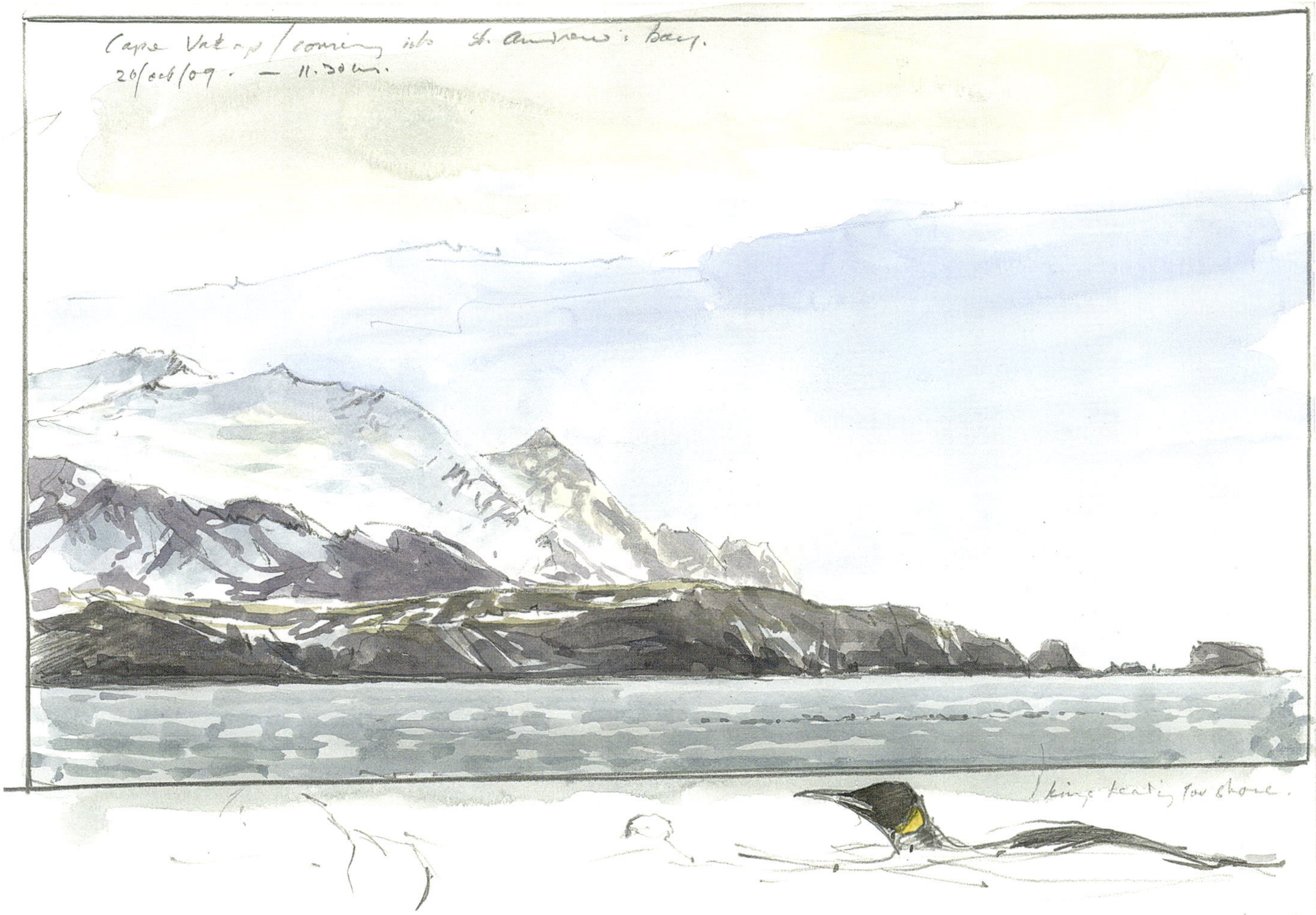

57 Passing down the north coast of South Georgia, October, 2009
30 × 42 cm · watercolour and pencil

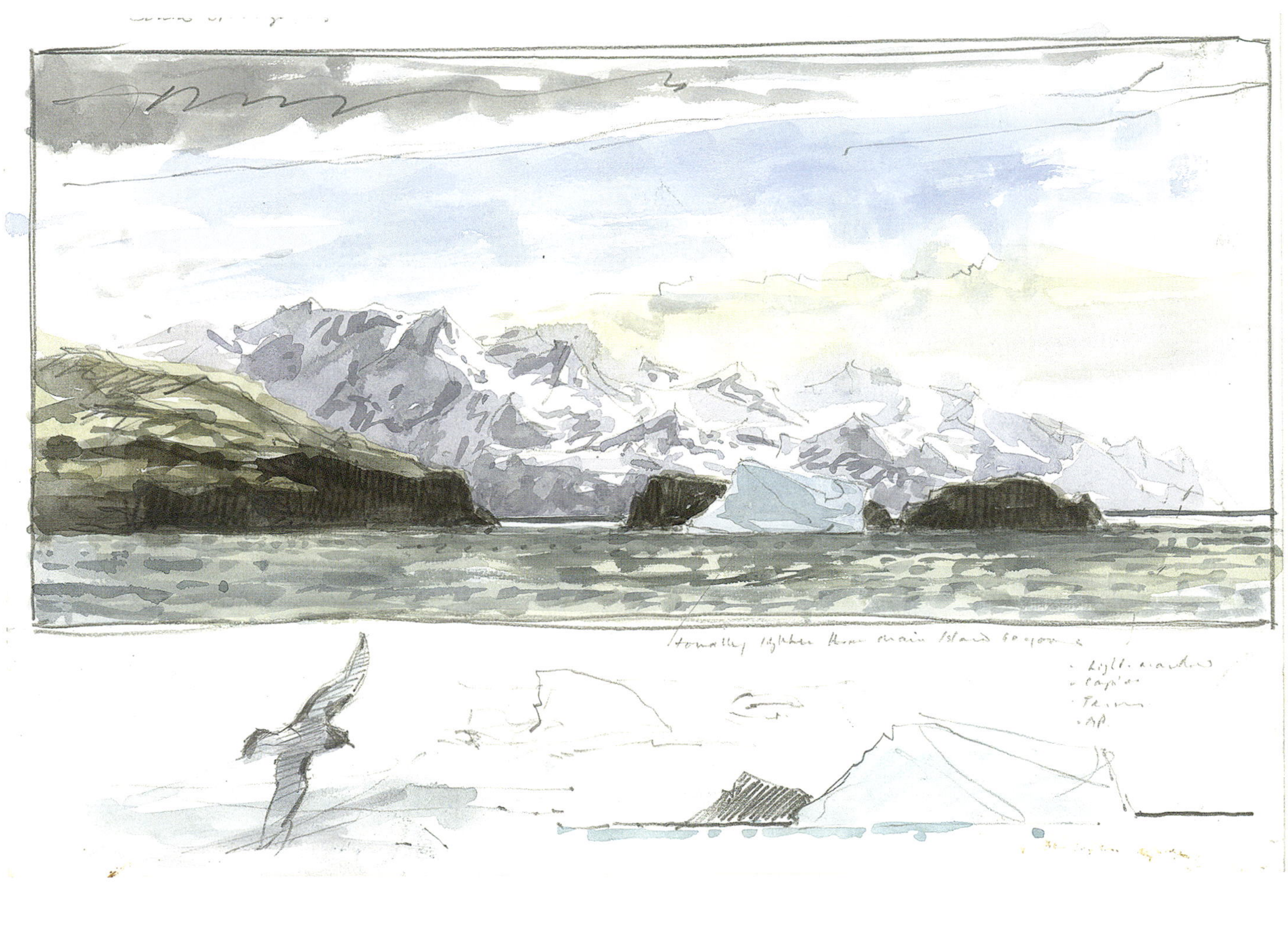

56 Passing down the north coast of South Georgia, October, 2009
30 × 42 cm · watercolour and pencil

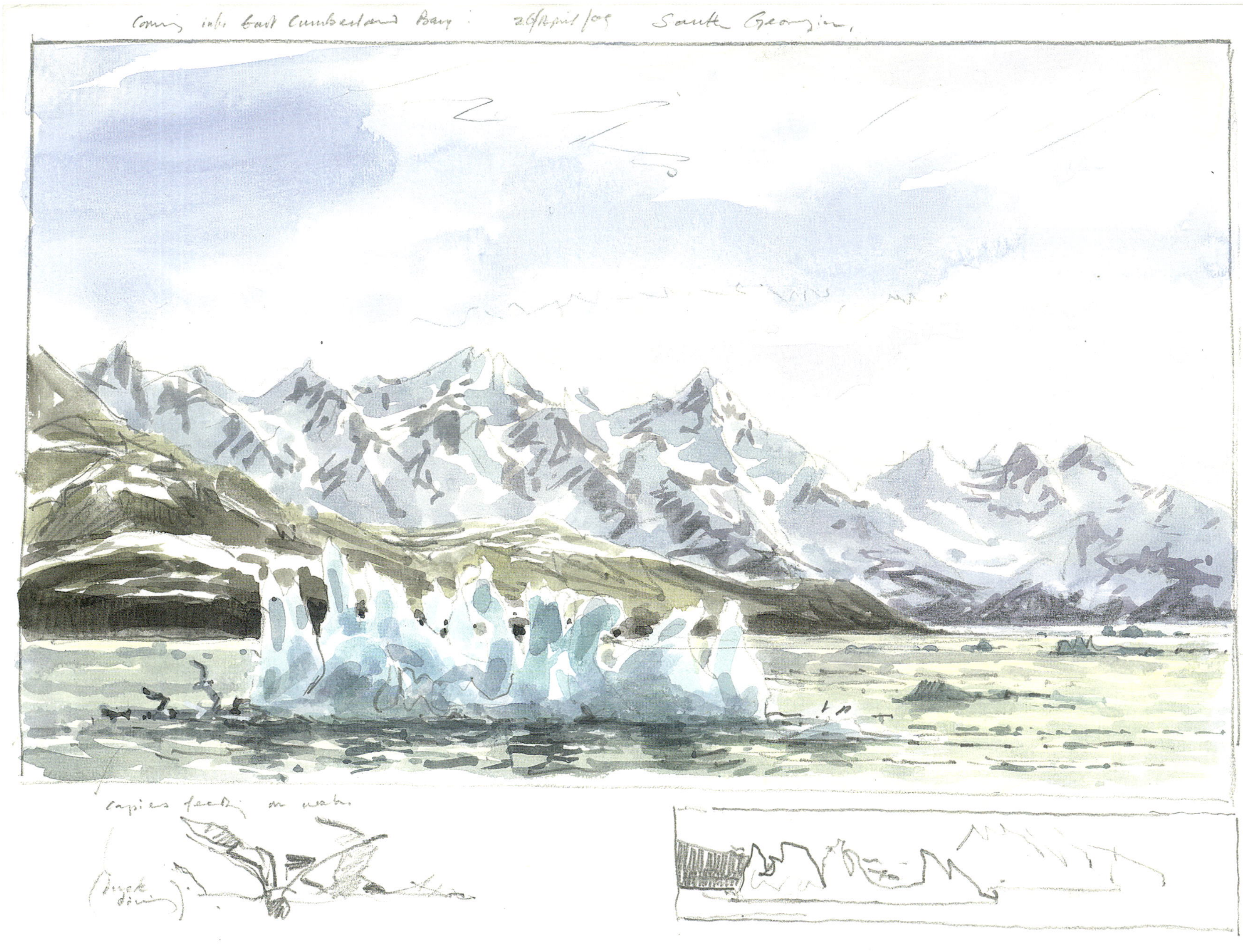

SOUTH GEORGIA ICEBERGS

The amount of floating ice around South Georgia varies from year to year. A few icebergs calve from South Georgia glaciers, but most are carried up and along ocean currents from the Bellingshausen and Weddell Seas. In some years the surrounding seas are crowded with spectacular sculptural ice forms.

Captain Cook appreciated that the amount of ice he saw around South Georgia could not have come just from the island and that there had to be a more ice-bound continent further south.

58 Entering Cumberland Bay, South Georgia, October, 2009
30 × 42 cm · watercolour and pencil

59 Ice against the shore, Cumberland Bay, South Georgia, October, 2009
30 × 42 cm · watercolour and pencil

60 Passing down the north coast of South Georgia, October, 2009
30 × 42 cm · watercolour and pencil

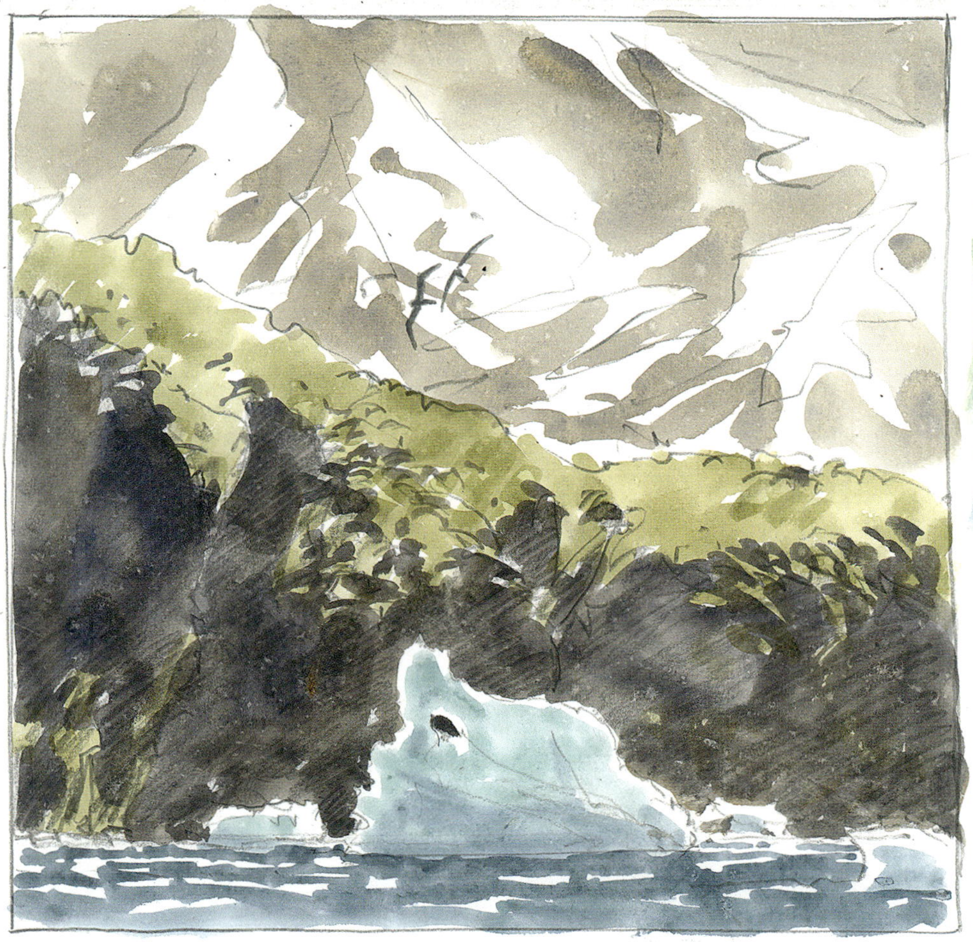

19/october '09.
South Georgia
leaving Cumberland Bay
against the light, heading into wind

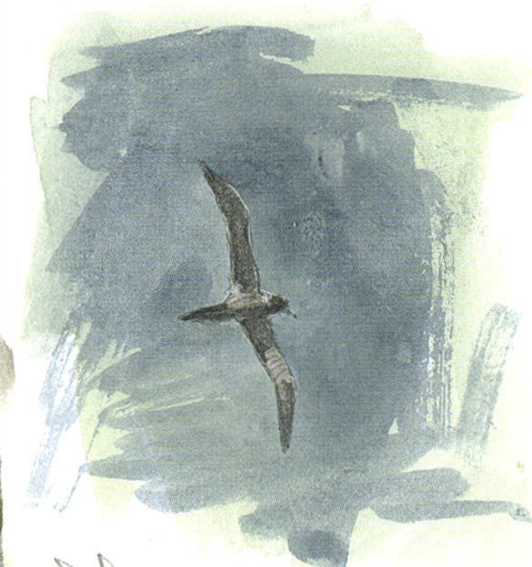

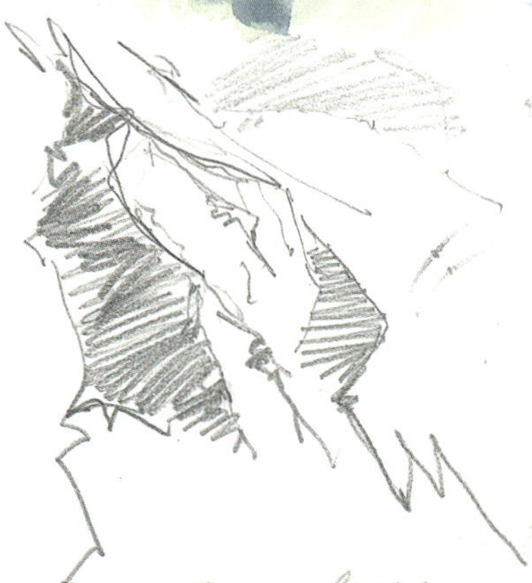

Bruce Pearson

Husvik — Bay of Isles (South Georgia).
27/06/09. c1130 —

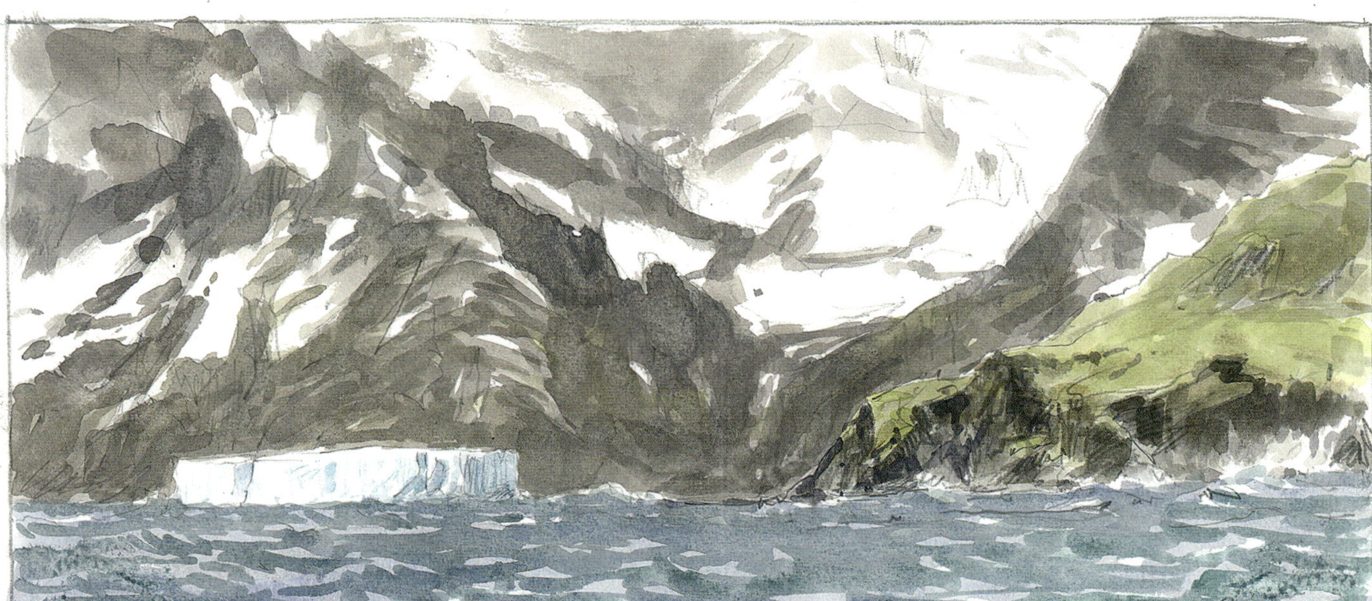

. light - marker
. capes
. white [illegible].

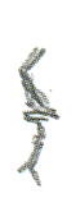

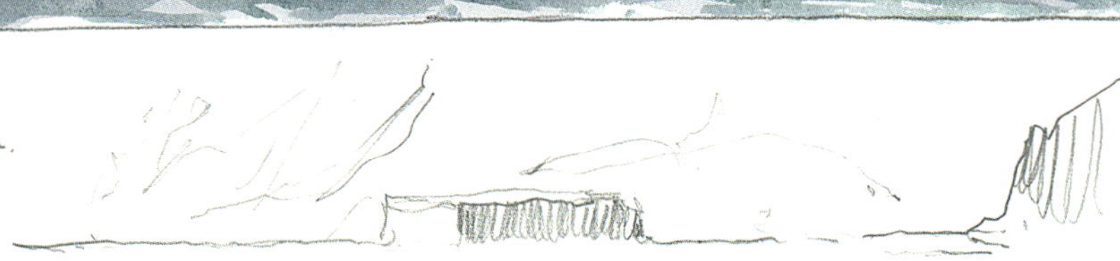

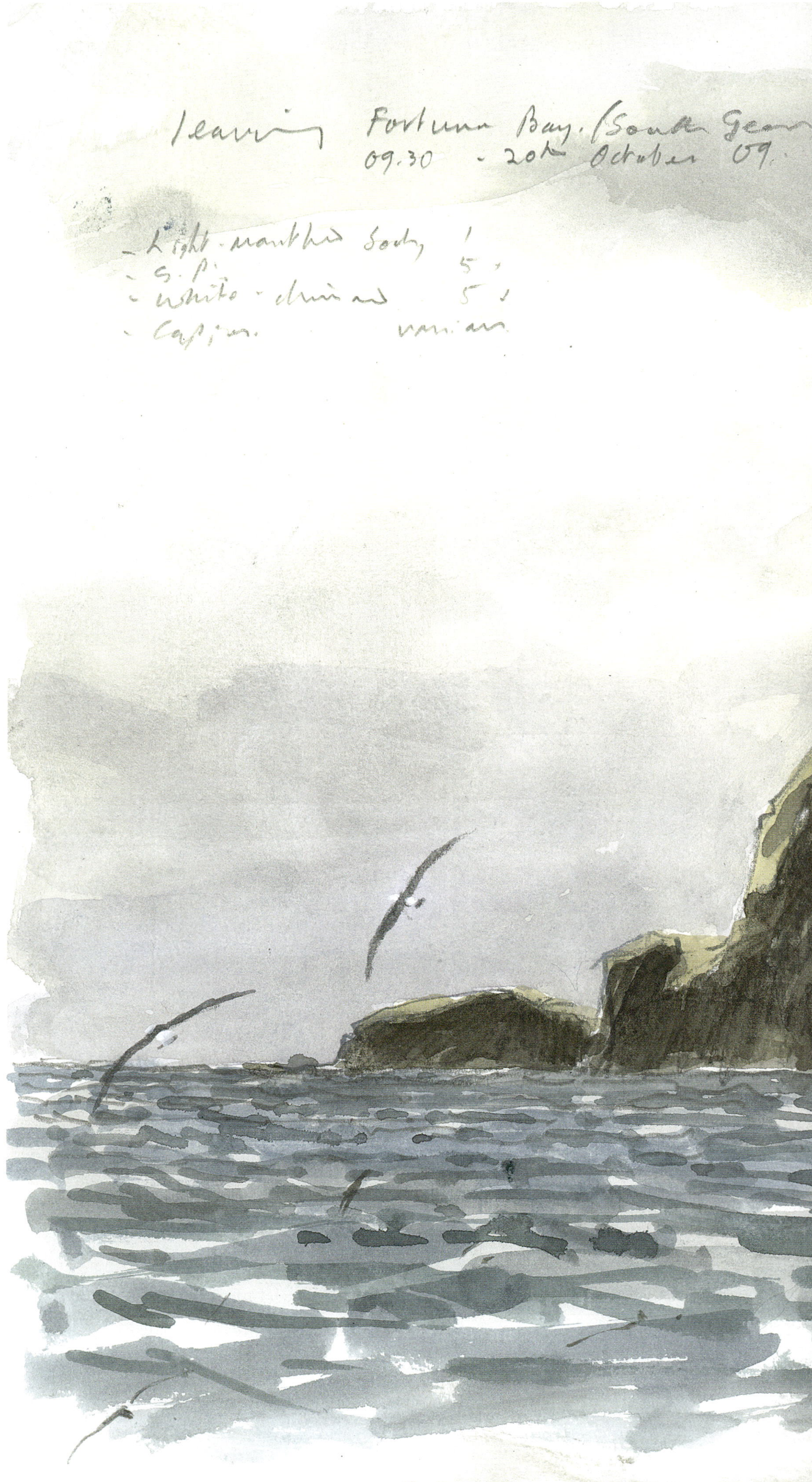

61 Leaving Fortuna Bay, South Georgia, 20th October, 2009
30 × 42 cm · watercolour and pencil

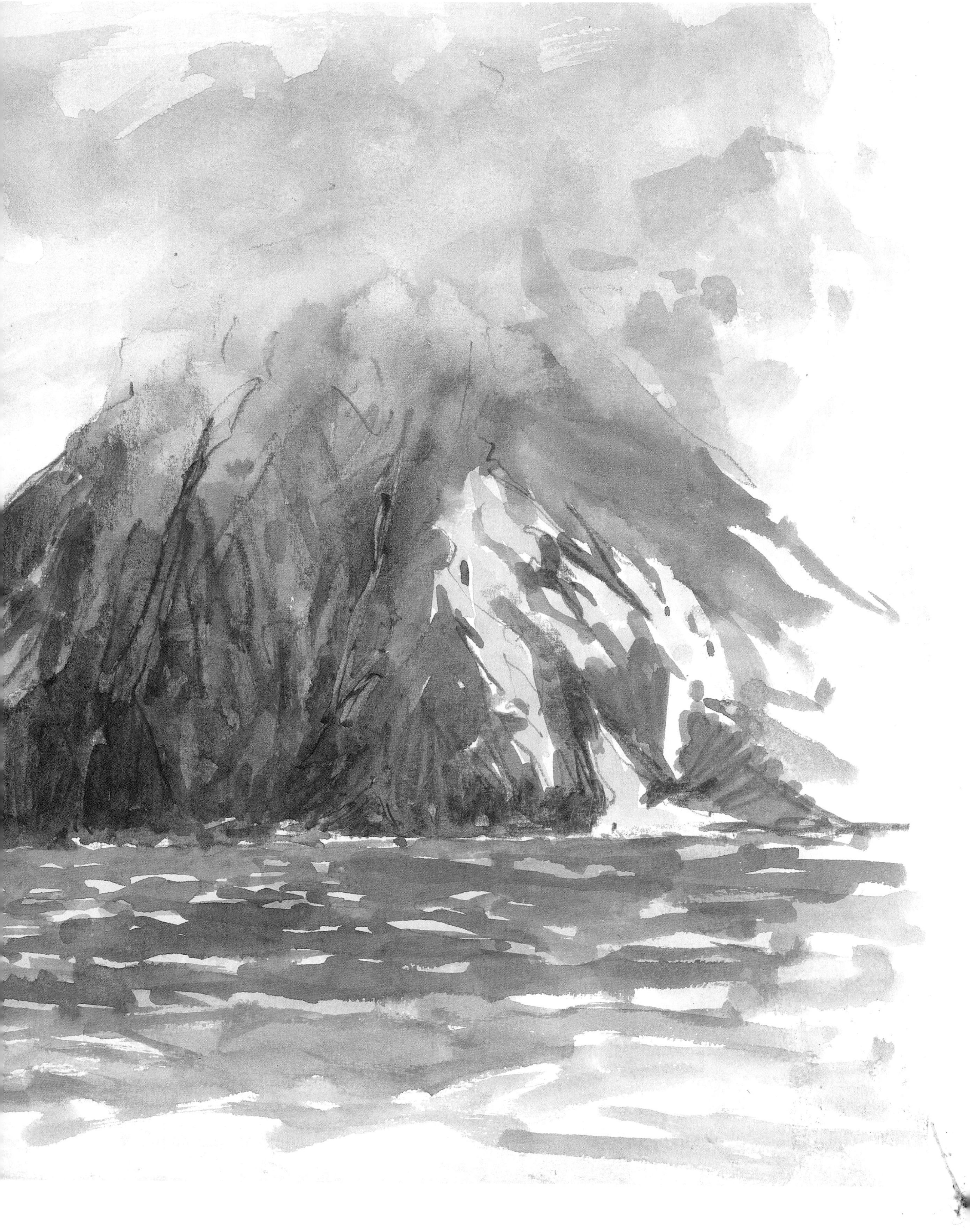

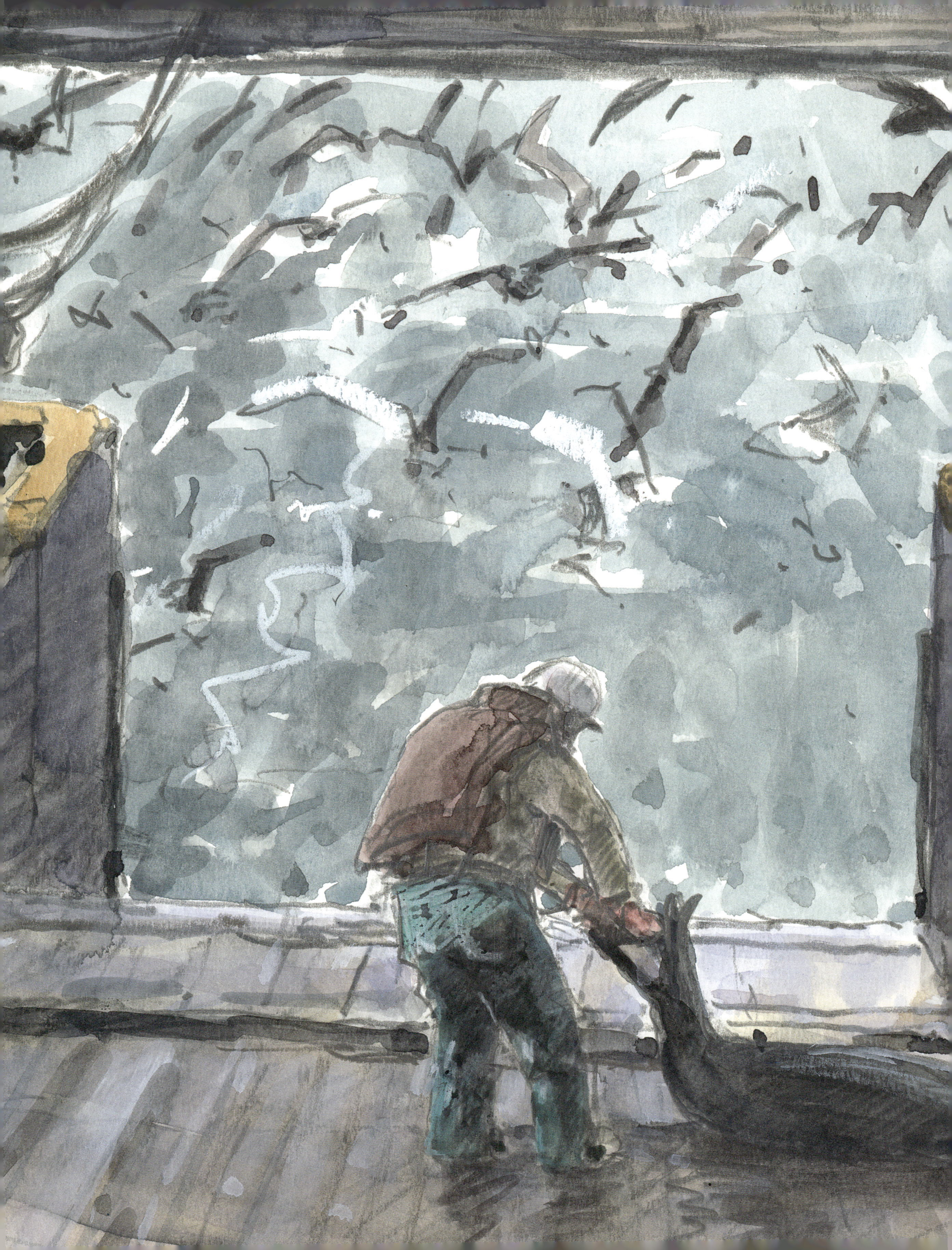

CHAPTER 5

Hooked and tangled

62 Bycatch. Removal of fur seal caught in the trawl net, *Marie Marine*, September, 2010 (detail)

It is October 12th and the day is bright with a strong gusting wind pushing loose bundles of cloud towards the south-west, and raising a swell on the surrounding sea. A choppy surface of sparkling indigo and turquoise colours is flecked with white breakers piling up and peeling-off cresting waves that leave trails of streaking foam. I am aboard a longline fishing vessel called *Ryoei* along with her crew of 12, the skipper, first officer, chief and second engineers, her cook, and 7 deckhands. We are over 100 miles offshore north-east of Durban at the extreme edge of the Eastern Atlantic – where the waters almost become the Indian Ocean. *Ryoei* was built in Japan 40 years ago and bought in 2005 by a South African company to operate out of Richards Bay on the Kwazulu-Natal coast to fish for tuna and swordfish.

We have been at sea for over a week and our position is 29° 28' S, 33° 55' E. Swinging to and fro in the wake behind *Ryoei*, there are white-chinned petrels with flesh-footed shearwaters mixed among them. Every now and then an Indian yellow-nosed or a shy albatross glides by and a passing Barau's petrel rises high and turns to hurtle downwind. Diminutive black-bellied storm-petrels are darting and trampolining over the tops of the waves. And way beyond all that activity there is the unmistakable form of a wandering albatross sliding gracefully upwind: the white diamond shape centred between two dark lines and speckled panels. When it passes nearby I can see the beautiful vermiculated and chequerboard pattern on the upper-sides of its wings before it rises high to show the pure white of the undersides with their contrasting dark trailing edges. The massive pink bill with greenish tip and the weighty look of the wanderer make me think it is possibly a male. I wonder where this bird is from? Is it on its way back to its island home to start breeding? Perhaps it is a South Georgia bird!

Since the last section of line was hauled an hour or so ago we have been drifting and the crew are taking a rest. The catch was disappointing: a few swordfish, four small yellowfin tuna, two blue sharks and six dorado – a beautiful sulphur-yellow, bull-headed pelagic species. After hauling, the skipper Jacques de Kock headed eastwards a few nautical miles to this new spot which – with his experience of sea temperature and currents – he sensed would be better fishing. It was important to set a good line tonight because of the full moon.

Jacques, a tightly framed and hugely engaging 39 year-old Afrikaaner has been longlining for 20 years and skipper of *Ryoei* for six. A few months earlier we had talked about the plan for me to join him on a fishing trip. 'No problem, it's all OK. Come in October and reckon on being here for 10 or 15 days either side of the full moon. The fishing is best then. Catches are good right now and the boat is running sweetly after the engine problems last year. We're looking forward to seeing you'.

For the Troubled Waters project to work, it was essential that I should explore the creative potential of a voyage aboard a fishing vessel. It is there that the lives of fishermen and seabirds intermingle, far too often tragically, and witnessing that collision would give the project a real focus, a potential conclusion, and a striking validity. Finding a boat willing to take me on-board was arranged through BirdLife International's Global Seabird Programme with the support of the Africa Co-ordinator, Ross Wanless, who works out of BirdLife South Africa's office in Cape Town. Ross put me in touch with Meidad Goren, an Albatross Task Force observer based in Richards Bay on the north-east coast. Meidad frequently sailed with Jacques, but could not go on every trip, so it was agreed that I could take his space for a voyage, if it was okay with the boat owners and, of course, with Jacques.

The day before I arrived at the quayside in Richards Bay, Jacques had docked and landed almost seven tonnes of fish. He also came ashore with an albatross lying dead in a freezer box! He had been hauling one of the last lines of the trip. 'It must have snagged, and been there a long while as it was exhausted. It was huge. And it had rings!' The albatross had swallowed a hook, was soaked and completely exhausted when retrieved. The hook was successfully removed and the bird put in a warm dark place and left alone to recover – but it died overnight.

With the dead albatross in front of me I looked at the icily inert and hunched form. It was a very sad sight. This was the first great albatross I had handled in 35 years. My mind's eye over the decades had turned albatrosses into ocean giants, but now this bird seemed small. Through the dampness and chill of the factory the utterly distinctive musky oily seabird smell instantly rewound the years.

I was feeling a little uneasy about joining a longliner to experience the clash between fishermen and seabirds, rather like, I imagine, a reporter heading for a war-zone. In both cases, the job is to get as close to the action knowing that witnessing mayhem and carnage might provide the scoop that makes the story and gets the headlines. Part of me wanted to witness the collision of birds and fishermen, and add a dreadful poignancy to my albatross story. But looking at this beautiful and memorably scented bird, I was hoping it would be the only fatality I'd see in the next few weeks.

Ringing recoveries and at-sea satellite tracking show that Tristan albatrosses rarely leave the South Atlantic Ocean, although a few do reach Western Australia. Although there is a 1959 ringing recovery from Port

63 Trawling and longlining locations

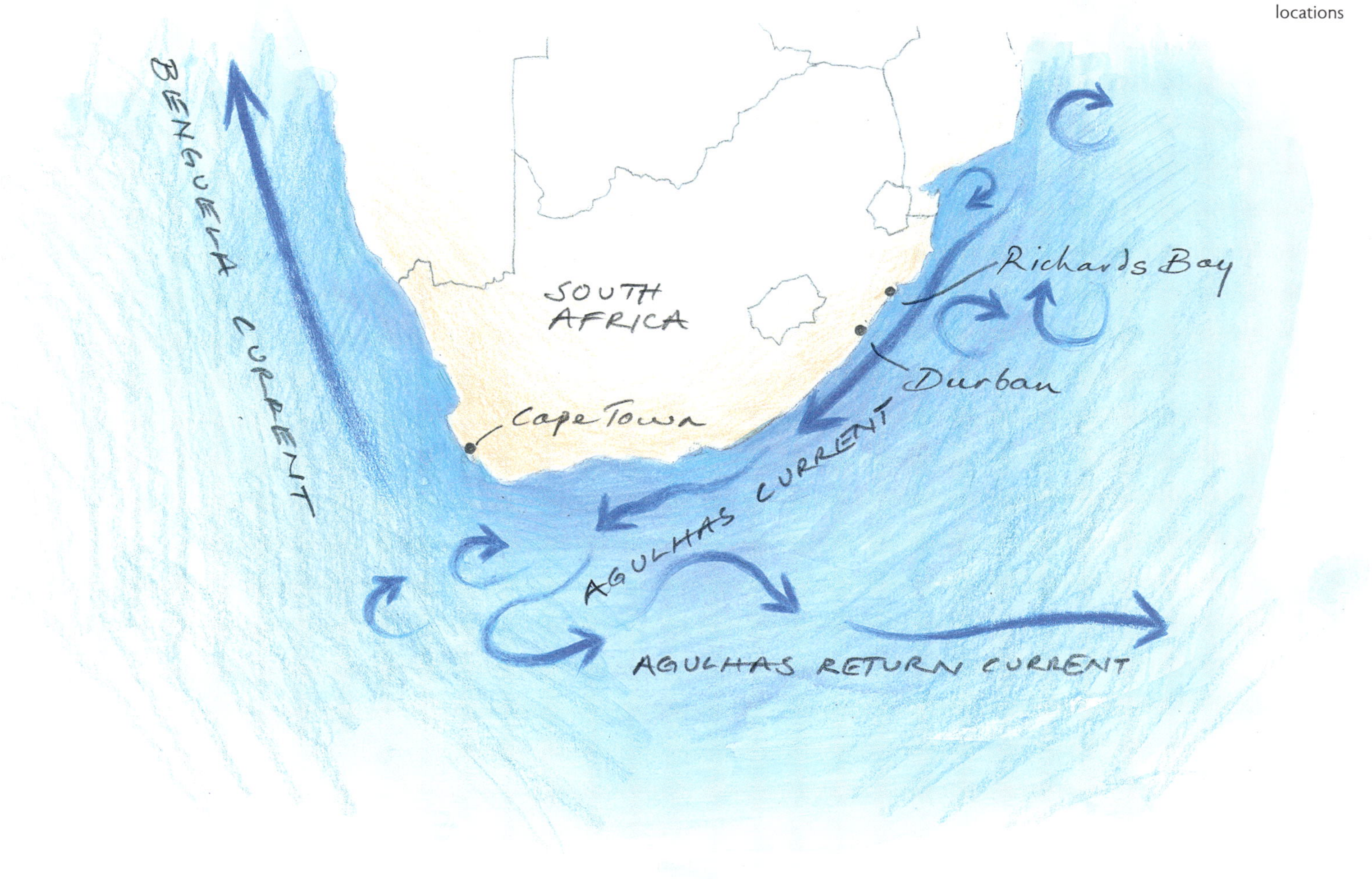

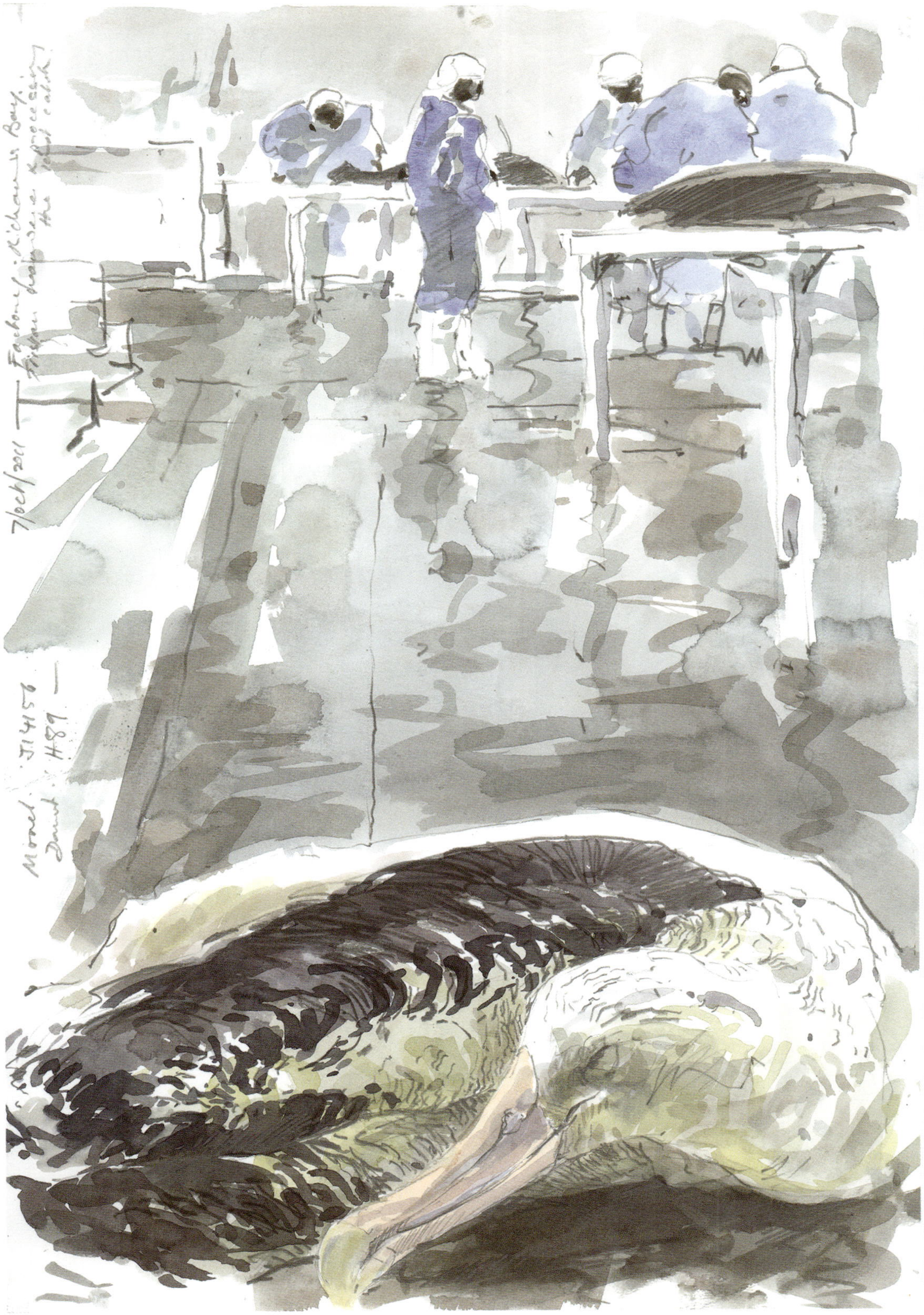

TRISTAN WANDERER (*DIOMEDEA DABBENENA*) J14156, YELLOW H89

On the quayside at Richards Bay, I talked to Tshikana Rasehlomi, the Albatross Task Force instructor who had collected the dead bird, and kindly offered to send me more background.

Tshikana later explained that it was a Tristan albatross, ringed as a chick on 29 October 2000 on Gough Island in the South Atlantic. Next recorded as a 'loafer' – a non-breeding visitor – on Gough in April 2004 and again in 2008, it was colour-ringed in January 2010, and identified as a male, probably breeding for the first time. Its chick had died by 12 July 2010, most likely after being attacked house mice that had been accidentally introduced by Gough in the 19th Century, and which notoriously attack and kill numerous albatross chicks. The young male had not bred in the 2011 season, so it had presumably been taking a year off and was travelling far from home.

64 The Tristan wanderer on floor of fish processing plant, Richards Bay, South Africa, October, 2011
30 x 42 cm · watercolour and pencil

Elizabeth, South Africa, the *Ryoei* bird represents a notable range extension for the species northwards in the Indian Ocean.

Back to the fishing operation: the wind was slackening and the sea beginning to settle as we drifted beam-on waiting for darkness. It was an opportunity to ask Jacques about the wait to start work: 'We can't shoot as there's too many of your friends out there', he replies, jokingly. One Albatross Task Force strategy to protect seabirds is to encourage skippers to set their lines after dark when it is much more difficult for birds to see the baited hooks going over the stern. Jacques tells me about longlining for hake on a larger vessel off the Namibian coast. 'We used to catch very many white-chins. The lights were the problem; two great beams lighting the sea all around the stern for no reason really. Then one of the bird observer guys said kill the lights. Given they weren't actually necessary, we agreed, and immediately we were catching only one or two birds. As you'll see, the guys can work fine with just fluorescent lights at the stern'.

In the half-light – as the sun heads towards the horizon – white chinned-petrels, two or three black-browed albatrosses and a few Indian yellow-nosed albatrosses start gathering around the boat. Some are preening and bathing as if gathering to roost. I head for the monkey island – my usual working spot on top of the wheelhouse – and settle down for a final short stint of watching and drawing for the day.

As darkness falls, *Ryoei* is underway again. In the muted glow of two fluorescent lamps, the crew begin paying out the longline from an open canopy at the stern. I watch from a slippery corner as the moon climbs over the sea, its reflections rippling and glowing along the horizon. White-chinned petrels arch through the darkness, their black forms showing distinctly against the moonlight. The crew works mostly in silence, wearing a muddle of oilskins, fleece jackets and woolly hats against the cold wind whipping around the bulkheads. The thud of engines and tumble of the wake below does not make for easy chatter. Under the brighter glow of light flooding the well-deck, a spool, like a giant cotton reel, spins out the line. It runs along the starboard gunwale to the stern where it passes through rollers down to the sea, drawn out by the forward motion of the vessel. To a regular beeping 10 second pulse that sets the spacing for the hooks, the crew work through a rhythmical sequence of snapping leader lines about 20 metres long with a swivel and weight three-quarters of the way down, and a light-stick lure and hook at the end. At every hundred metres they attach a buoy, and every 5 kilometres fix a radio-marker buoy. By about 1 o'clock in the morning, when the last radio buoy goes over the side, the crew will have set 1,500 hooks on 60 kilometres or more of line.

The wind gets up in the night and by first light it is blowing 20 knots and filling the air with a fine salt haze. With the day warming rapidly and brightening with

LONGLINE FISHING

A combination of buoys along the main line, calibrated weight and length of leader set the hooks at a predetermined dept for the targeted species. All the bait used on *Ryoei* is frozen squi from the Falkland Islands.

65 Noita sorting snaps and hooks alongside at Richards Ba 18th August, 2010
30 × 42 cm · watercolour and pencil

66 Dokter feeling the line as it comes in, *Ryoei*, October, 2011
30 × 42 cm · watercolour and pencil

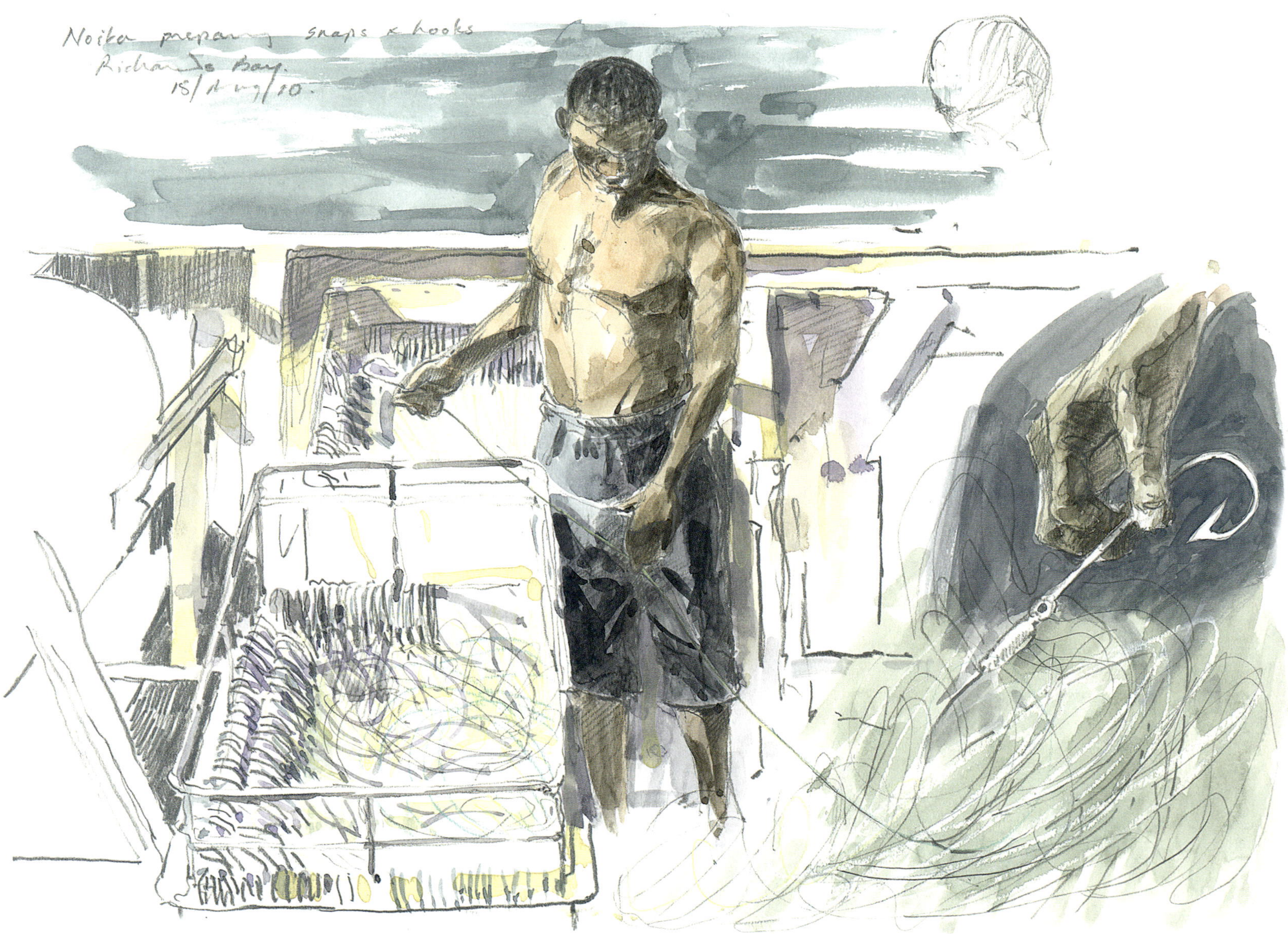

banks of clouds sending purple-blue shadows racing across the heaving azure sea, there are white-chinned petrels all around, as well as hordes of flesh-footed shearwaters, cape petrels, and storm-petrels – Wilson's and black-bellied. Jacques moves *Ryoei* upwind towards the signal from the first radio buoy, and the hauling starts. The conditions are difficult, but I try to work from my monkey island perch. I secure a few bits of kit, but a gust soon whips away the pencil parked behind my ear. The drama of the crew hauling the line into the heaving seas and the wheeling seabirds presents such exciting creative opportunities I carry on as best I can. Spray crashes over the bows and drifts high and down the length of the ship. Even so it is warm, and my sketchbook dries enough between dousings that I can keep working to try and capture the intense activity all around me.

Moving steadily forward into the weather and oncoming sea, the lightweight monofilament line – as thin as spaghetti, and immensely strong – slices through the sea 20 metres off the starboard beam. Like the noise of wind through telegraph wires, one moment it is roaring through the water, then moments later hissing close in front of the bows. Even though the ship pitches and rolls the line appears steady, and rises out of the water to a pulley above the gunwale edge. Standing beneath is Dokter, his hand up and thumb hooked over the line – fingers resting lightly along it. In touch with the ocean, he is feeling for rising hooks, sensing whether there is a catch. One after another, he unsnaps the leader and assembly of failed bait, hook, lure, and weights, and passes them back to the crew behind him for sorting and stowing. Then, without a word, Dokter signals to the skipper watching from the open wheelhouse window. Jacques spins *Ryoei* to starboard pivoting her around a cauldron of surging water and tightening line, as if snagged on a submarine volcano. He cuts the engine. In a few moments, where the white of the line vanishes into the deep colours of the ocean below, there are flashes of

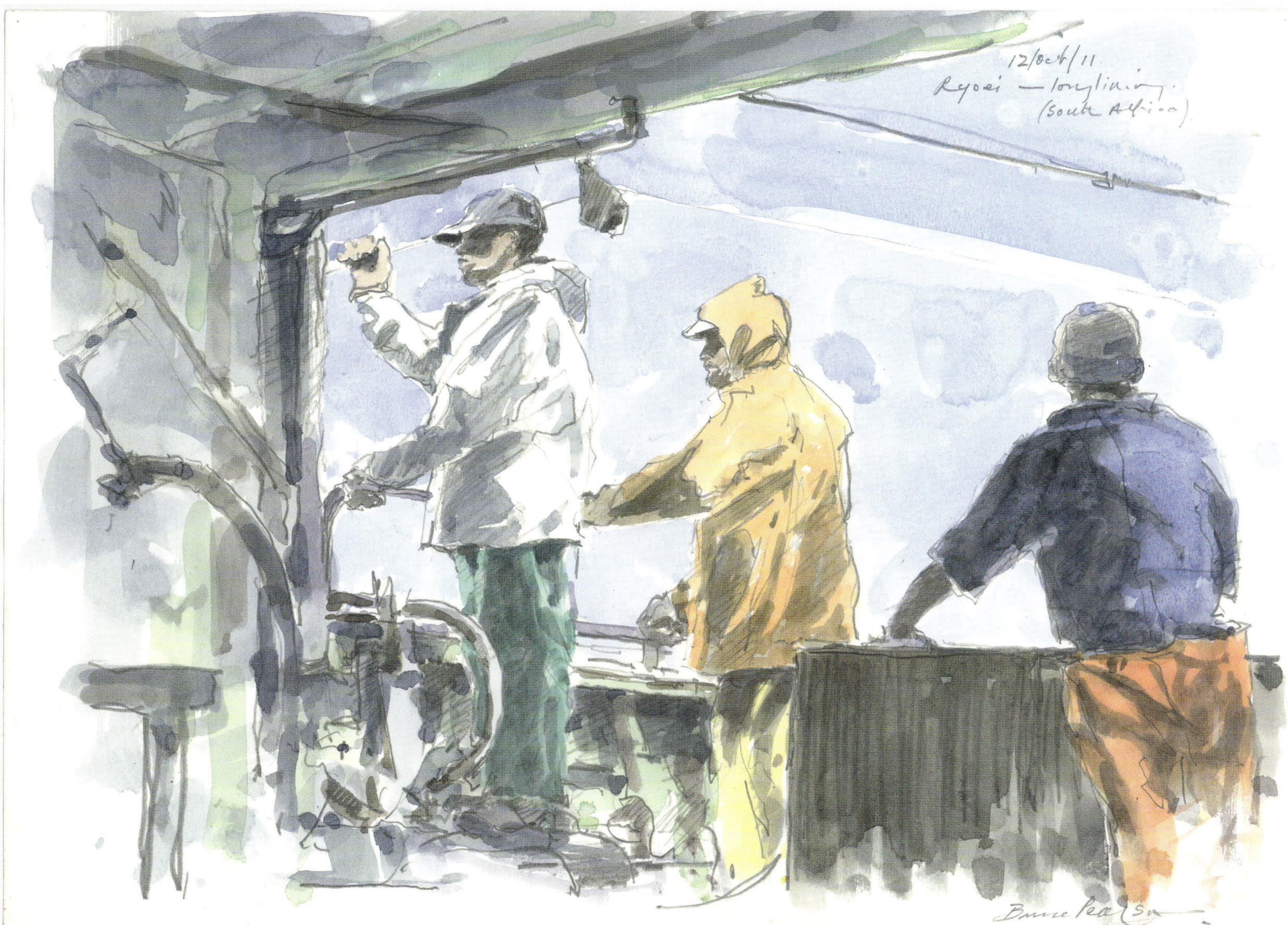

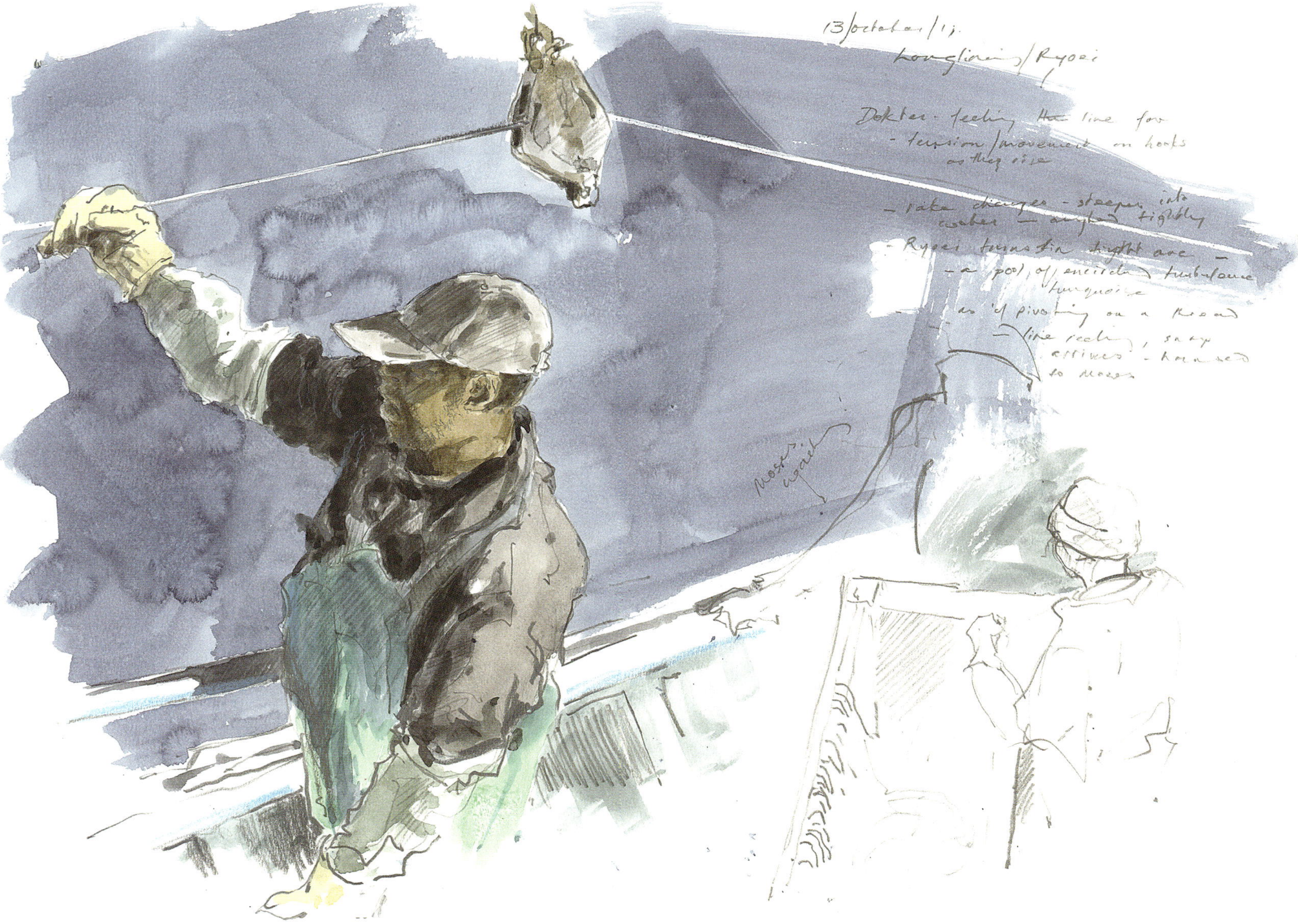

iridescent blue and silver, and dazzling yellow. The snap comes up, Dokter releases it passes to Moses, who starts hauling. With feet braced against the gunwale and back arched using his whole upper body, he pulls hard. The other men gather like warriors with pole-hooks standing ready as Moses brings the fish alongside. The gaffs catch, and a stunningly beautiful 60kg yellowfin tuna is suddenly lying on the deck, slapping and gaping.

As *Ryoei* gets underway again, the tuna is systematically skewered and sliced, cleaned out and washed, docked and tagged, measured and wrapped, and heaved down a foredeck hatch into a water tank just below freezing. The whole process takes perhaps ten minutes, and meanwhile another two yellowfin tuna and a swordfish are landed. But the line hauling is quite often slowed, and sometimes held-up for a while, by the accidental catch of non-target species. One hook has snagged a small shark which, with a real fish market value, is hauled and brought on board, but sadly another hooks a massive manta ray, and another a leatherback turtle. Both these species are hauled in as close as possible before the line is cut and they are released back to the sea.

Through the morning hours of hauling, the barometer rises steadily and the wind slackens, settling the sea. There are more tuna and swordfish on the line, and more bycatch – another shark, and two dorado. A massive tangle of line the size of a shredded football is extremely frustrating for the crew. 'Sometimes fish like swordfish fight and the stays get bunched along the line, perhaps ten or twenty hooks together, and then the tangle floats', explains Jacques, when I join him in the wheelhouse for a coffee and a break. 'That's when hooks, if some are still baited, get carried to the surface, and when birds grab them and get caught'. Perhaps that is how the Tristan albatross was snagged?

By mid-afternoon, the end of the line is in sight. For

the previous eight hours or so the work of gutting the catch has been leaving an intermittent trail of offal in our wake – a floating feast for the birds. Once overboard, the discarded head and fins sink quickly, but the entrails and great handfuls of gills float for much longer. First the white-chinned petrels, perhaps 15 or 20 that seem to have been following us all along, drop eagerly. And then flesh-footed shearwaters, and a grey petrel, crash into the throng of bickering birds. Larger mollymauks arrive, two yellow-nosed and a black-browed, and finally a much larger shy albatross. Together they dominate the feeding frenzy. Then, as the offal going overboard dwindles, the birds spread out until there are almost none nearby just a straggling line of feasting bunches of birds stretching towards the horizon like way-marks along *Ryoei's* passage.

On some days the swordfish catch is much better, with some weighing over 100kg. And there are days when the tuna fishing is excellent and more crew switch to processing the catch. At the same time, there are sections of line that are extremely frustrating for Jacques. He hauls six tuna and each has a neat jaw-sized semicircular lump missing from its central belly – evidence of shark attack. Jacques also loses fish to the fearsome killer whales that have learned a long-line holds easy pickings. 'What the heck can you do?' he says, 'We have to share the ocean with these things. The best thing is just to steam as far away as possible in the hope they'll miss your line, or go somewhere else'.

I know Jacques feels bad about the Tristan wanderer caught the previous trip, and I can see that working these seas is not easy. This is his sixteenth trip in 10 months and he still doesn't know whether he will return to Richards Bay with a hold of fish that breaks even, let alone turn a profit. He tells me a good catch is over 2 tonnes a day. When killer whales find his line or when the weather is bad, a day's catch might be only a couple of hundred kilogrammes.

Ryoei is only one of many vessels and she operates within the jurisdiction of South African fishery authorities. Her owners and skipper work in full cooperation with the Albatross Task Force and do what they can to mitigate seabird losses. Frustratingly, however, throughout the world's oceans, there are pirate longliners

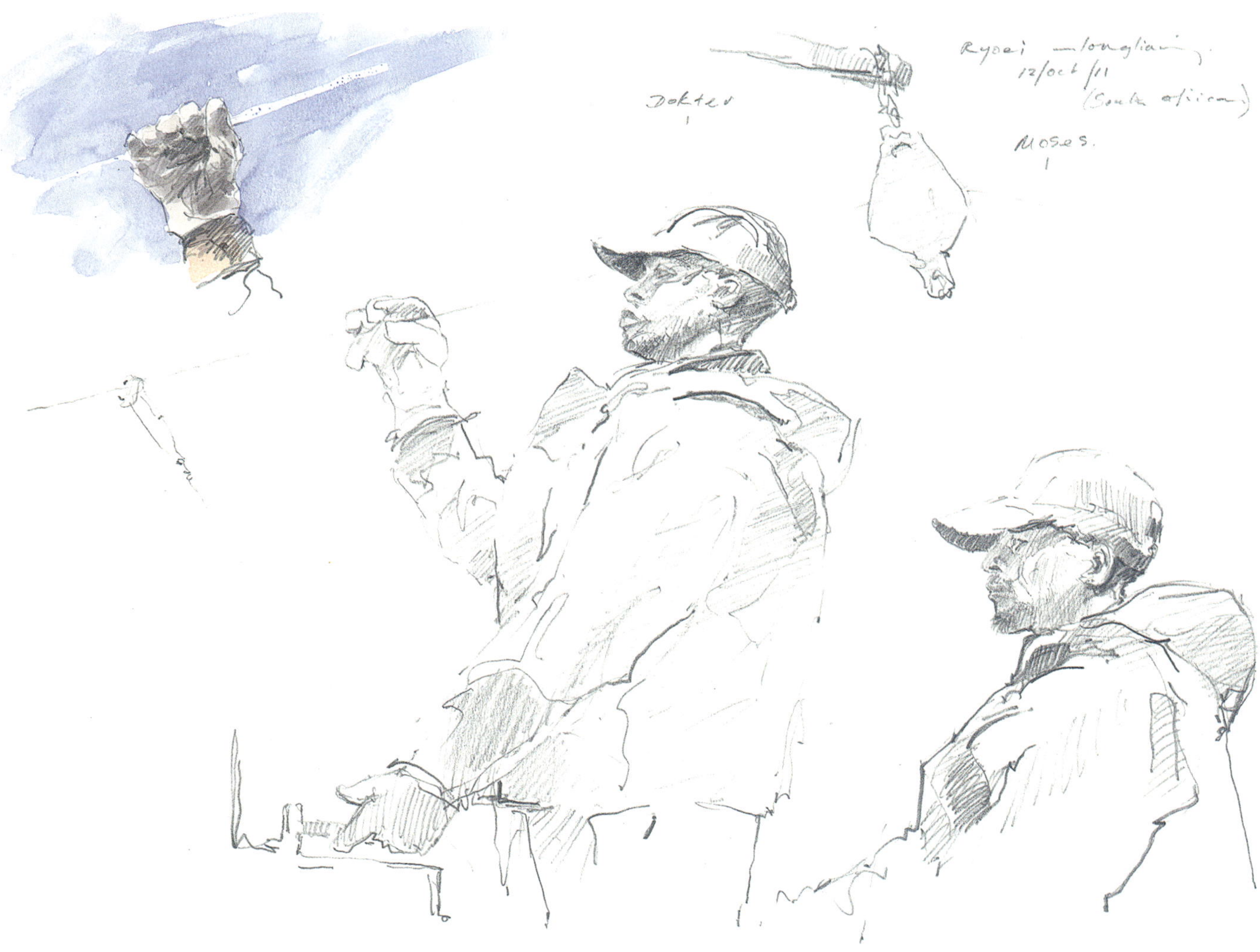

67 Dokter and Moses at work, *Ryoei*, October, 2011
30 × 42 cm · watercolour and pencil

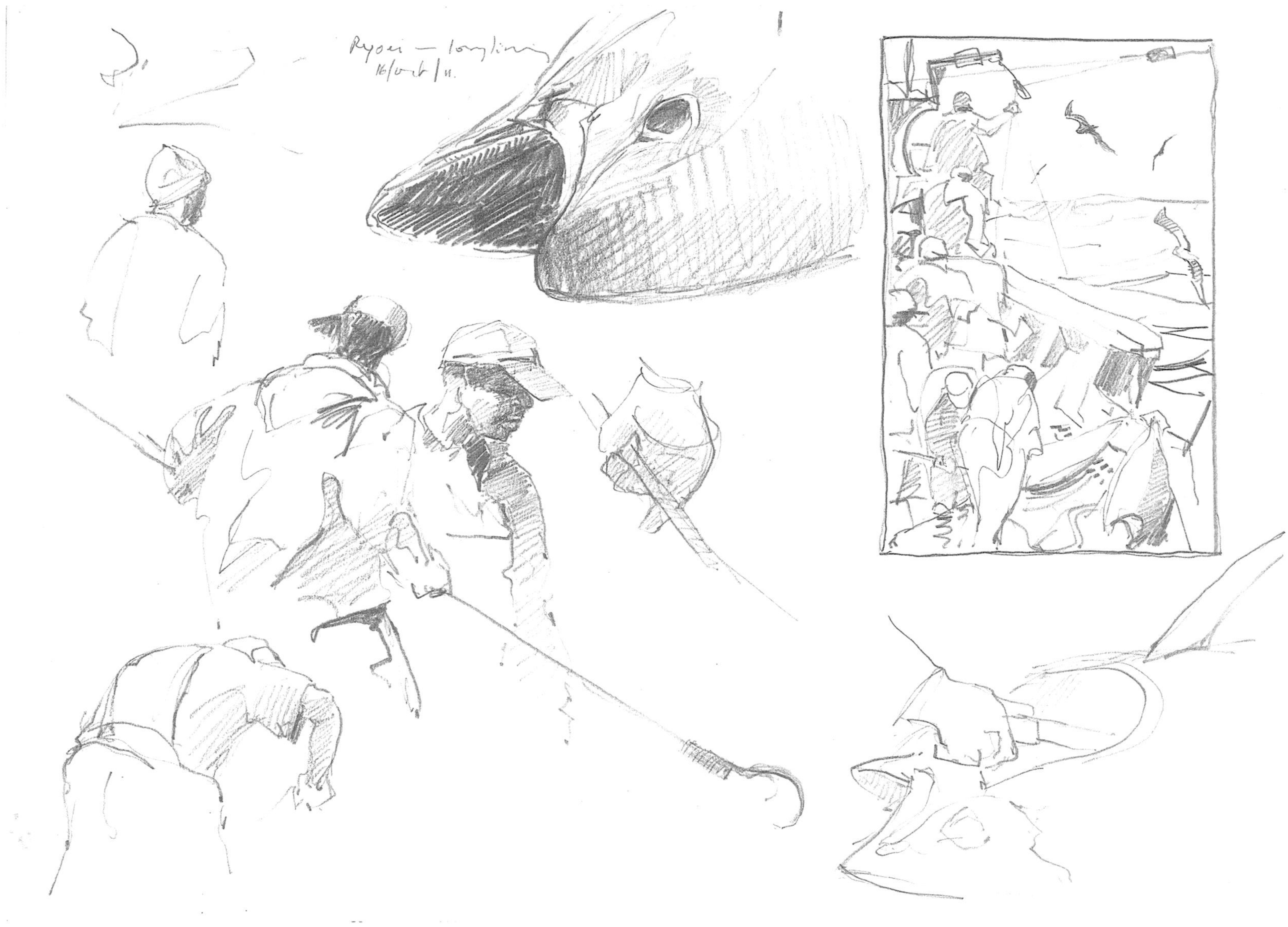

exploiting legal loopholes. Operating under 'Flags of Convenience', they plunder fish stocks with no regard for regulation, national sovereignty or bird protection, and leave devastation in their wake. Although they still cause significant losses, a combination of both catch certification schemes and more effective patrolling means the number of such vessels has dropped substantially in recent years.

Jacques gives me his perspective; 'Two years ago I tried out there, about 600km offshore. Every day another two or three ships were around – Spanish, Taiwanese, Japanese, French. You need a bigger ship to be successful out there, twice the size of *Ryoei*. You need to increase the effort and be setting 2500 to 3000 hooks a time'.

The principal objective for my time with the Albatross Task Force had always been longlining, but in the BirdLife South Africa office in Cape Town I was told by the Task Force's Ross Wanless, and Bronwyn Maree, about the significant seabird bycatch in the trawl fishery, particularly off the south and western coasts. I learned that not only albatrosses and petrels but also coastal species like cape gannets, are killed in large numbers by the warp cables that attach the trawl net to the fishing vessel. They entangle the long-winged albatrosses in particular, and drag them underwater. For the past five years, the Task Force has been working successfully with the trawl fleet to reduce this mortality. Before 2006 it was estimated that about 18000 birds were killed each year in the South Africa hake trawl fishery – now it is half that number. 'At first there was a resistance, particularly from one or two of the older skippers', Bronwyn explained. 'They would tell me that, 'there are hundreds behind my boat, and we only catch a few; why is there a problem'? Through workshops and showing how mitigation works

68 Crew of *Ryoei* and catch, October, 2011
30 × 42 cm · pencil

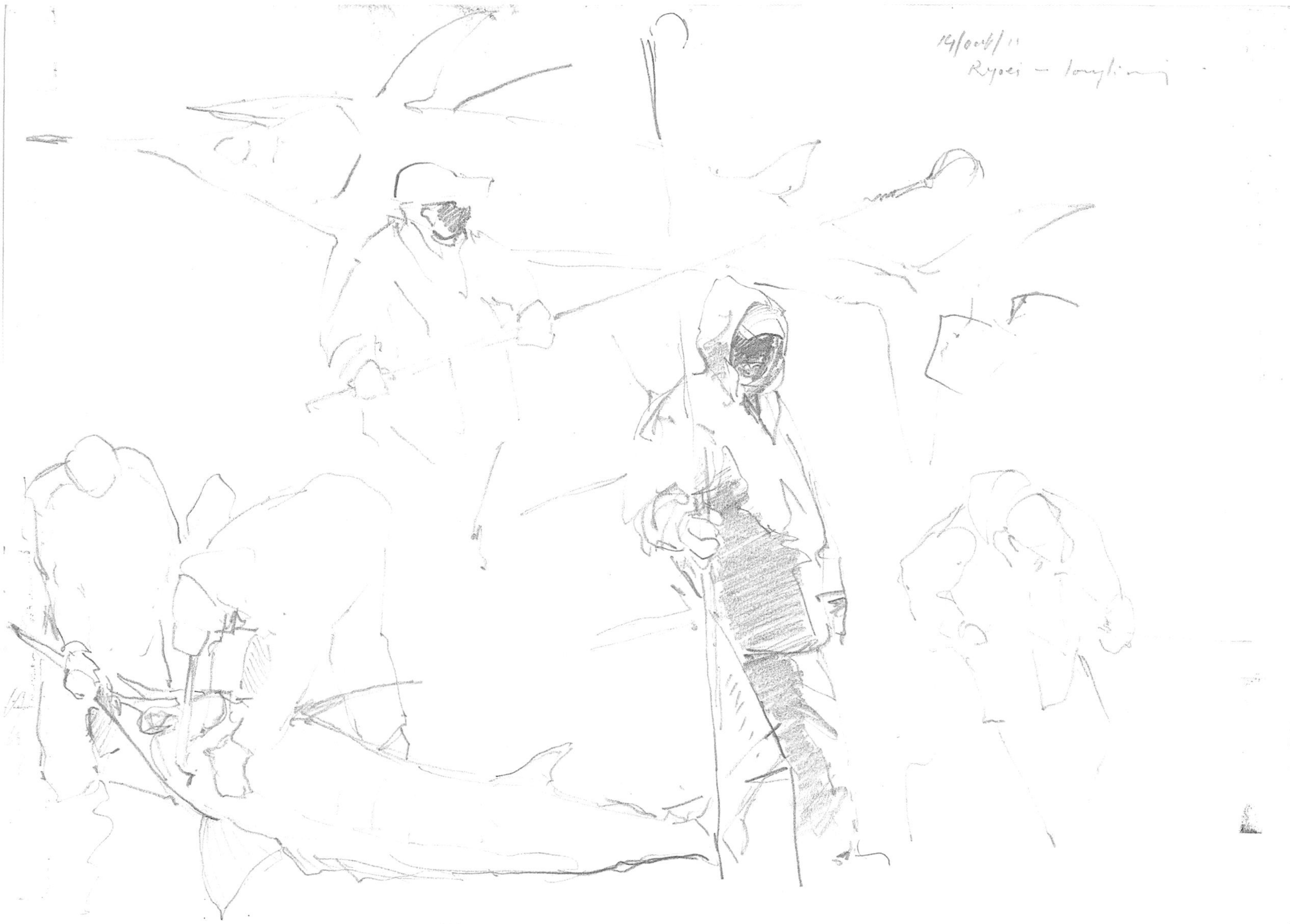

to everybody's advantage, we gradually began to turn things around'. I was eager for an opportunity to witness this significant part of the bycatch story.

Within a few days I was aboard the *Marie Marine*, a 650 ton stern-trawler sailing out of Cape Town for a six day voyage into the southern end of the Benguela Current. The cold waters of the current run northward along the west coast of southern Africa, pushed by prevailing winds that keep it inshore. We were heading for the edge of the continental shelf where colder nutrient-rich waters well up from the deep ocean to make it one of the most productive ocean areas in the world.

I get up on deck at first light and head for the safe vantage of the gantry platform that arches over the stern. The only access is across the main working deck so it is essential that I am up there and out of the way before the trawl net is hauled. The day is bright with a light breeze, and a calm rolling indigo sea. Around the horizon are other trawlers: two or three a long way off, another crossing a few miles ahead, and one on a course running close and parallel. It is entirely subjective, I know, but in two weeks at sea on *Ryoei* there was never a sight of any other longliner. Only two days on *Marie Marine* and we are surrounded by industrial-scale fishing. I have an overwhelming sense of the intense pressure facing the ocean's resources.

Behind one of the distant trawlers I can see a sprinkling of birds stretching a long way downwind. Another vessel in the middle distance has a loose cloud of birds around it. The nearest has a mass of flashing white and dark seabird forms milling around the stern. I can make out cape gannets and kelp gulls, white-chinned and cape petrels, sooty shearwaters, shy and black-browed albatrosses. The density and activity of the following birds indicate the different trawling stages, the greatest numbers gathering around a net brought to the surface or a vessel discharging offal.

Heading up wind at a steady 4 or 5 knots, *Marie Marine* has had her nets on the bottom since the early hours. The two warp cables hauling the net were payed out from enormous winches. They run down the length of the trawl deck on each side – through giant pulleys, over the stern and down into the wake below. The steely grey warps, as thick as soup cans, cut through the water like an armoured slicer. Dangling over them are the 'tori' lines – two curtains of red hosepipe trailing from ropes fixed to the gantry rail. They slope and twist down the wake and end at two traffic cones that create just enough drag to keep them taut.

Inside the safety zone of the bird-scaring lines, numerous fur seals are swimming lazily, sometimes stopping to roll and scratch. Above them drift kelp gulls and cape gannets. Outside the 'tori' lines, elegant black-browed, shy and yellow-nosed albatrosses pass through streams of cape petrels and Wilson's storm-petrels. There is a sense that all the birds are just cruising along keeping company with us in anticipation of the nets appearing at the sea surface.

At night, the drama of congregating birds and the crew

BY-CATCH

Highly productive areas of the global oceans, such as upwellings and fronts, are of key importance to the world's commercial longline fisheries. They are also the rich foraging grounds for seabirds vulnerable to being caught as bycatch, particularly albatrosses and petrels.

Effective action to reduce seabird bycatch involves five key steps: recognising the problem, setting requirements for mitigation measures, collecting representative bycatch data, establishing systems to monitor compliance, and evaluation and refinement of measures. Since 2004, significant progress has been made in the tuna commissions: all five now have requirements for their longline vessels to use bycatch mitigation measures in areas overlapping with albatrosses, and all five are establishing bycatch data collection programs.

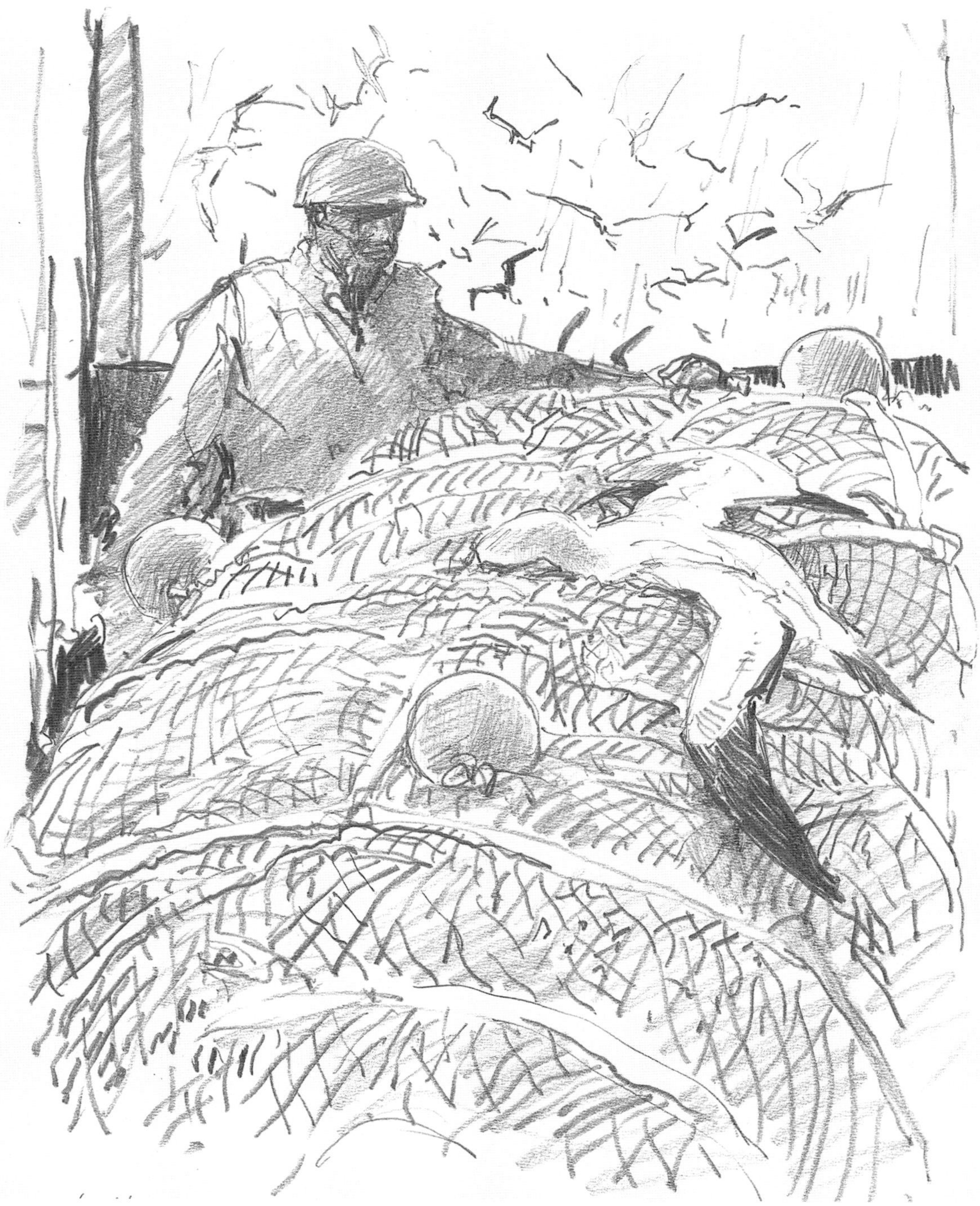

69 cape gannet – bycatch in the trawl net, *Marie Marine*, September, 2010
42 × 30 cm · pencil

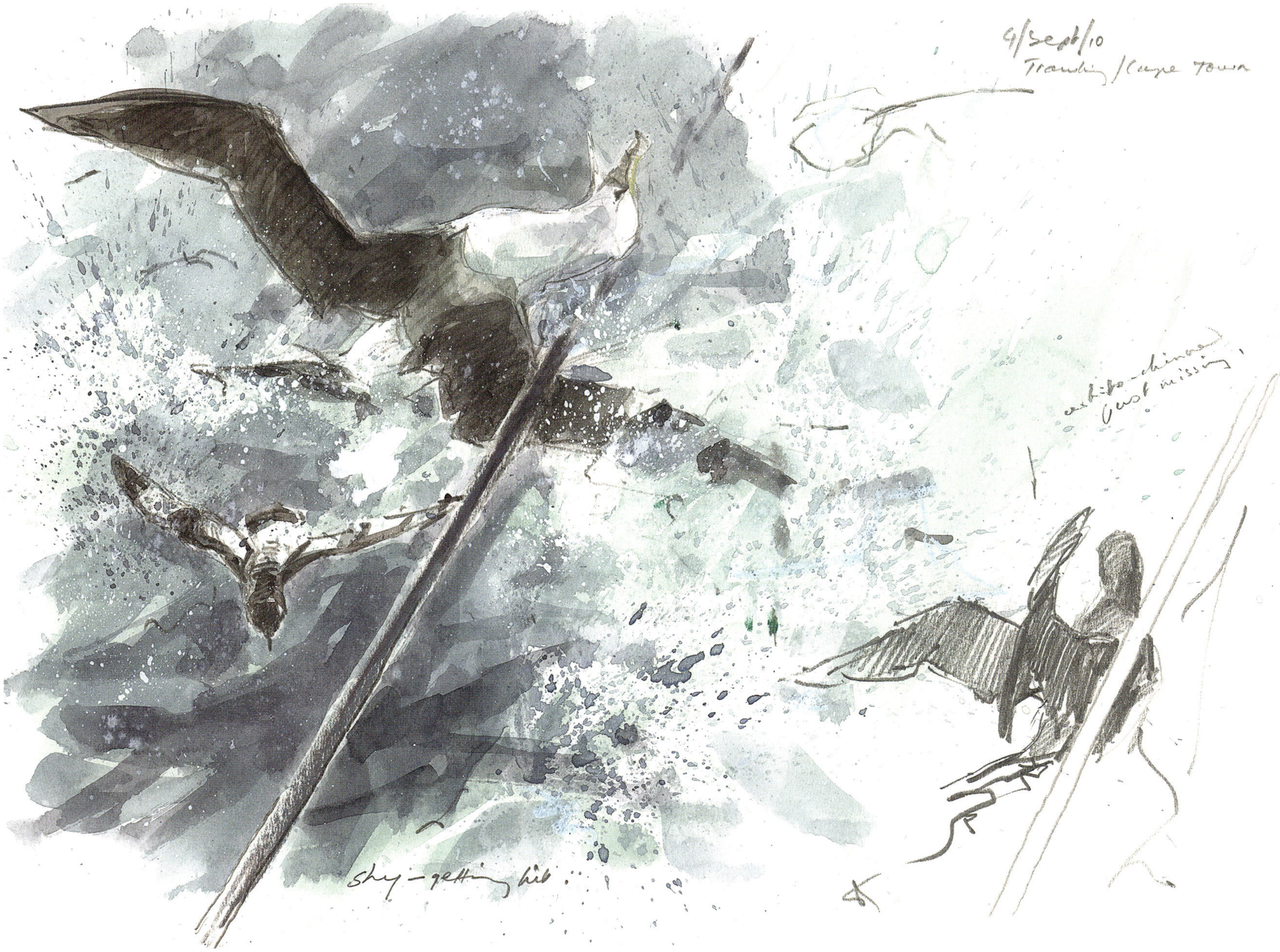

70 Collision: shy albatross and trawler cable
Watercolour and pencil
42cm × 30cm

hauling nets takes on much more of a theatrical feel. From high up on gantry beams and bulkheads lamps throw a harsh orange glow over the deck. Spotlights on gunwales and gangways pick out winches and capstans, and huge coils of cables and chains stand like theatre props in the deep shadow of the wings. The stern ramp and opening under the gantry form a stage where the deckhands move like actors in a synchronized sequence of tasks and procedures while the ship heaves to the sound of waves, grinding winches, and thumping engine noises. The backdrop is the vast curtain of ocean blackness flecked by the patterns of massed birds crossing through the beams of light.

The first indication of the spectacle about to unfold is one of the crew hauling in the 'tori' lines, and a general readying of cables and rope lines on the main trawl deck. The bird-scaring lines have to be out of the way so they do not get entangled when the warp cables are wound in. The whole ship shudders and shakes to the noise of thundering and clanking cables and chains as it slows and the enormous winches start hauling. This is a signal for all the birds and seals for miles around to gather around us, as if we are at the centre of a vortex sucking in every living thing in sight. From my high vantage point I can see streams of birds turning in our direction. Seals become more active and start clustering around the stern. An ever-growing mass of birds cluster above me, and gather on the sea surface all around *Marie Marine*.

Ten minutes later, with turbulence showing that the net is approaching the surface, the plunging and diving starts. The net breaks the surface and a chaotic tangle of albatrosses, petrels, gannets, gulls and seals plunders the

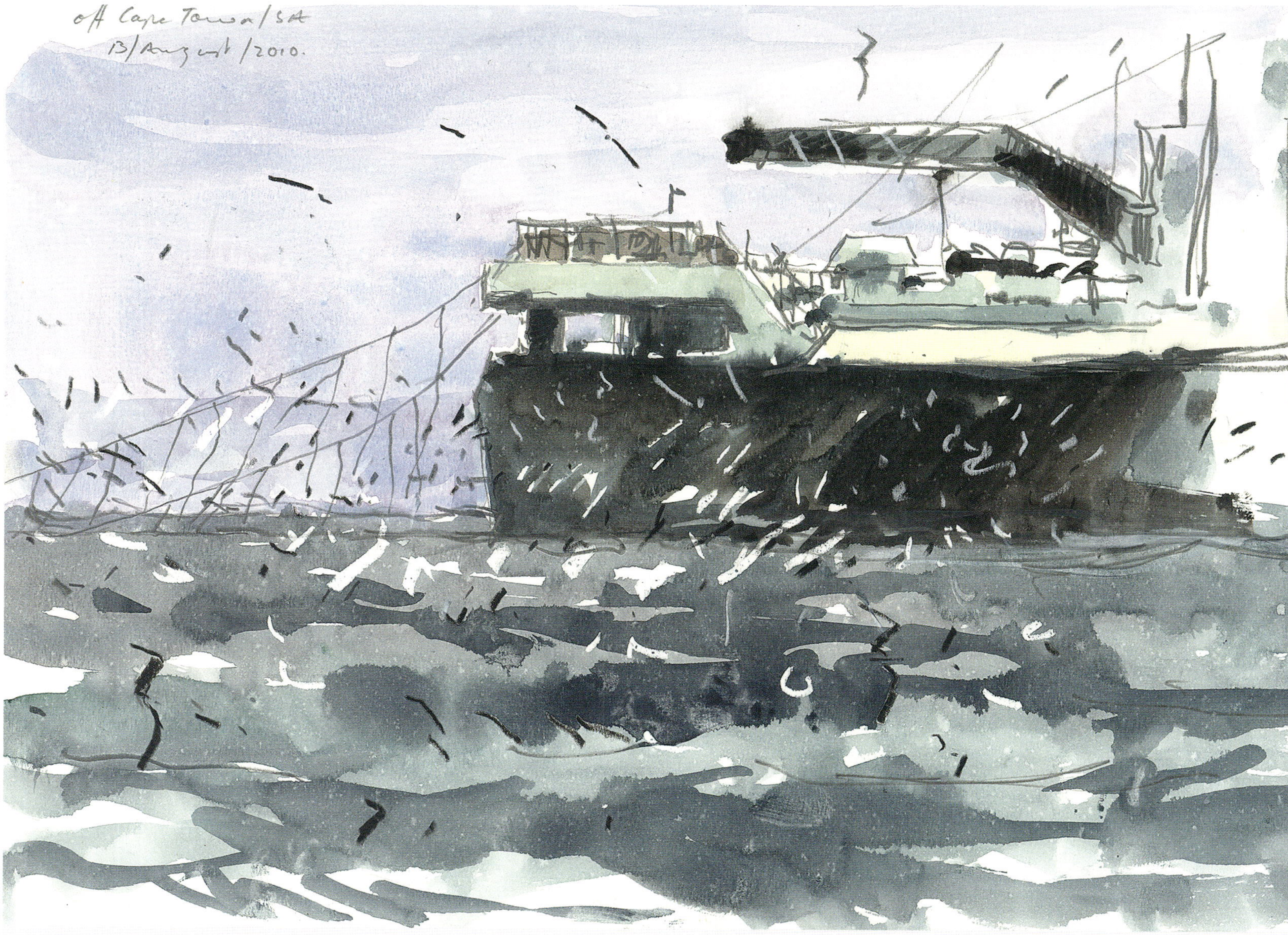

BIRD SCARING LINES / 'TORI' LINES

Streamer lines, also called 'tori' or bird-scaring lines, are one of the most effective devices for mitigating losses of birds. They are lengths of rope with brightly-coloured streamers of different lengths spaced at intervals. The lines are towed behind vessels from port and starboard to create an effective 'cordon sanitaire' around the area of most danger to seabirds. The key to their effectiveness is having the lines fixed high enough on the stern to achieve a curtain of height and sufficient length to cover the warps. Critically, they must also be set before the discharge of waste and offal overboard attracts large numbers of birds.

Used on their own, 'tori' lines can reduce seabird bycatch significantly. However, they work even more effectively – particularly in longline fisheries – when used in combination with other mitigation measures, such as setting at night, weighting lines so that baited hooks sink rapidly out of reach of the birds, and carefully managing how offal is discharged overboard.

bounty spilling from the net. There are gannets landing on it jabbing between the meshes, seals colliding with albatrosses, yellow-nosed and shy albatrosses snatching fish from each other, cape petrels darting about, squabbling giant petrels threatening white-chinned petrels, and Wilson's and black-bellied storm-petrels fluttering in between plunge-diving shearwaters. Floating low in its collar of buoys, the net is hauled towards the stern and up the slipway. Gannets are still thrashing at it as the bulging whale-like form is dragged to a halt on the trawl deck. Then the net is hauled high into the gantry, before its bloated neck unlocks over the chute, and the catch disgorges in a cascade of struggling silver onto the processing deck below.

Only 15 or 20 minutes after it appeared on the surface, the net is dragged back down the slipway and the ship gets underway again. The massive warp cables tighten as the nets sinks – and it gets much more

71 Seabirds, 'tori' lines, and the stern of a trawler off South Africa, August, 2010, 30 × 42 cm · watercolour and pencil

SAVE THE ALBATROSS CAMPAIGN / ALBATROSS TASK FORCE

The BirdLife Save the Albatross Campaign was launched by HRH Prince Charles in 2000. The focus of the campaign is reducing seabird bycatch through a combination of 'grass roots' action and advocacy.

To promote the uptake of mitigation measures, in 2005 BirdLife International and the RSPB (BirdLife in the UK) formed the Albatross Task Force (ATF), with their first team based in South Africa. The ATF is the world's first team of dedicated mitigation instructors and the team works at the frontline of seabird conservation in seabird bycatch 'hotspots' to develop and test new mitigations measures and demonstrate the adoption of 'best practice' mitigation.

One of the ATFs great strengths is the local knowledge that underpins its international focus. Recruiting and training local mitigation experts provides a unique response to the urgent need to reduce seabird bycatch on a global scale. Working in partnership with industry and government, the ATF has achieved reductions in seabird bycatch of up to 80% in some target fisheries and is now active in eight countries throughout southern Africa and South America. They now plan to mirror this success in other regions of the worlds where bycatch is a major cause of seabird population declines.

72 Chaos of birds around the stern of a trawler, September, 2010
30 × 42 cm
watercolour and pencil

dangerous for the foraging birds. The 'tori' lines cannot deploy until the trawl is on the bottom, but the catch processing below deck is already firing a broadside of offal and discards from a pipe just above water-level on the starboard side, sending a stream of waste swirling around the cable and down the wake. In the few minutes before the bird scaring lines go out, I watch as white-chinned petrels swerve or flap furiously to get out of the way, I see shy albatrosses struggling sideways to escape, see gannets hurtling around the warp cables and glimpse a black-browed albatross strike the cable and vanish in a tumbling tangle of wings.

In the all chaos and confusion of the contact between seabirds and fishermen I have observed and drawn

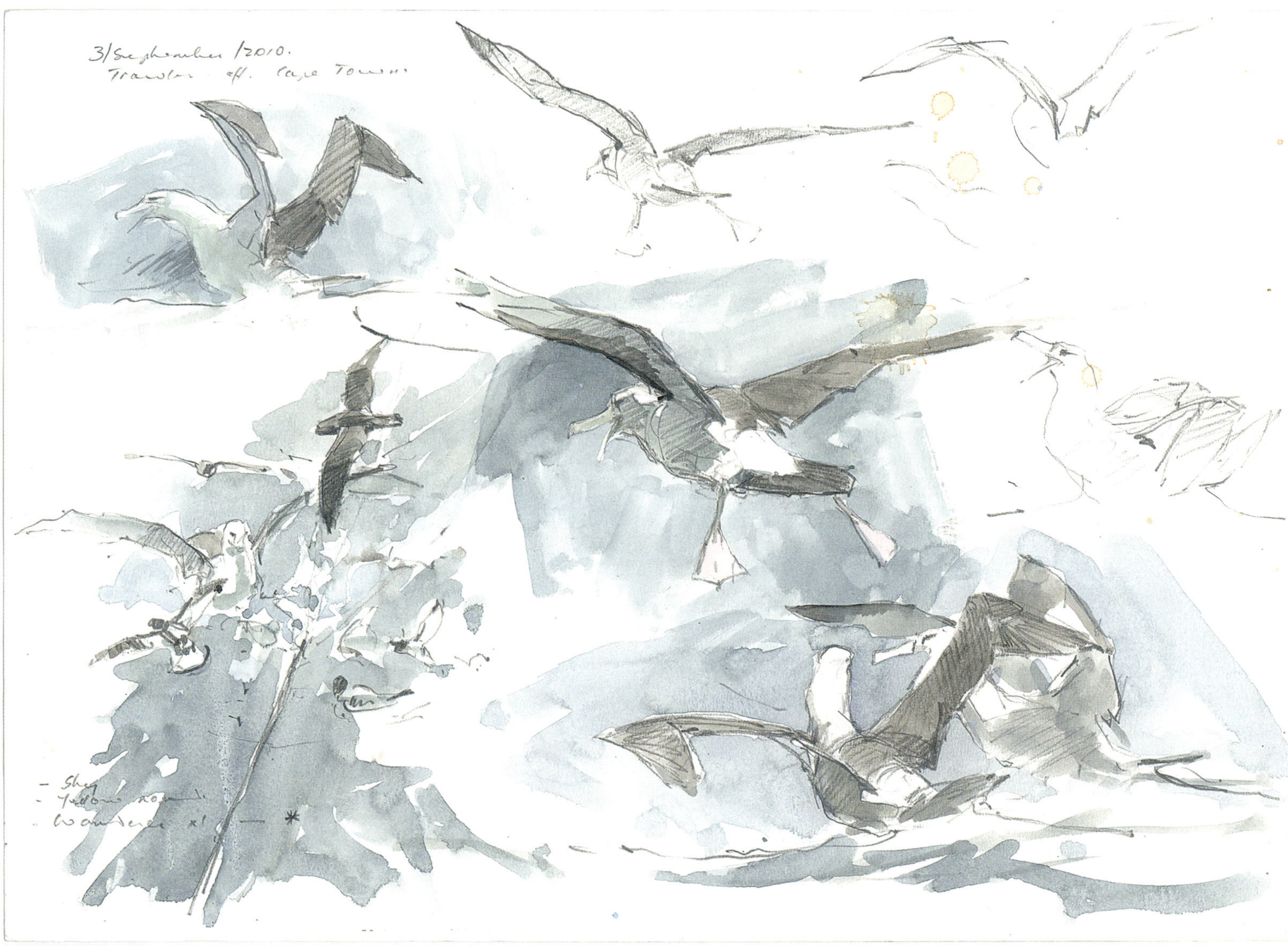

There are two forms of yellow-nosed albatross that can be seen in waters around South Africa; the western or Atlantic yellow-nosed (*Thalassarche chlororhynchos*), and the Eastern or Indian yellow-nosed (*Thalassarche carteri*). They are difficult to tell apart, and Atlantic birds especially, can sometimes be confused with grey-headed albatross.

They are the smallest mollymauks in the Southern Ocean with a distinctive slender appearance due to their small heads tapering to narrow black bills. Yellow-nosed derives from the distinctive and characteristic yellow streak that runs down the bill-top ending in a reddish-pink tip.

Atlantic adults have a bluish-grey head and neck forming a clearly demarked hood that contrasts with the otherwise white underparts. The forehead and crown are slightly paler and some may show white on the chin and throat. In general, the light grey hood allows ready separation from Indian yellow-nosed albatross which have entirely white heads.

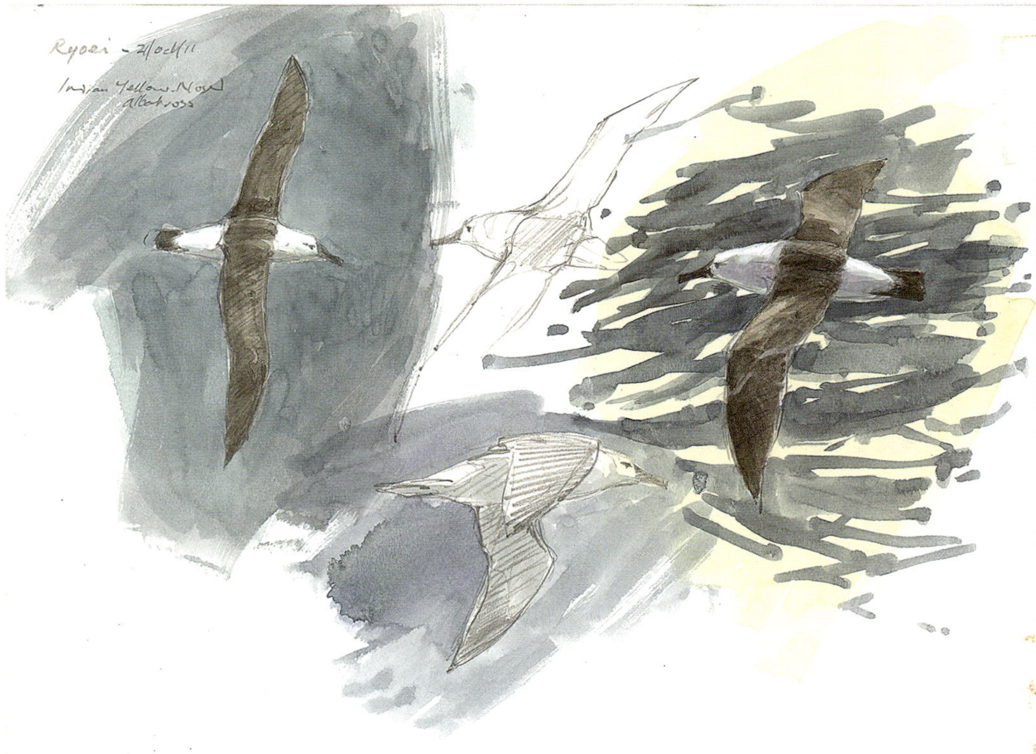

73 Indian yellow-nosed albatross, *Ryoei*, October, 2011
30 x 42 cm · watercolour and pencil

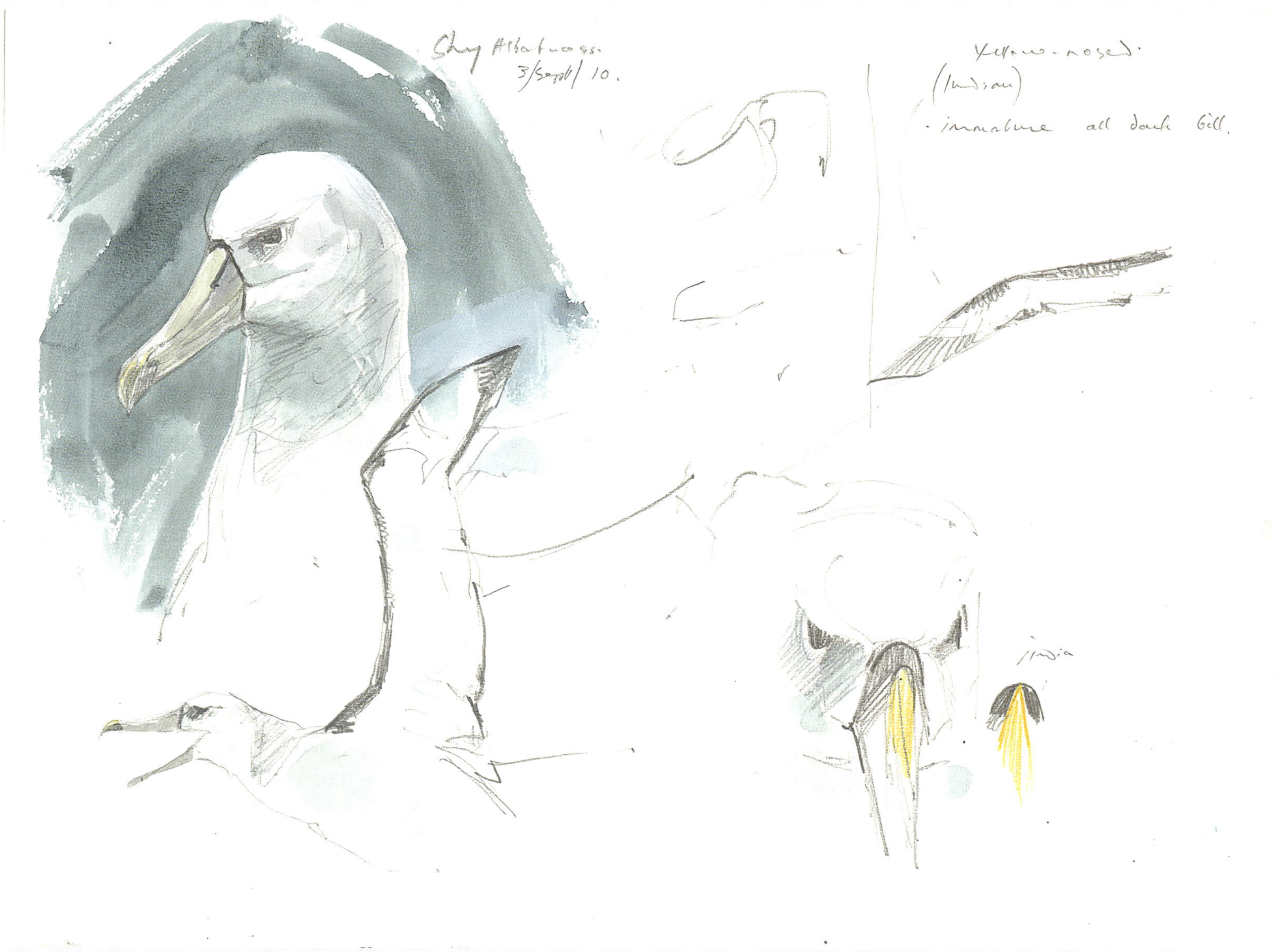

74 Shy albatross (left) and Indian yellow-nosed albatross, (right), September, 2010
30 × 42 cm · watercolour and pencil

during my time in South African waters, I cannot say I definitely witnessed the death of an albatross – but I know it happens. Spending time at the cutting edge of the collision point, I was able to see how and why it happens, and how surprisingly simple and inexpensive mitigation techniques can be highly successful in preventing seabird losses. At sea, I experienced the daily challenge the Task Force faces in bridging the gap between fishermen trying to avoid catching seabirds, and proving to captains and their commercial backers demanding financial return, that mitigation does not affect catches. There is still much to do on the wider international front negotiating with governments, fishing communities and, commercial fish companies for positive conservation outcomes. Meanwhile, a global review of the impact of longline fisheries on seabirds has been published recently. Despite all the efforts to reduce seabird deaths, the estimate remains that upwards of 300,000 birds are being killed every year, and some experts consider this to be too low by a third.

Saving albatrosses and other seabirds depends entirely on the goodwill and practices of fishing masters and their crews, who need the guidance and support of policies and actions at national, regional and international levels, in both territorial and high-seas waters. We have to do all we can to prevent these magnificent birds from slipping away into extinction – and conserve the majesty and abundance of the whole marine ecosystem. Not just for the albatrosses, but to give all seabirds – and fishermen – a future.

75 cape gannet, September, 2010
30 × 42 cm · watercolour and pencil

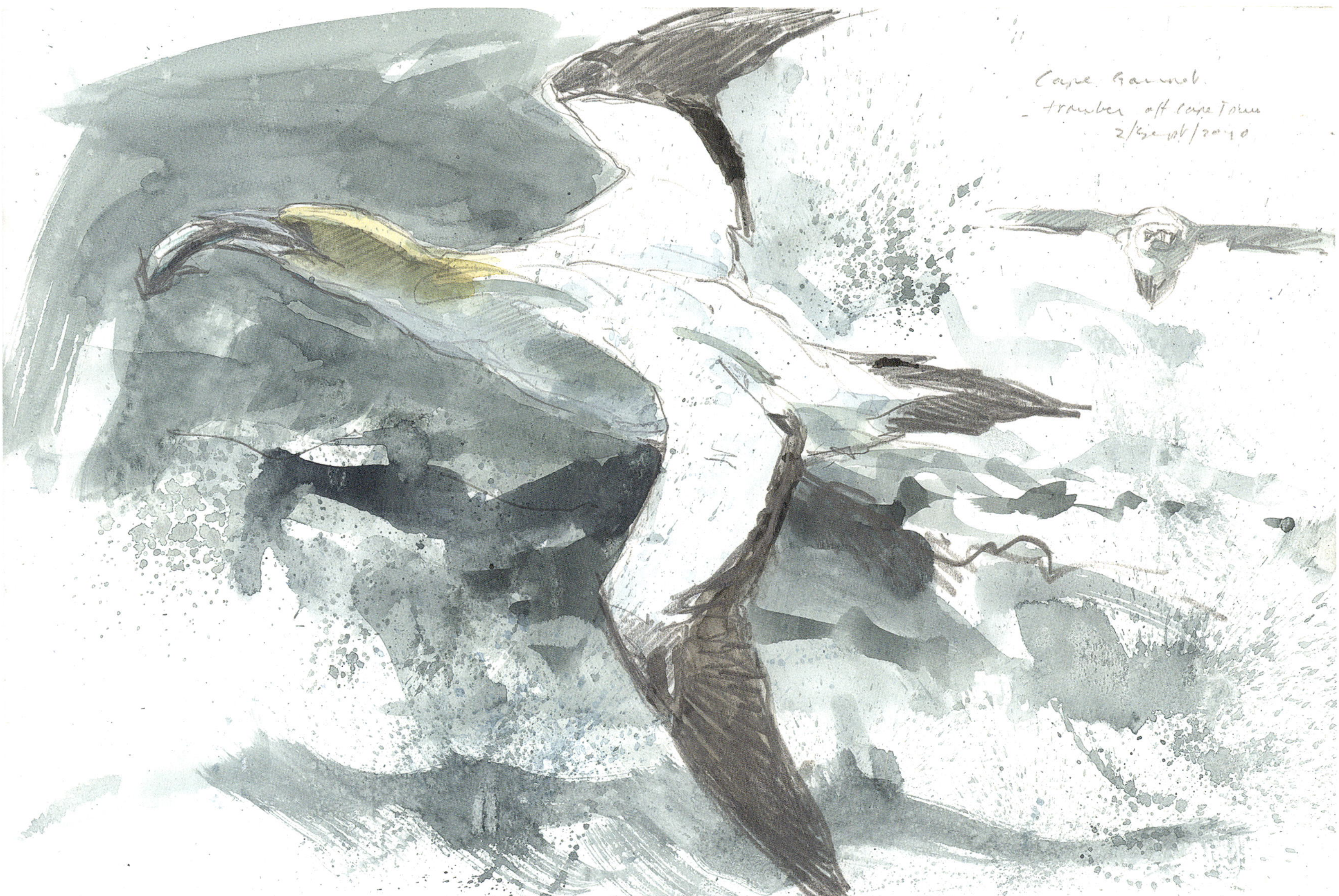

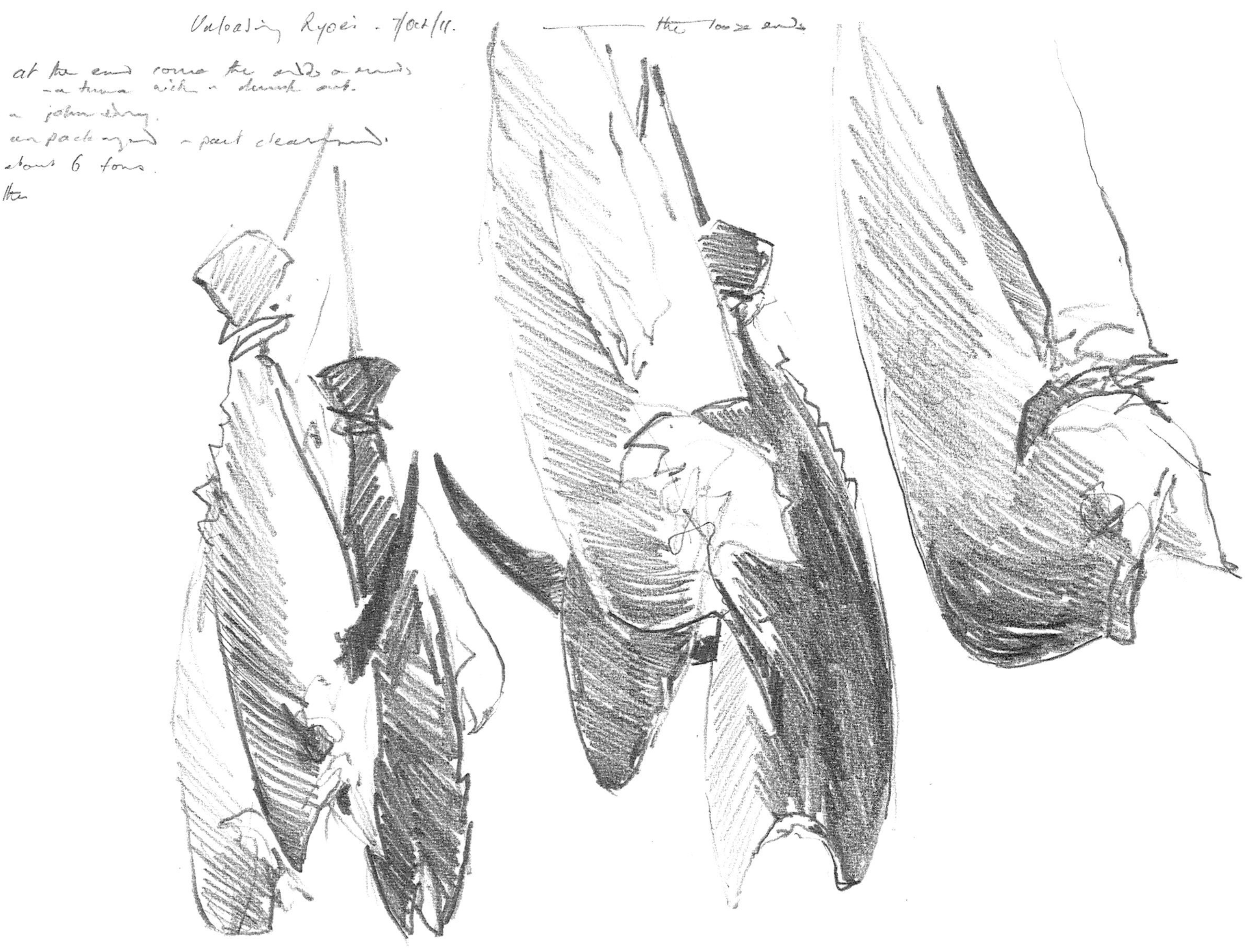

76 Dorado and yellowfin tuna being unloaded, October, 2011
30 × 42 cm · pencil

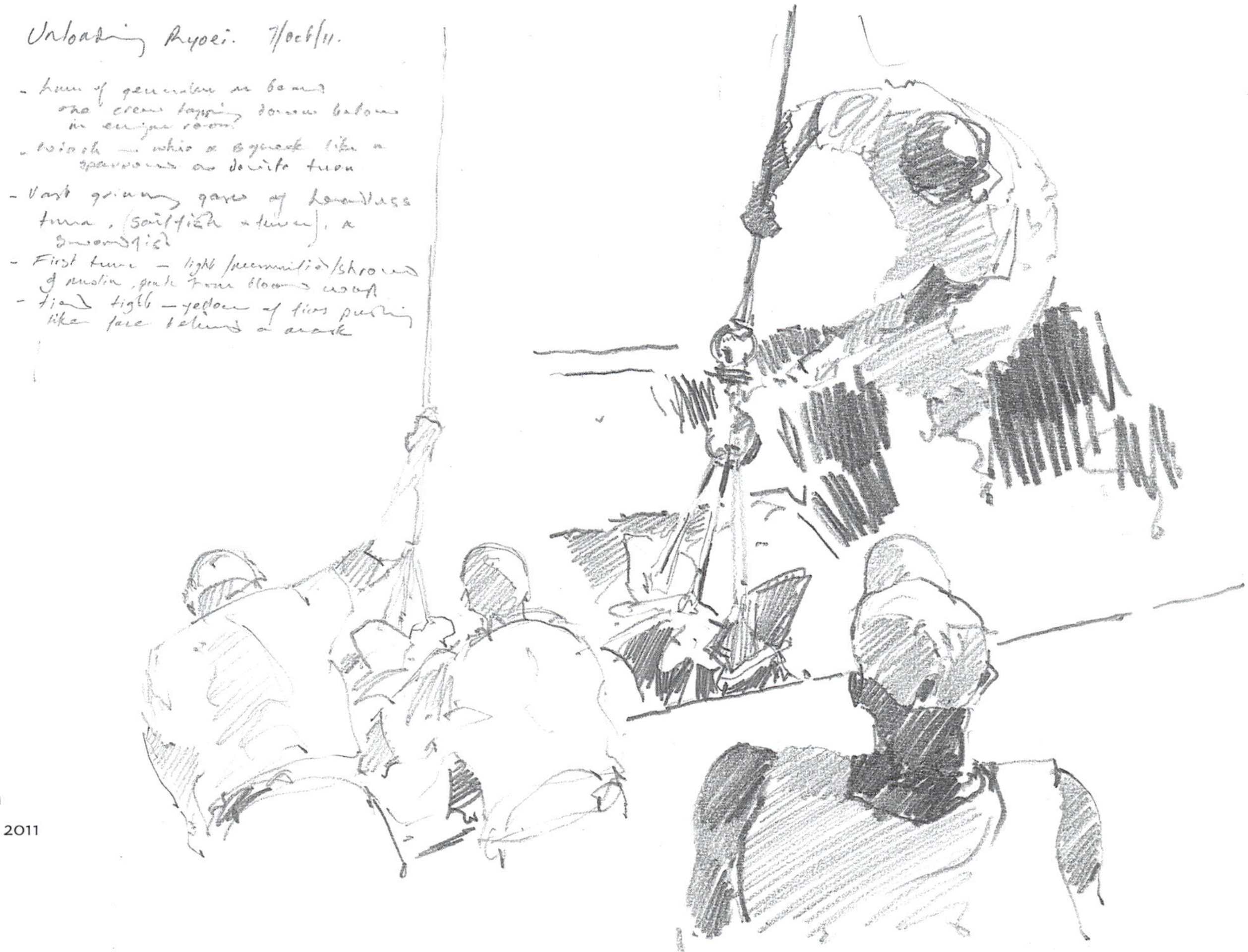

77 Unloading the catch, quayside in Richards Bay, South Africa, October, 2011
30 × 42 cm · pencil

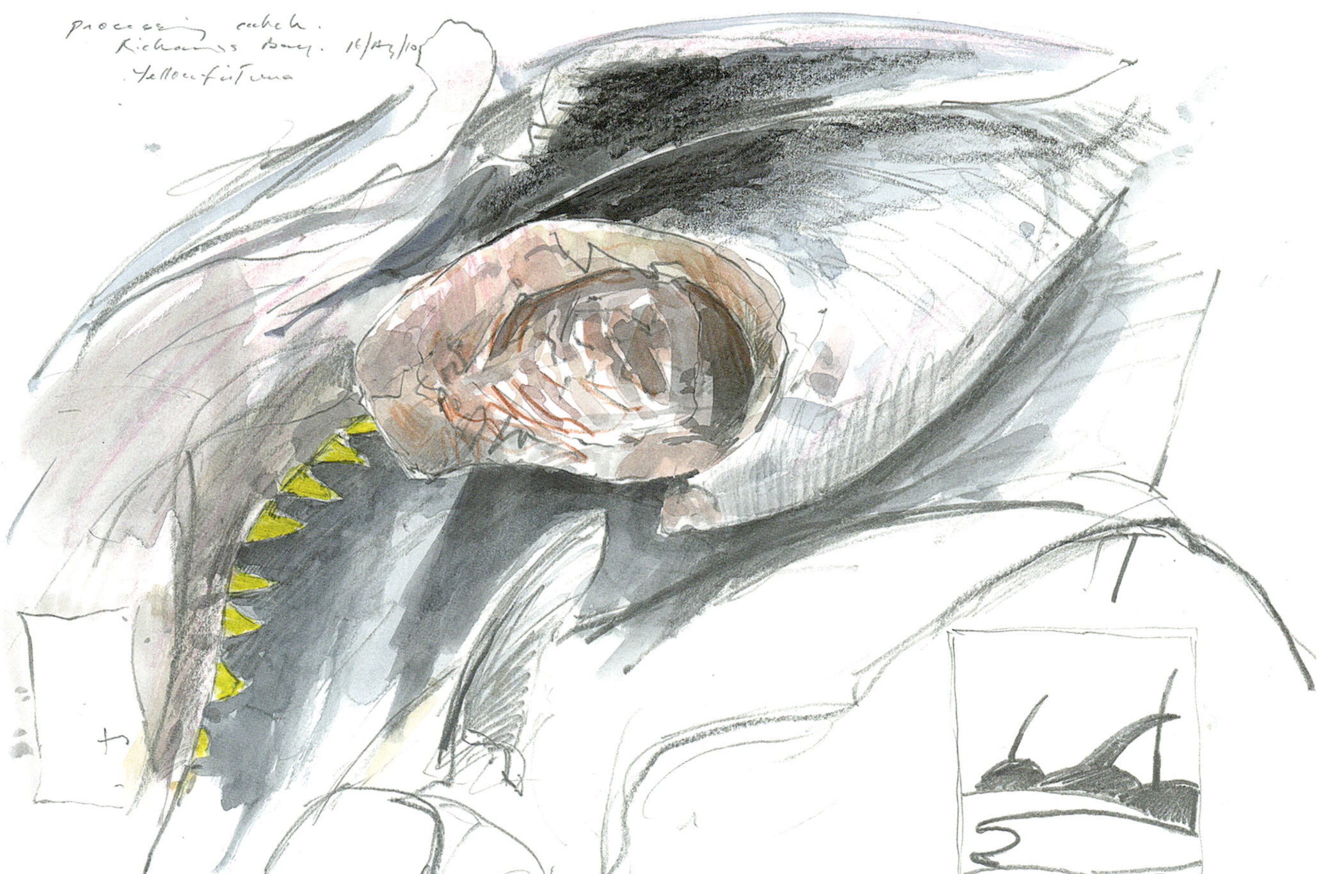

78 Yellowfin tuna in the processing plant, Richards Bay, South Africa, August, 2010
30 × 42 cm · watercolour and pencil

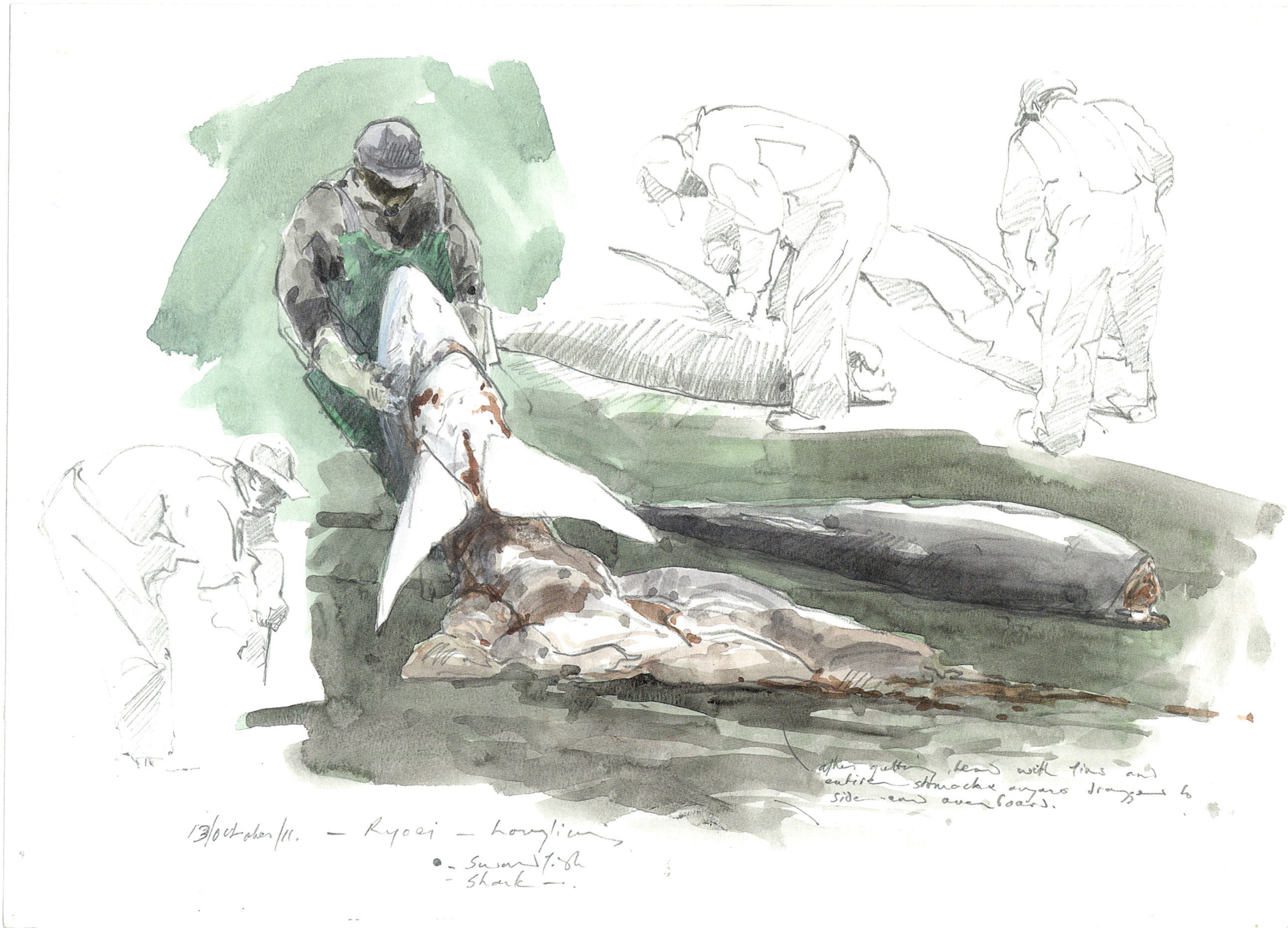

79 Shark bycatch, *Ryoei*, October, 2011
30 × 42 cm · watercolour and pencil

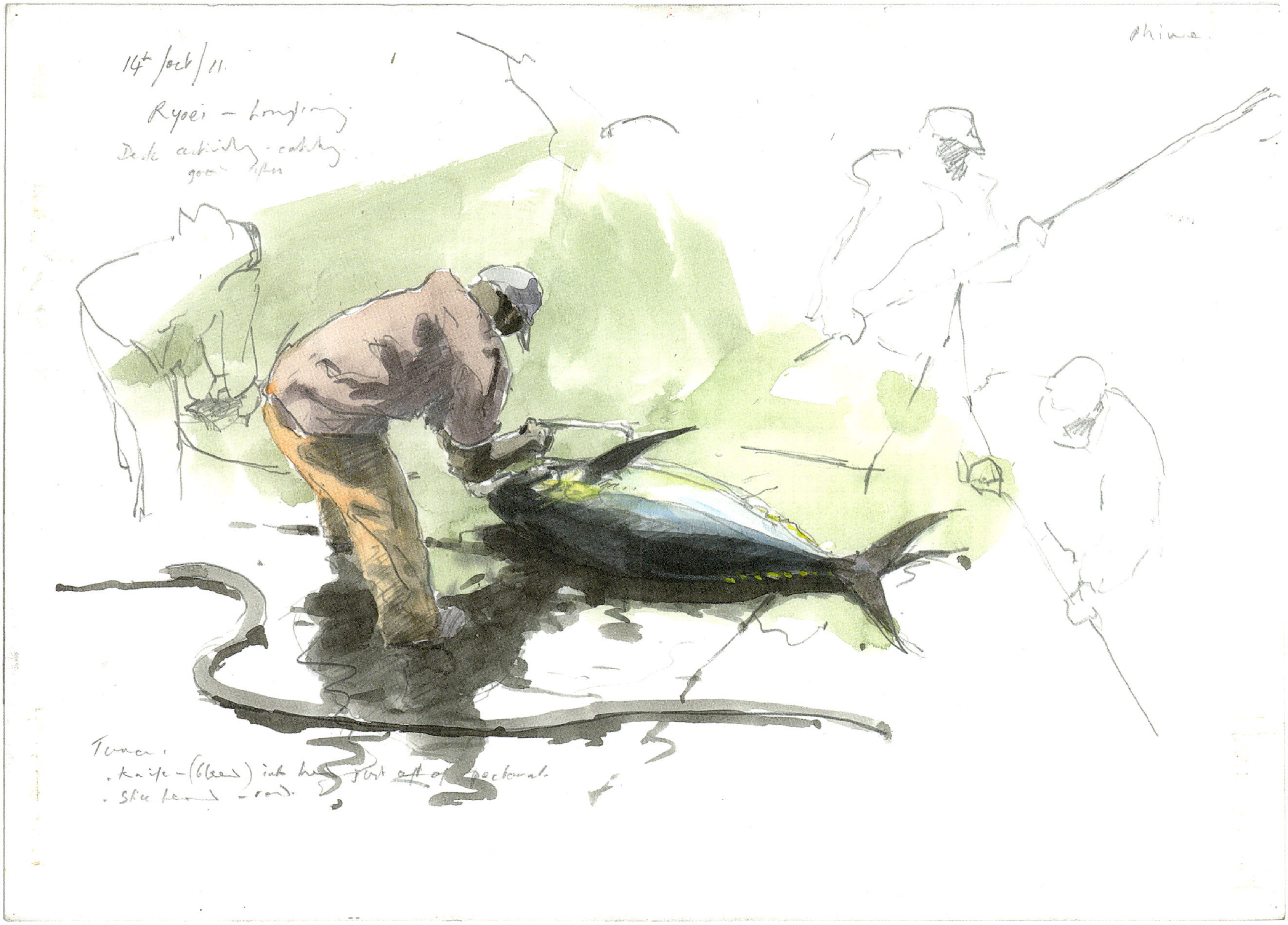

80 Processing tuna, *Ryoei*, October, 2011
30 × 42 cm · watercolour and pencil

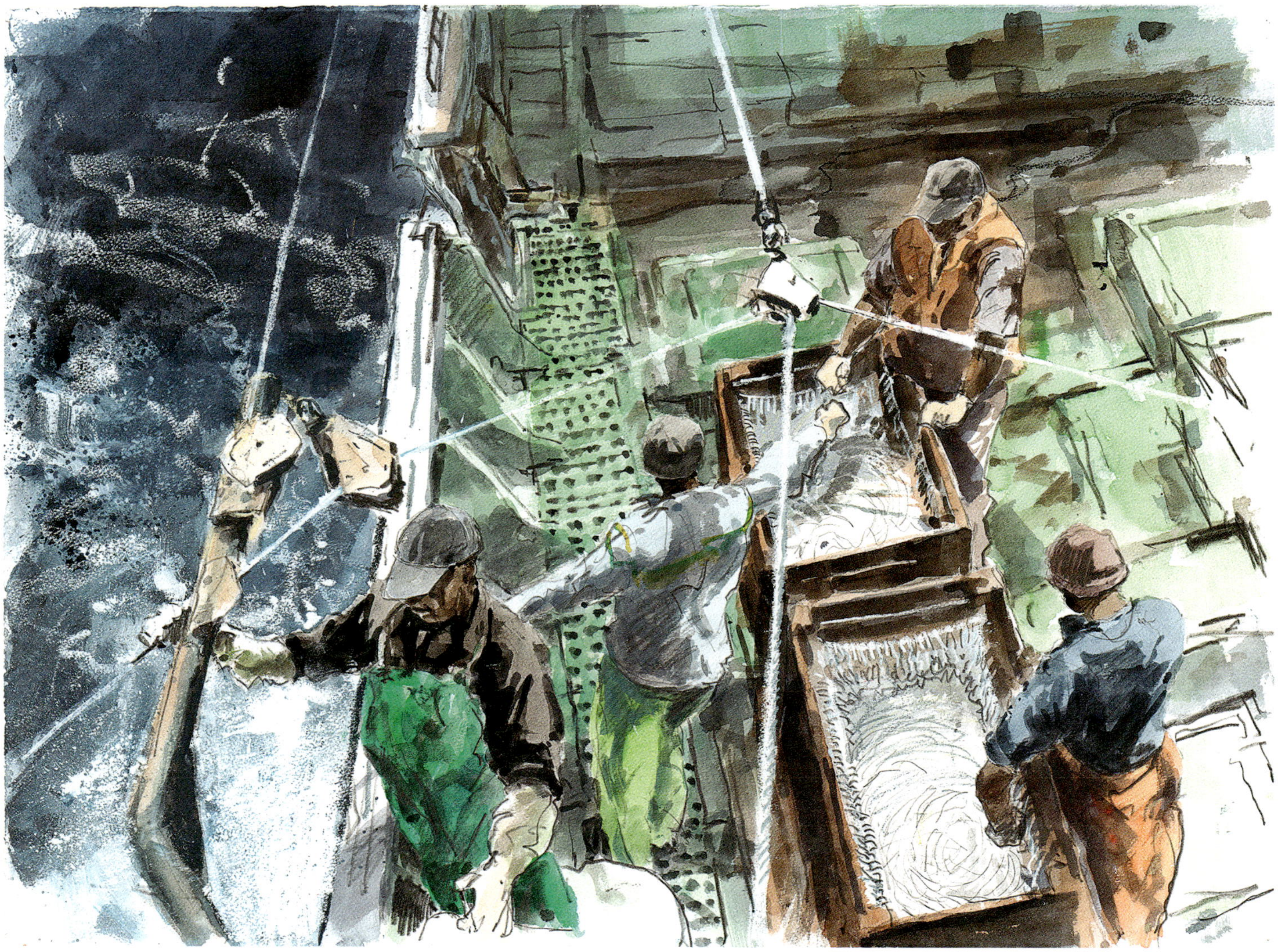

82 Crew at work, *Ryoei*, October, 2011
57 × 77 cm · watercolour / mixed media

81 Longlining off South Africa, 2012
76 × 76 cm · oil

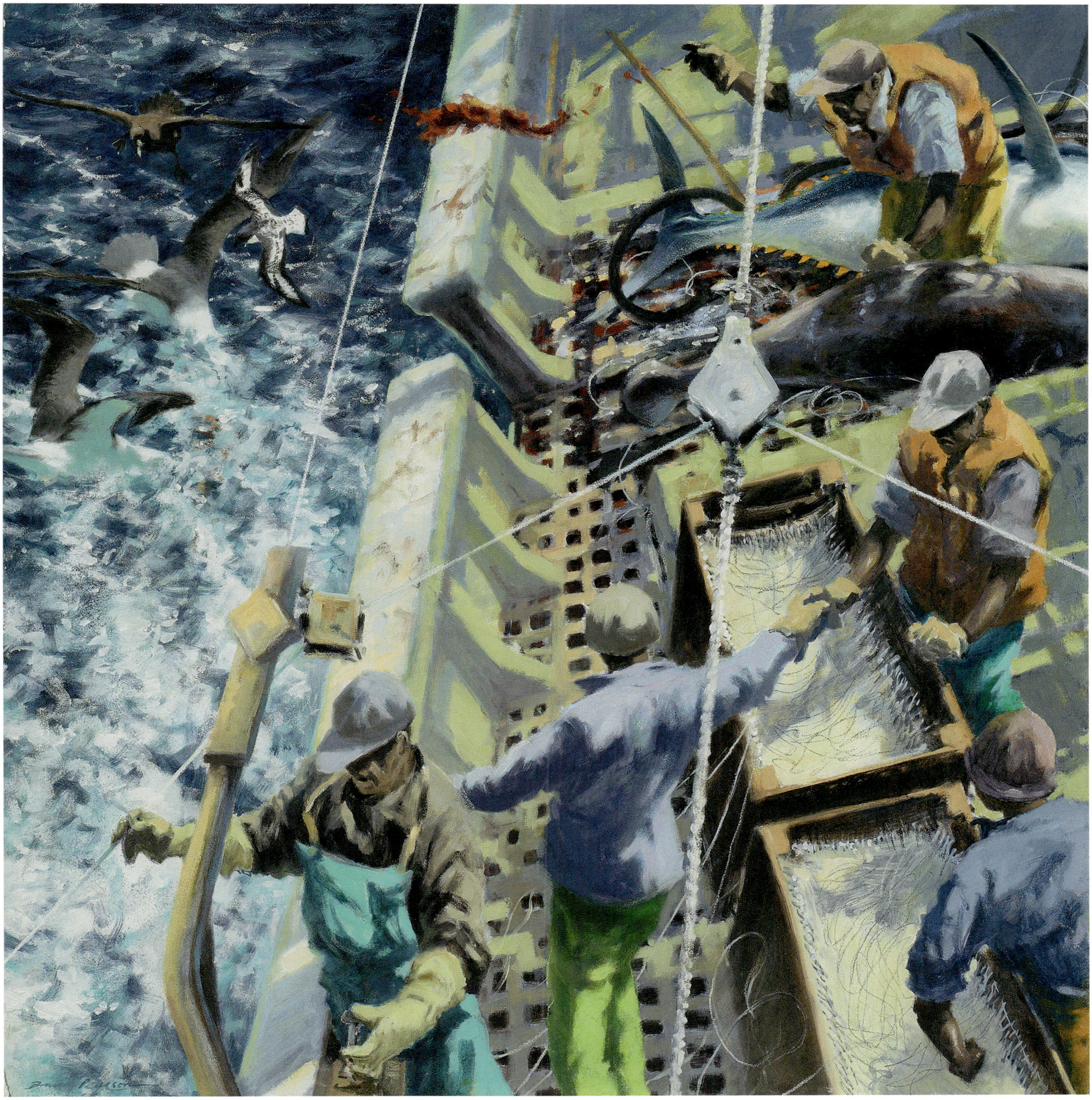

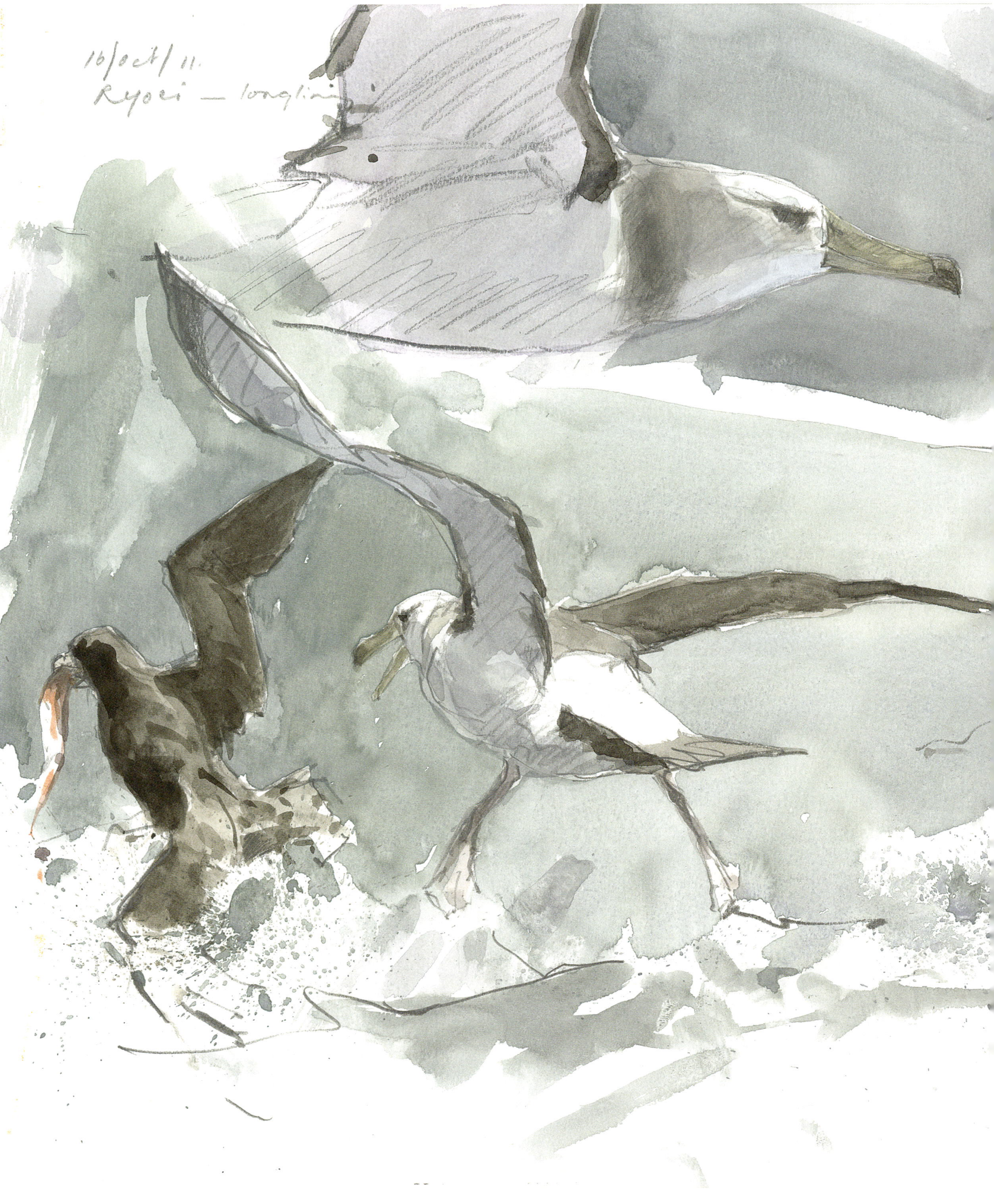
16/oct/11.
Ryoei — longlin

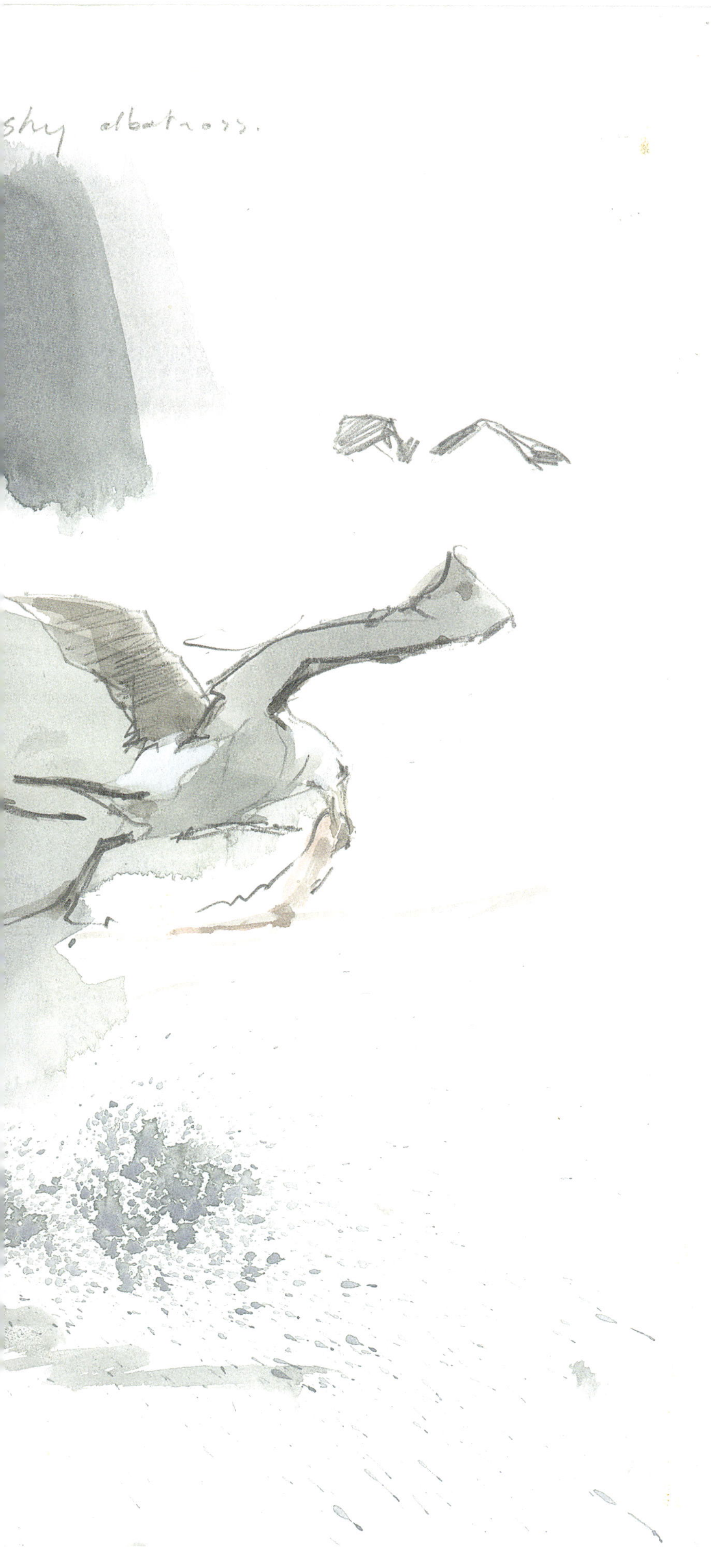

83 White-chinned petrel and shy albatross activity as offal goes overboard, October, 2011
30 × 42 cm · watercolour and pencil

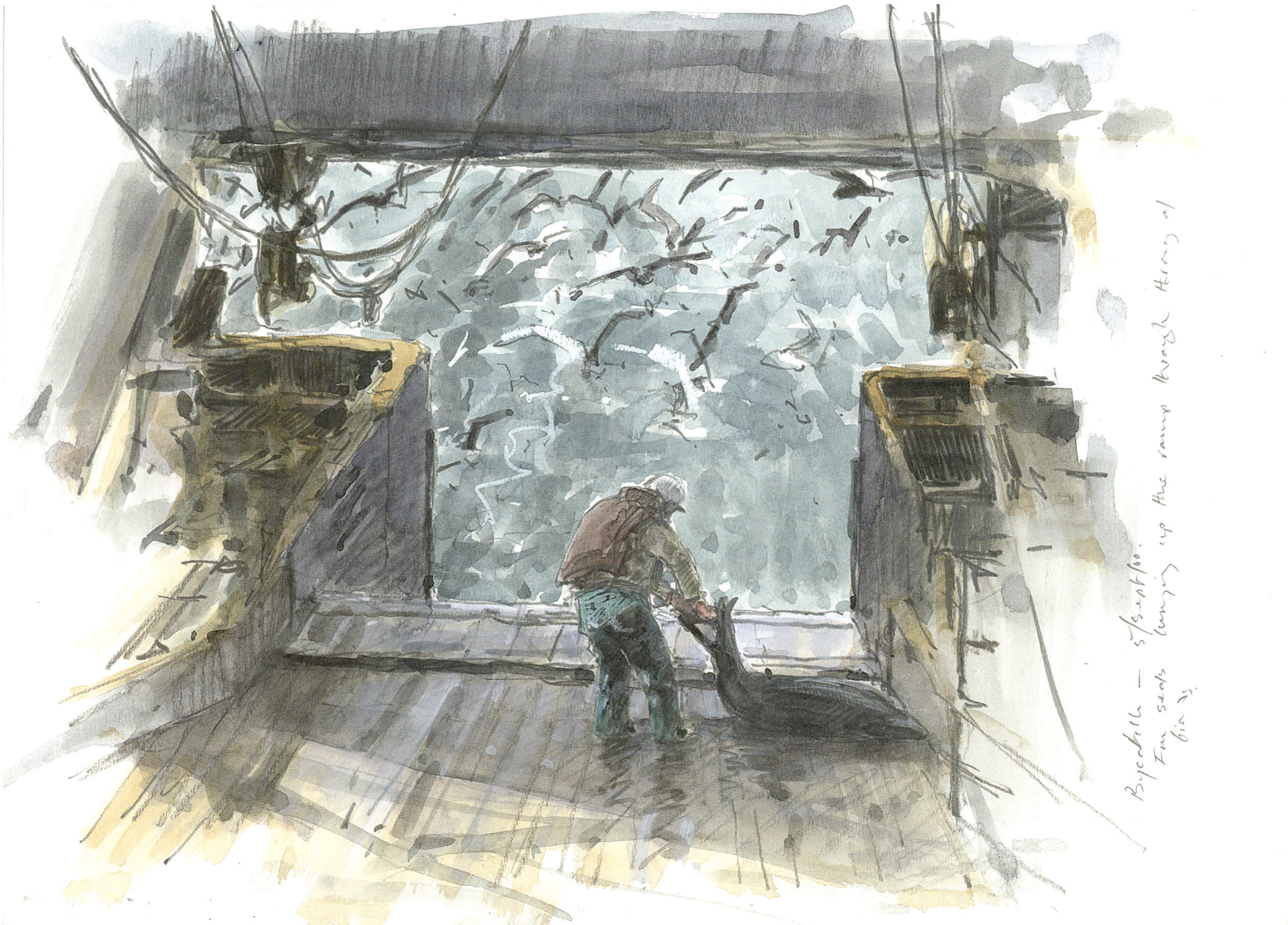

84 Bycatch. Removal of fur seal caught in the trawl net, *Marie Marine*, September, 2010
30 × 42 cm · watercolour and pencil

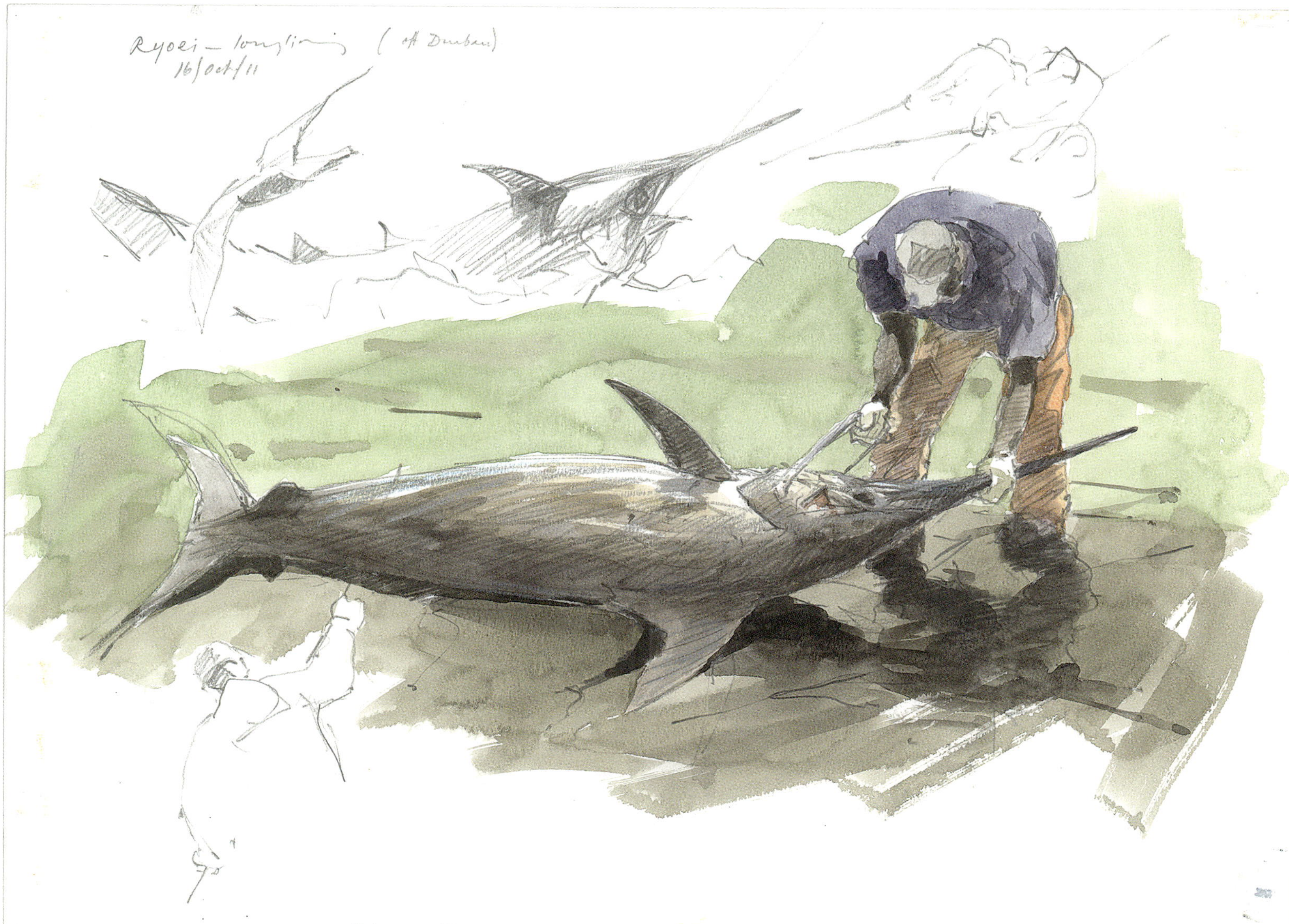

85 Processing a swordfish, *Ryoei*, October, 2011
30 × 42 cm · watercolour and pencil

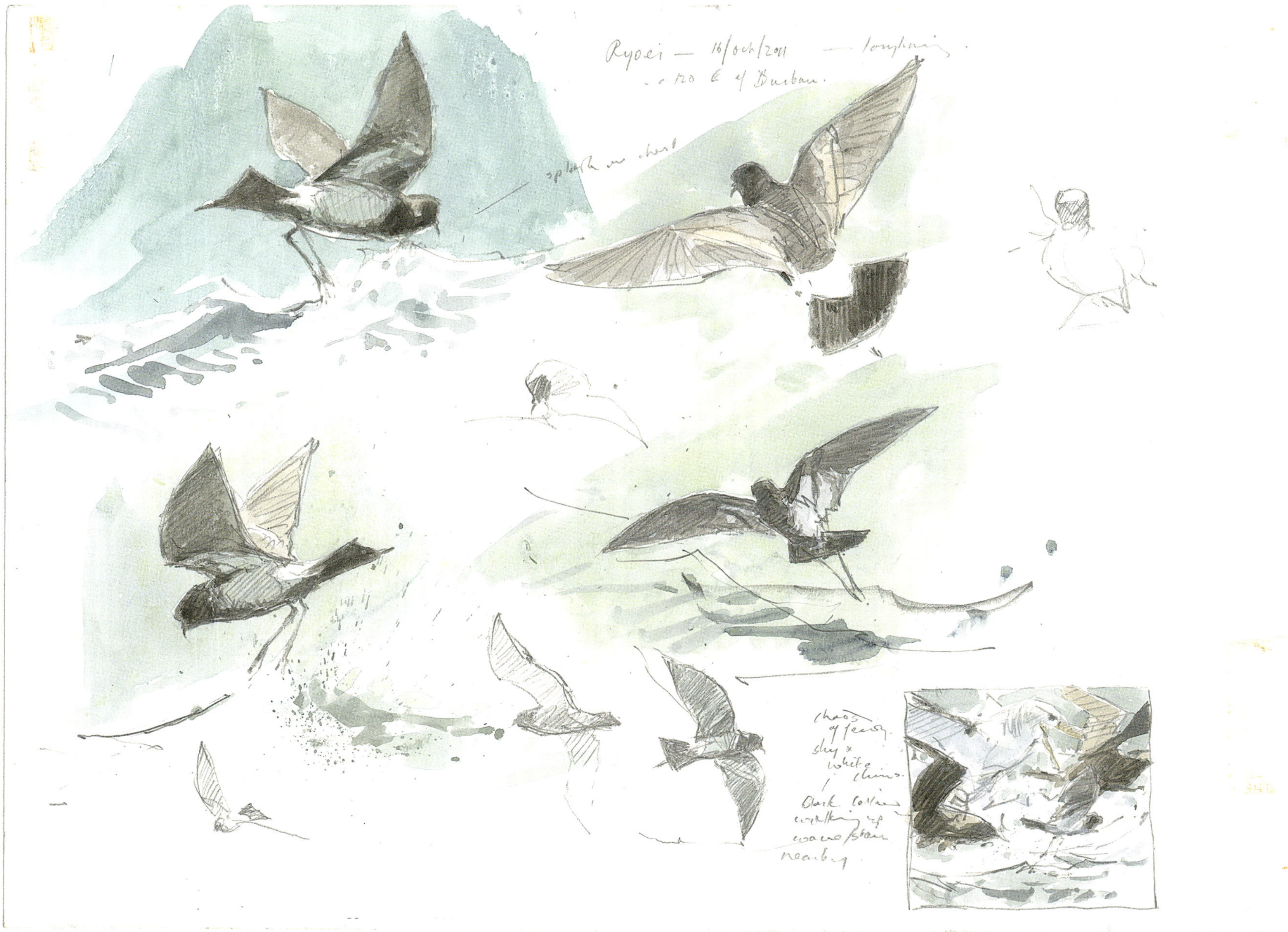

86 Black-bellied storm petrels, *Ryoei*, October, 2011
30 × 42 cm · watercolour and pencil

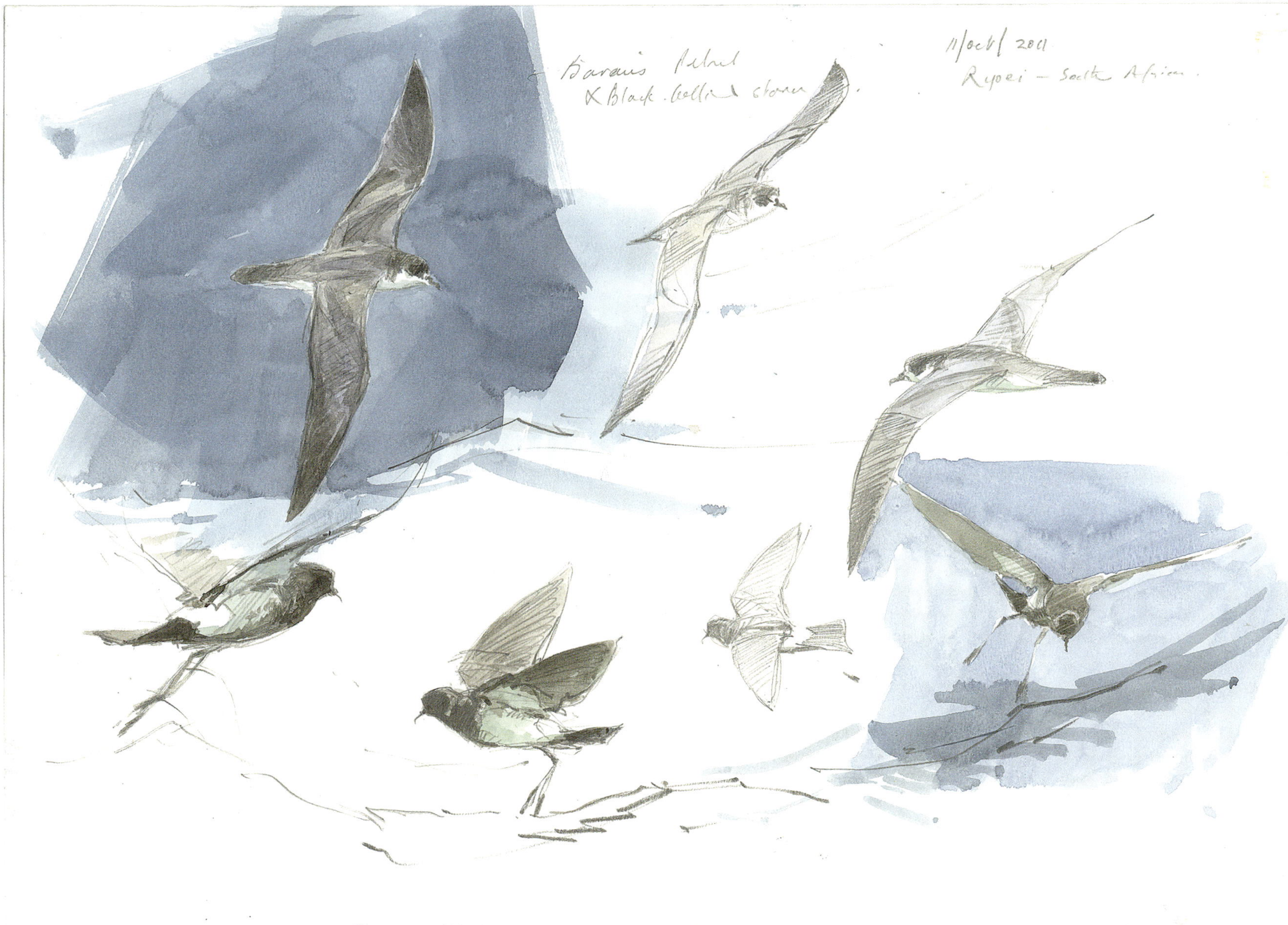

87 Barau's petrel and black-bellied storm petrels, *Ryoei*, October, 2011
30 × 42 cm · watercolour and pencil

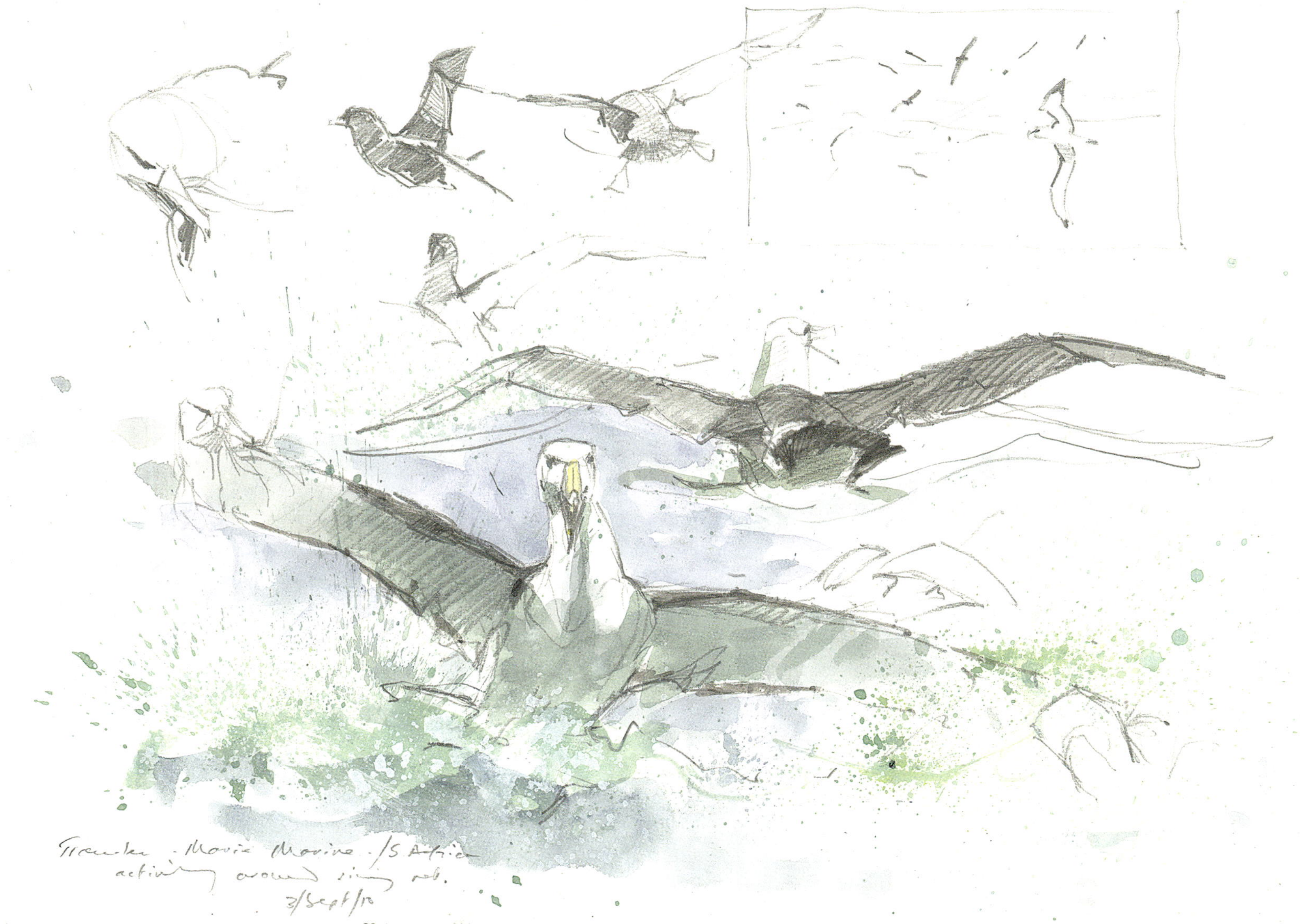

88 Chaos of birds around the stern of a trawler, September, 2010
30 × 42 cm · watercolour and pencil

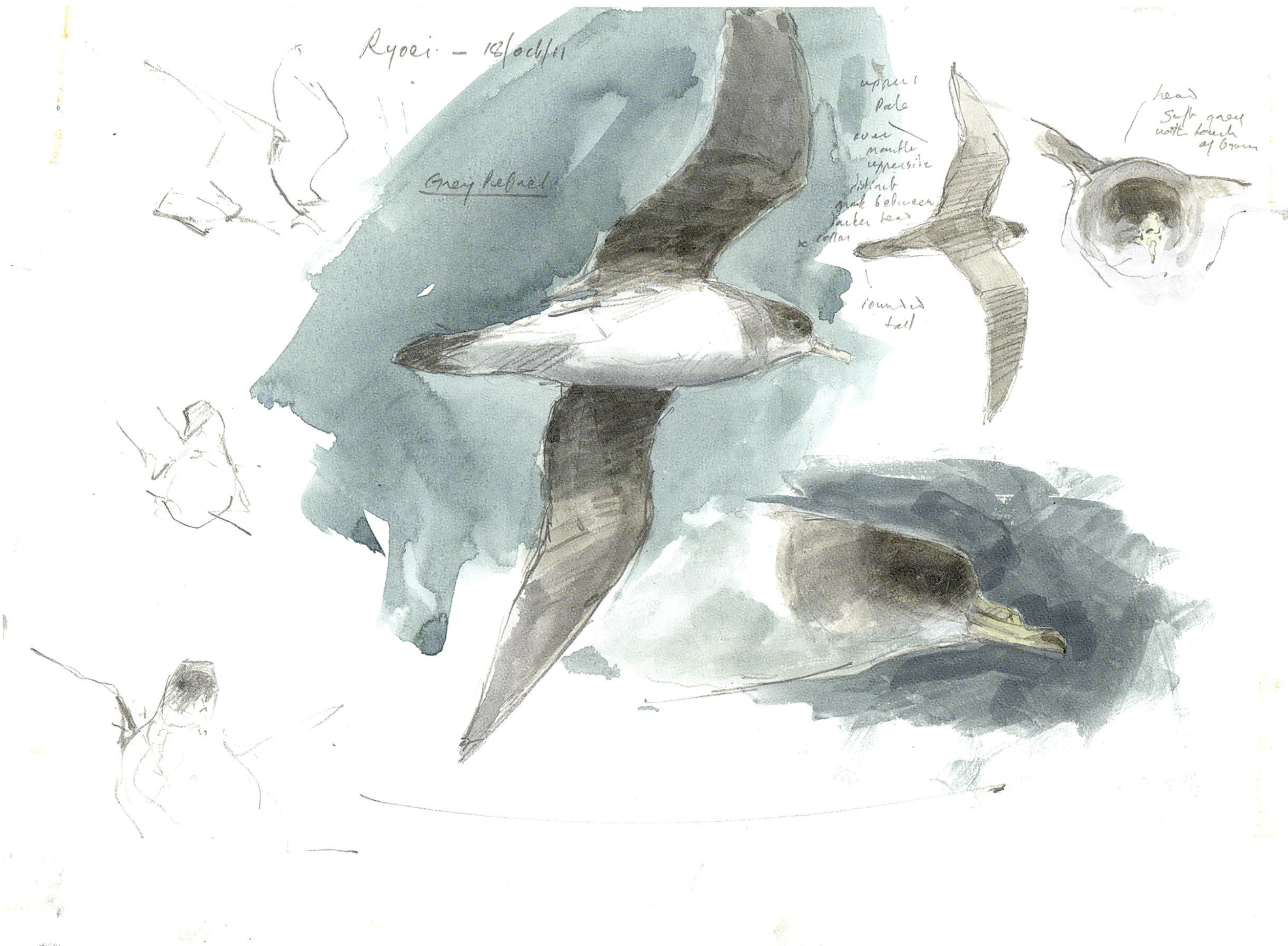

89 Grey petrel, *Ryoei*, October, 2011
30 × 42 cm · watercolour and pencil

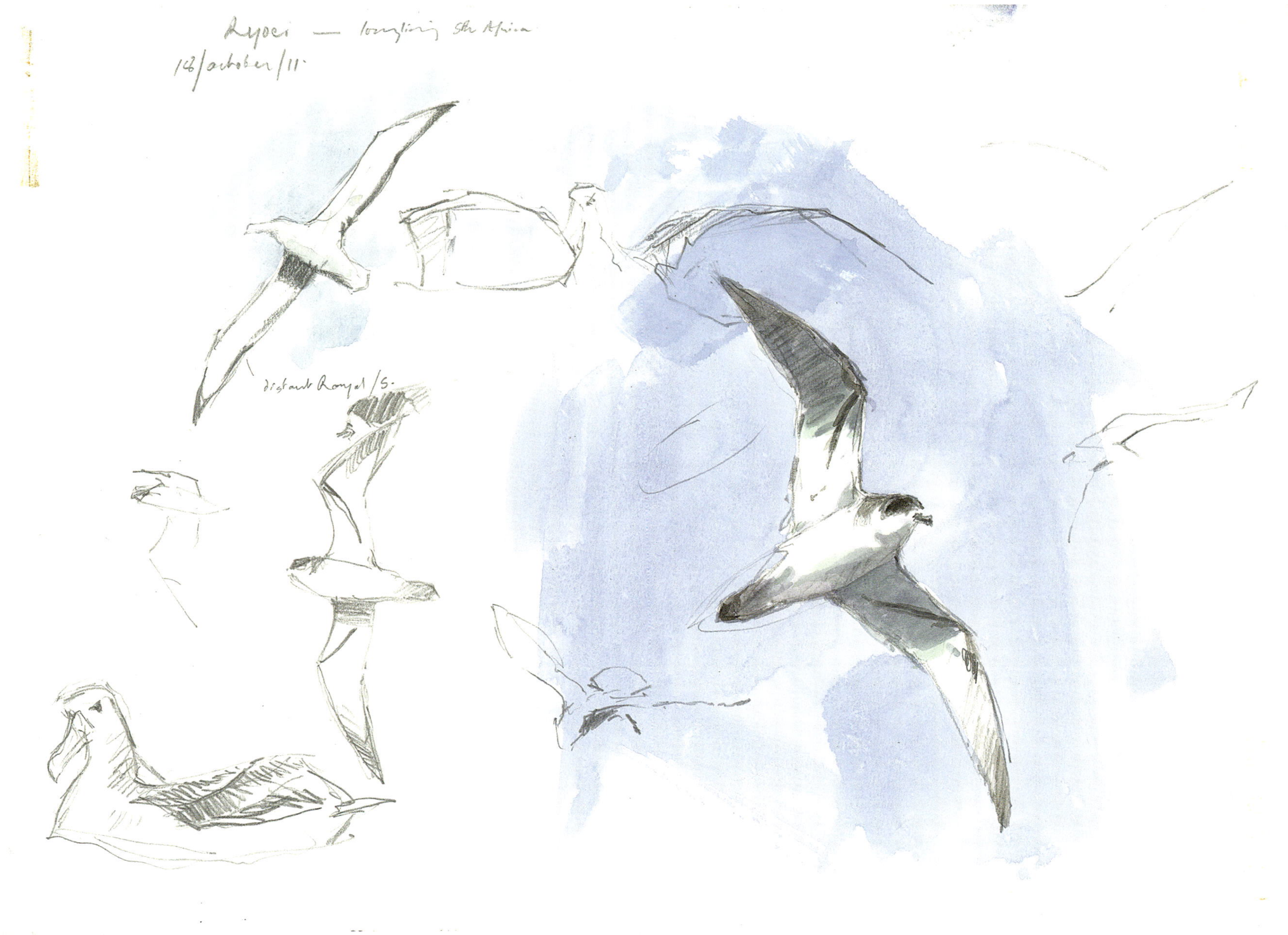

90 Barau's Petrel, *Ryoei*, October, 2011
30 × 42 cm · watercolour and pencil

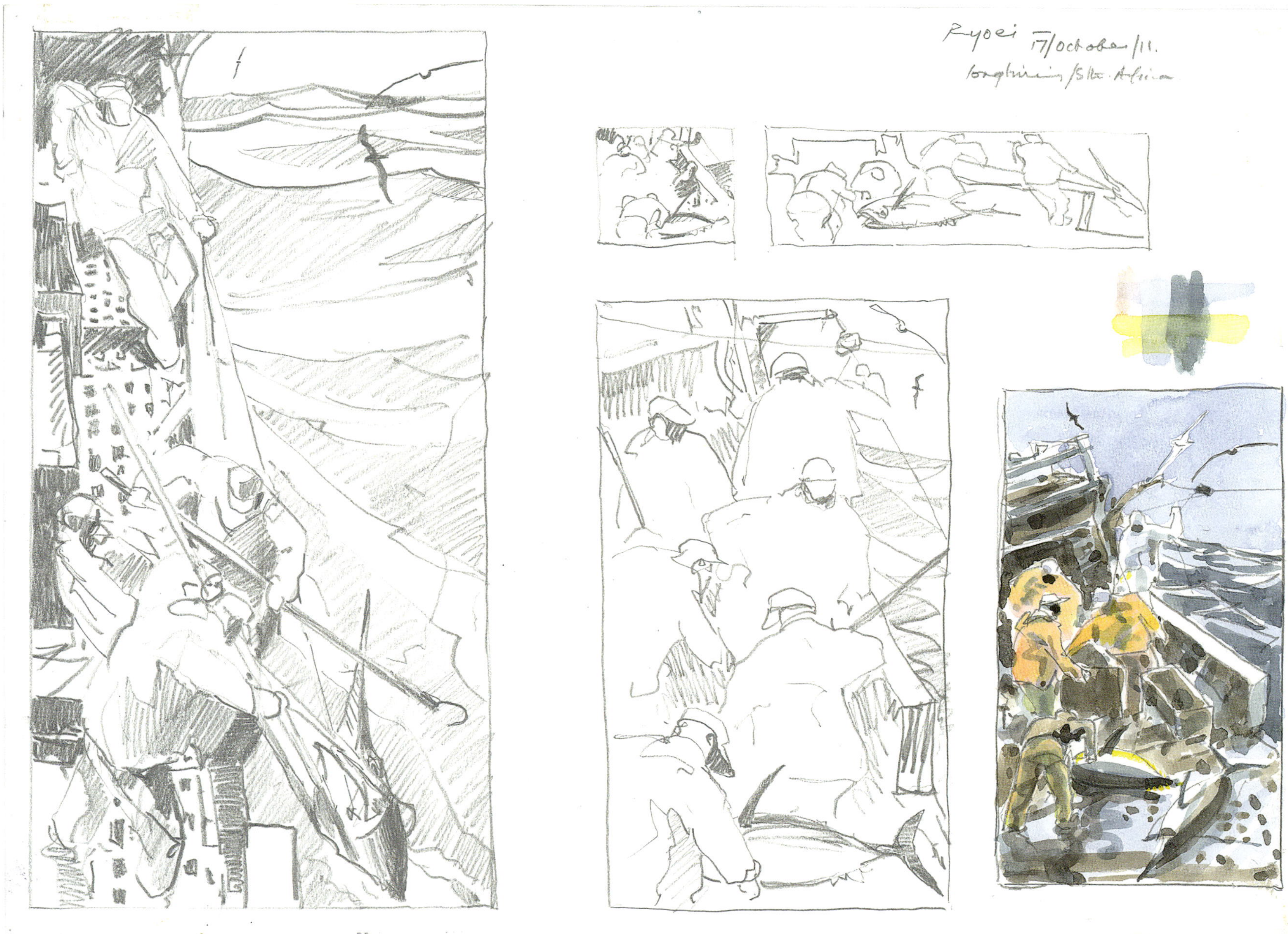

91 The crew at work, *Ryoei*, October, 2011
30 × 42 cm · watercolour and pencil

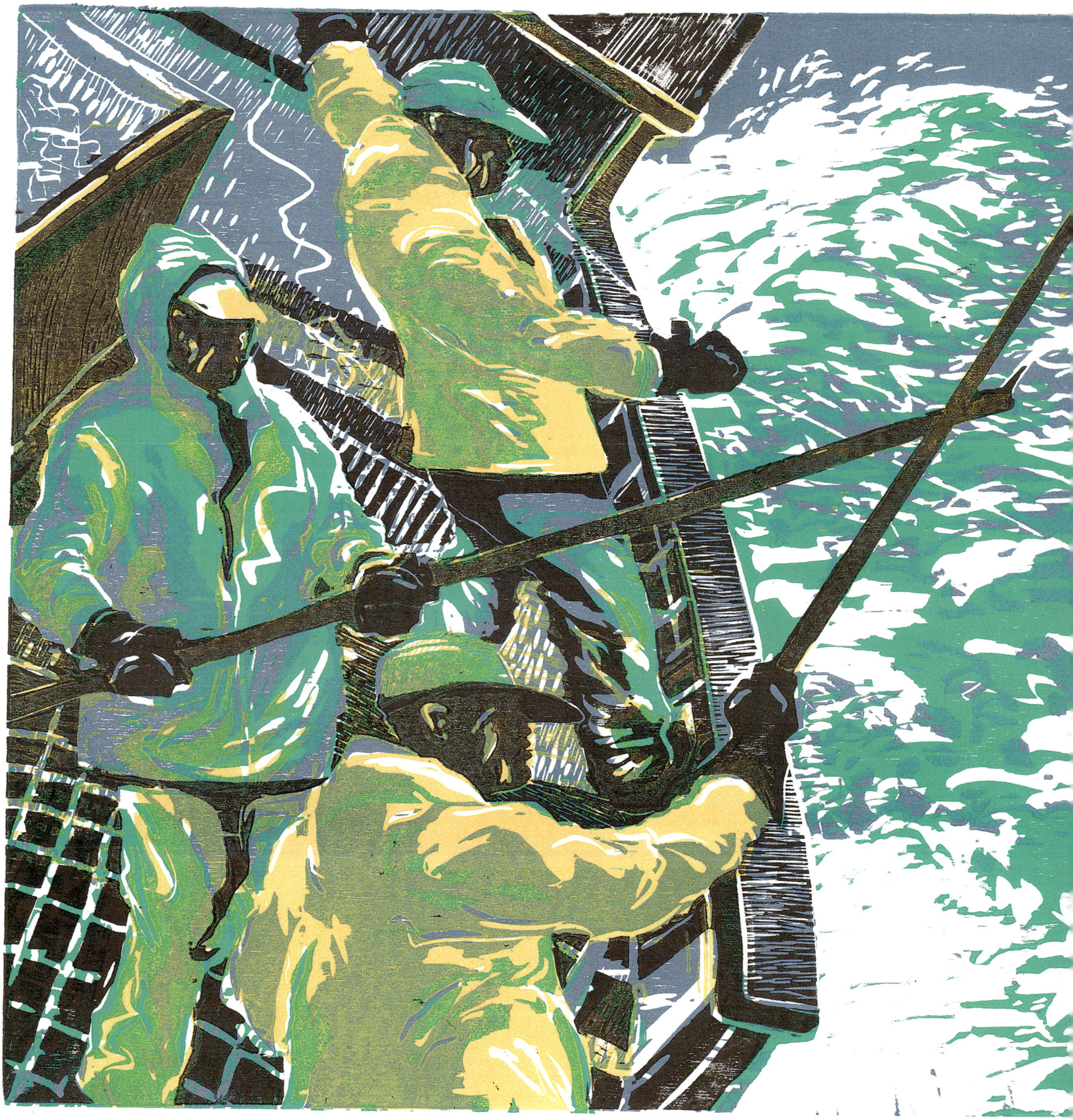

92 Hauling In, 2012
44 × 90 cm · woodcut print

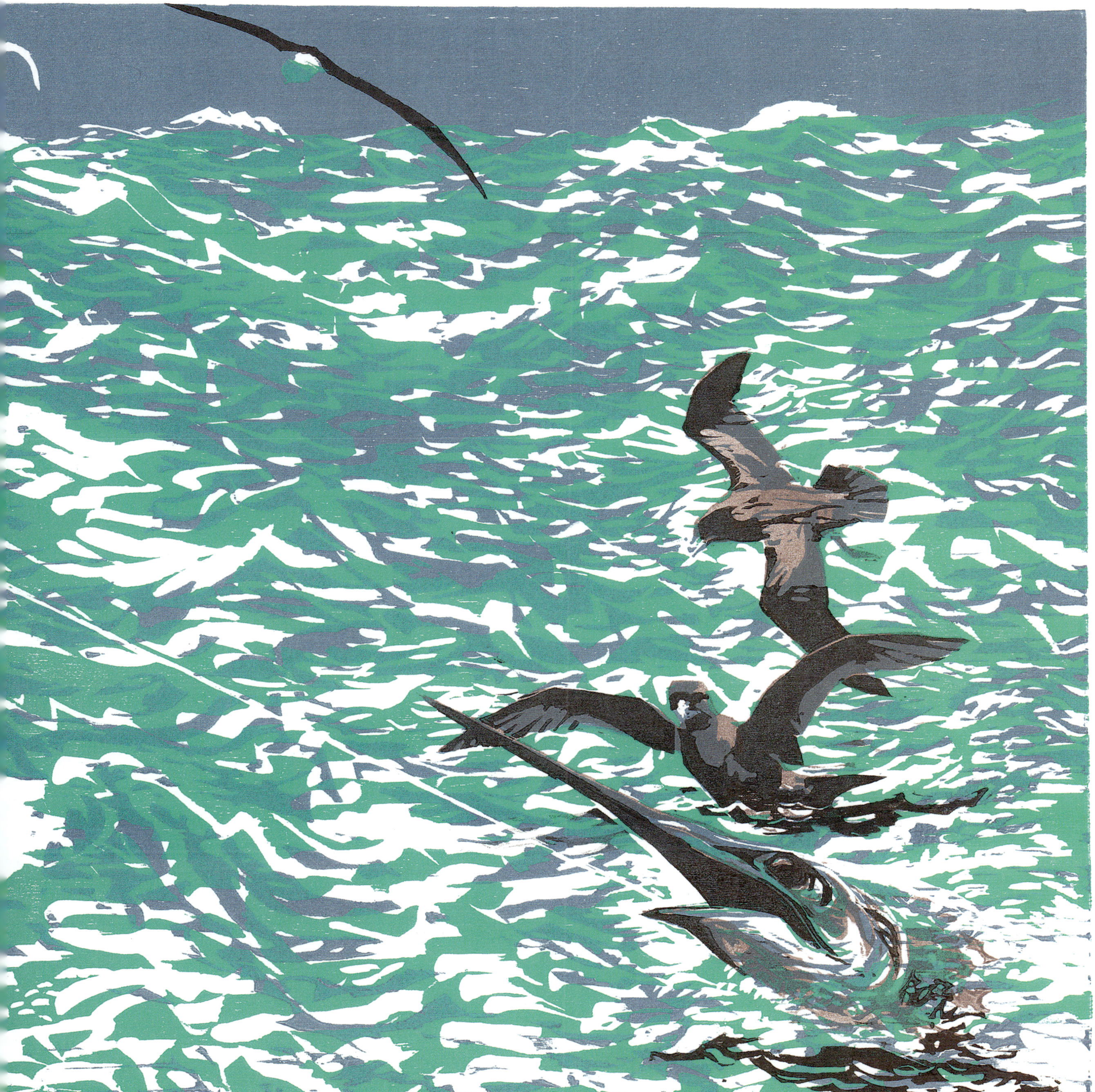

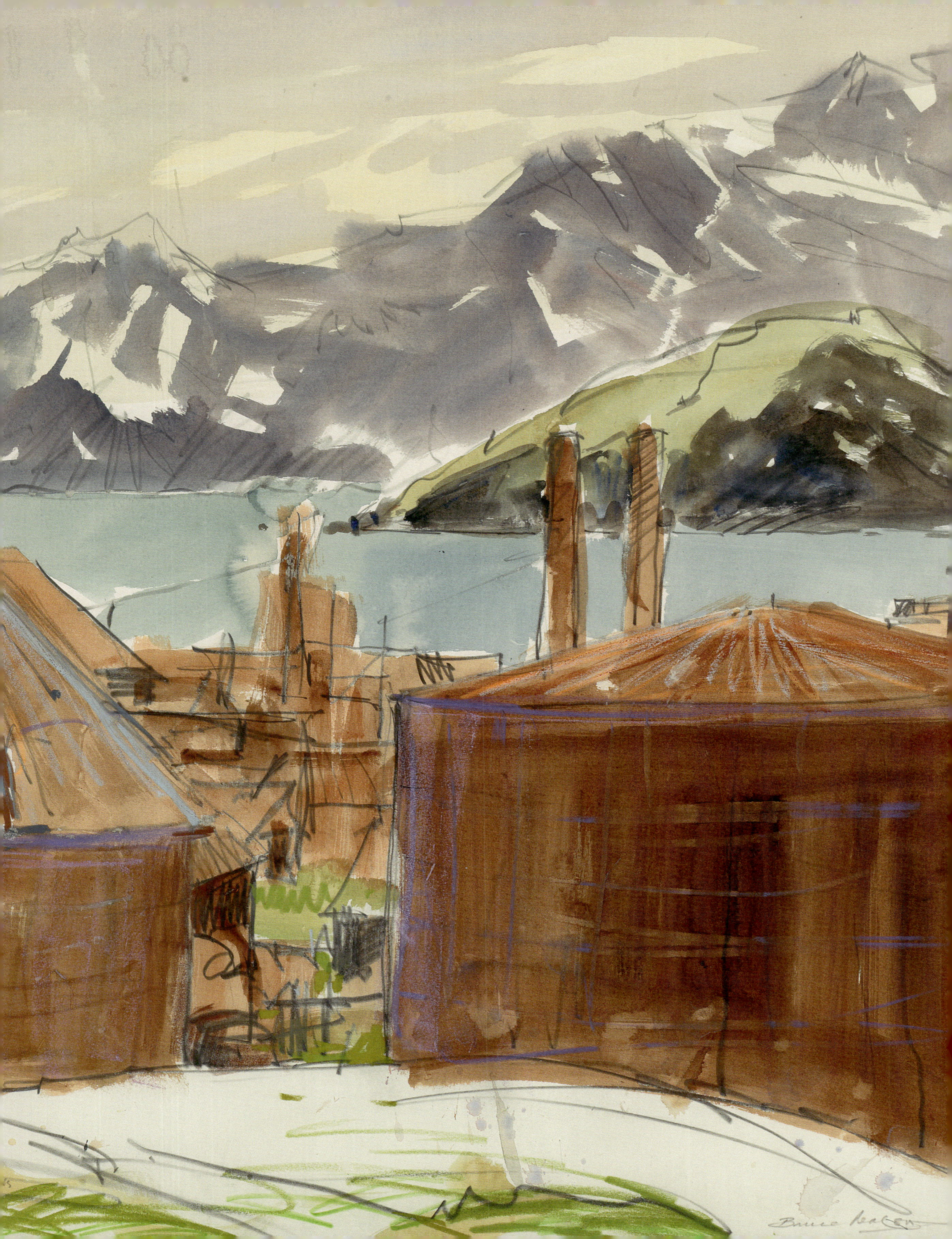

CHAPTER 6

Drawn south again

93 Leith Harbour whaling station, South Georgia, October, 2009 (detail)

It is still dark and my turn on watch; first light is a couple of hours away. It is bitterly cold with a strong wind and occasional snow flurries. A three-quarter moon shows between broken clouds. Small petrels and prions whisk across the moonlight reflections on the sea and vanish suddenly into the darkness. The only sound is the wind in the sails, the run of waves along the hull, and the hiss of spume trailing down the wake. Then out of the darkness comes the unmistakable whickering bark of a fur seal – the sound instantly rewinding the years. The last time I was heading for Bird Island and South Georgia was thirty-five years ago on board a 1600 tonne research ship. This time I am on *Pelagic Australis*, a 22 metre aluminium yacht designed for polar sailing and adventuring. We are on a month-long expedition to South Georgia. Most of us are already familiar with the island, and eager to revisit the places that captured our hearts and imagination. For me it is a tremendous opportunity to get to know albatrosses again and gather a wealth of new artwork that hopefully reflects their lives and captures the changes.

The four days crossing the Southern Ocean from the Falkland Islands had reawakened all the old enthusiasm for oceanic seabirds and seascapes. I had forgotten just how exhilarating is a life at sea. And my way of painting in difficult conditions has evolved over the years. The drawings I made from these latitudes in the mid-1970s were mostly in small sketchbooks. Now, when the opportunity arises, I reach for a very large sheet of fine watercolour paper. I keep the paper rolled up and protected in an easily portable sandwich of tough, lightweight polycarbonate sheets. A sheet of paper can easily be slipped from the sandwich, clipped to the plastic working surface and then laid on the ground, or tied by the corners to any convenient support to hold it in place. Although large sheets are difficult to handle in the wind, I get a special excitement from not letting the physical difficulties of wild locations prevent me from creating work in the field. All this reminds me of advice from the Renaissance scholar and humanist, Leon Battista Alberti: 'Practice by drawing things large, as if equal in representation and reality. In small drawings every large weakness is easily hidden: in the large, the smallest weakness is easily seen'.

Working on the big sheets of paper encourages a boldness of expression and freedom of thinking that I hope gets reflected in my work. There is no time to fuss over detail, so the response has a directness that is impossible to replicate in the studio. And sometimes the elements play a part: waves splash the paper, it often gets wet with rain, and freezing temperatures have once or twice created interesting crystal shapes in the colour washes. Finding a corner of the yacht in which to sketch at a smaller scale was easy enough, but trying to spread metre-wide sheets of paper as the wind whined in the rigging and the yacht tossed about in the waves, was more of a challenge.

Brightening weather at first light reveals icebergs ahead. In the strong, gusting wind, a handful of tilting, curved, split and sculptured masses the size of office

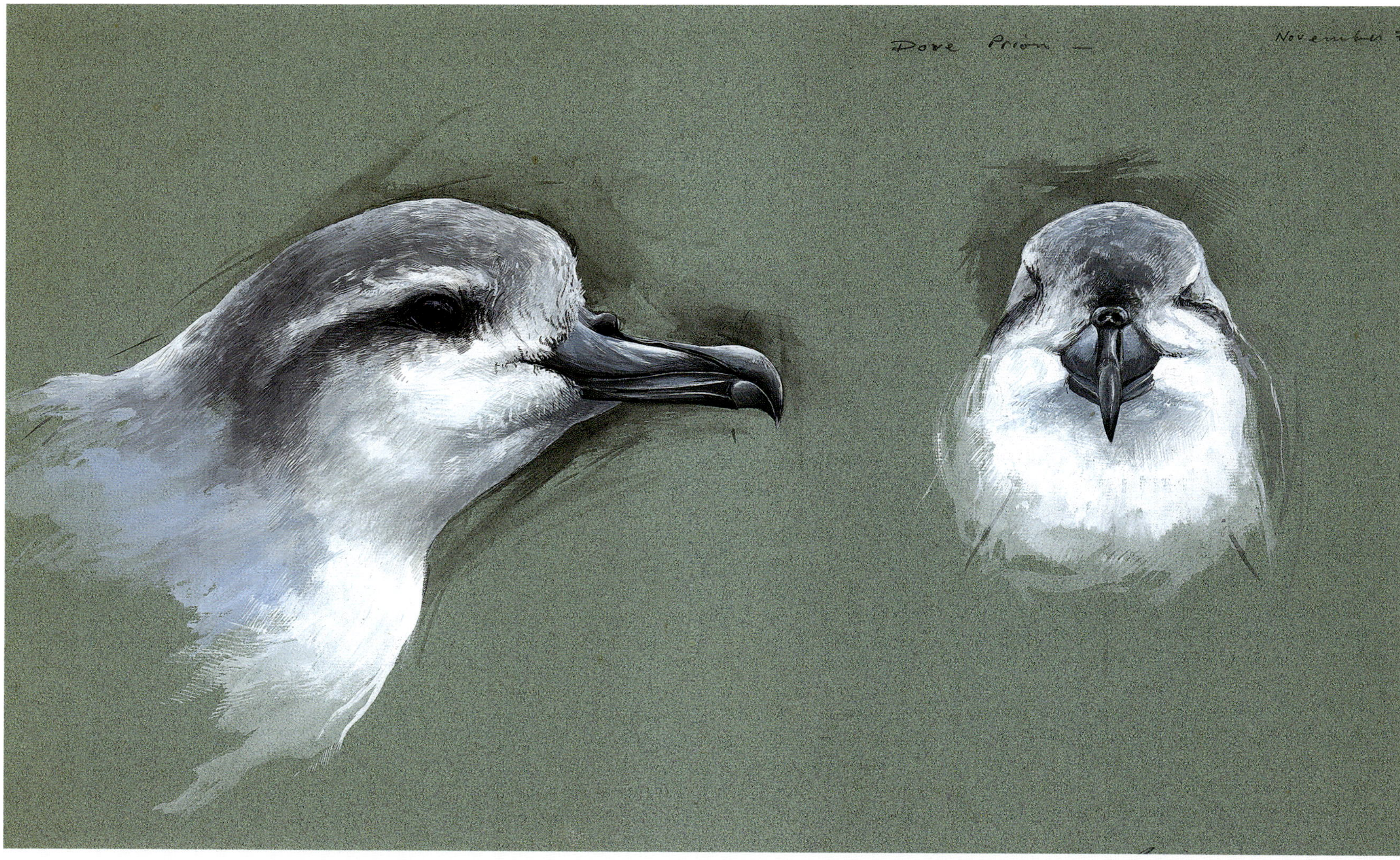

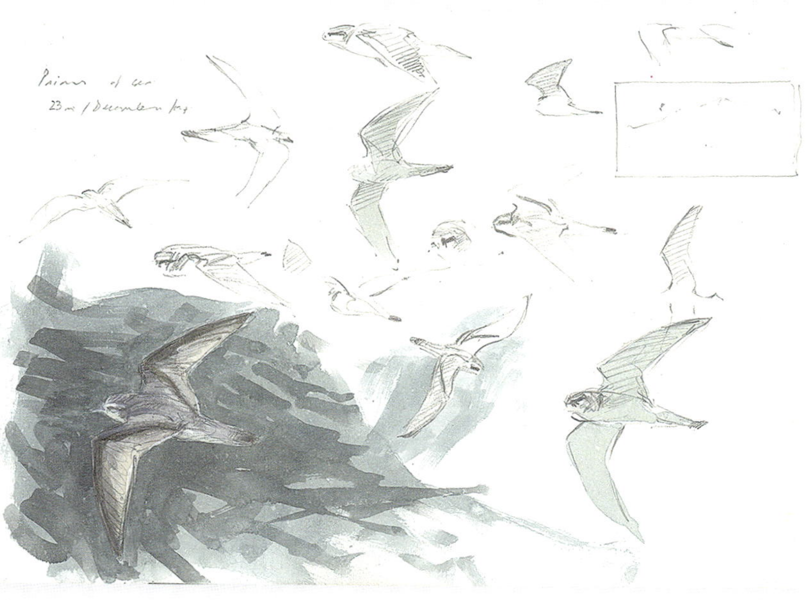

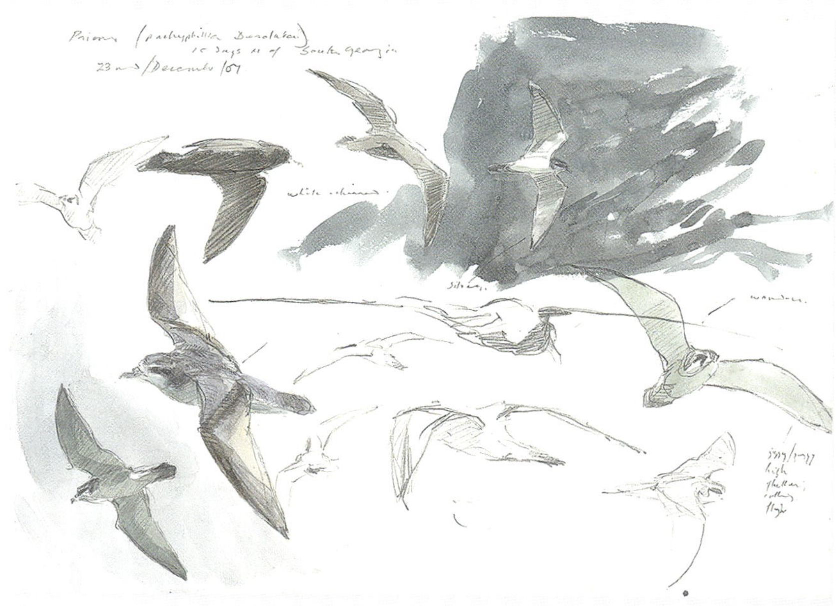

WHALE-BIRDS

The prions, and closely related blue petrels, have bills set with rows of lamellae, fine plates for filtering – like the baleen plates of whales. These birds were once known as 'whale-birds'. The name comes from their close association with whaling and the way they gathered in huge flocks to feed on discarded offal, and not from the form and function of their bills as might be suspected. Yankee whalemen sometimes called them 'scoopers'.

94 Specimen study, Antarctic prion (*Pachyptila desolata*), Bird Island, 1976
38 × 57 cm · watercolour and ink

95 Antarctic prions at sea, Southern Ocean, December, 2007
30 × 42 cm · watercolour and pencil

96 Antarctic prions at sea, Southern Ocean, December, 2007
30 × 42 cm · watercolour and pencil

MARINE IBAS

The Important Bird Areas (IBAs) Programme of BirdLife International seeks to identify and conserve sites that are critical for the long-term viability of bird populations. IBAs are chosen using quantitative, standardised, globally agreed criteria. Since 2005 BirdLife has been working to identify IBAs in the marine environment and promote these sites as priorities for site-based seabird conservation efforts. Marine IBAs information has already helped achieve new Marine Protected Areas in Europe and is informing many regional policy mechanisms, as well as global agreements like the Convention on Biological Diversity.

Over 40 BirdLife Partners are now working on marine IBAs, pulling together a range of data, such as those collected from tracking studies, at-sea surveys, and colony monitoring, to identify key sites. These include seabird breeding colonies, critically feeding areas around breeding colonies, non-breeding concentrations, migratory bottlenecks and foraging areas for pelagic species. Around 3000 sites have so far been identified, and can be viewed and queried via an electronic atlas – www.birdlife.org/datazone/marine.

blocks glisten in the distance. There are black-browed albatrosses passing, a lone grey-headed, and a few giant petrels. But closer in towards the bergs, we are suddenly surrounded by smaller petrels – lots of cape petrels, a few Wilson's storm-petrels and snow petrels, and increasing numbers of prions and blue petrels.

Now close to a berg we can see even greater numbers of birds nearby. The wall of ice underwater causes an upwelling of marine life that attracts scores of birds to feed in the turquoise waters crashing around its cliffs. Loose swarms of 'whale-birds' settle lightly on the water with wings half-open, thrusting their heads below the water and scooping food. Waves of birds dip and dive through the cold blues of the turbulence, each fluttering wave overtaking the next as they work their way upwind. The whole area of sea twinkles with the powder-blue and grey of blue petrels and prions, and the pure white of snow petrels. A few black-browed albatross pass but do not approach the berg and the abundance that is attracting all the smaller petrels. A lone adult wanderer sweeps by, its plumage warm-toned white against the berg-wall backdrop of cold blues and hard icy whites. With the bergs far behind but a few petrels still around, a south-westerly flurry of sleet and rain carried on furious gusts of wind passes through and leaves an early afternoon of soft cloud with the sun breaking through.

Eventually, across the horizon ahead, we catch sight of a dark-greyish line capped with an intangible whiteness blending with the soft sky. It is the north-west end of South Georgia. In a while headlands and islands become increasingly familiar. Rounding Johannesen Point on the southern side of the Willis Islands, the great sloping wedge-shaped form of Bird Island comes into view. Beyond, across Bird Sound, the dark slopes of the Paryadin Peninsula fade into the low cloud and distant mountains of South Georgia.

As with any return to a place that was home a long while ago, finding things as they are and not as they were can be disappointing, even unsettling. I remember how the same sight thirty five years ago generated a tremendous sense of adventure and anticipation. Then there seemed to be albatrosses absolutely everywhere. They were the most striking part of the experience and dominated first impressions. Seeing Bird Island again all these years later, the sense of anticipation about the creative adventure ahead, and the excitement about being 'down south' again, are still equally profound. But my entirely subjective impression is that there are fewer albatrosses now. Is it a genuine reaction, or just an assumption coloured by everything I have read on their rapidly declining populations?

A landing, if only for a few hours, to renew my acquaintance with the albatrosses and see for myself what has happened would complete my return. But I know and fully appreciate that all the closeness and intimacy I once had is absolutely unrepeatable. To preserve the Bird Island's fragile natural environment it has to be vigorously protected from damage and disruption. So landing is not permitted. As we pass the island on its southern side we catch a glimpse of the field station. The original garden shed, and even my old home Lönnberg House, have long gone, and been replaced by Prince House named for my old friend and which now provides luxurious living and working conditions when compared with the old days. Up to ten people work there during the summer months and typically four stay on through the southern winter. We make radio contact with the current BAS team as we run through Bird Sound to our first anchorage at Elsehul on the north-west tip of South Georgia.

Bird Island has been a base for seabird research almost continuously for the past 54 years. That continuity has enabled long-term population monitoring studies on the albatrosses. Lance Tickell's work in the 1950s

THE AGREEMENT ON THE CONSERVATION OF ALBATROSSES AND PETRELS (ACAP)

The Agreement on the Conservation of Albatrosses and Petrels (ACAP) is a legally binding international agreement that entered into force in 2004. It requires signatory states to take specific action both on land (in breeding colonies) and at-sea to improve the conservation status of albatrosses and petrels. Measures include research and monitoring, reduction of incidental mortality in fisheries, eradication of non-native species at breeding sites, reduction of disturbance and habitat loss, and pollution reduction..

The Agreement is significant because it brings together the main breeding and fishing range states responsible for halting the decline of so many albatrosses and petrels populations. ACAP is an instrument that facilitates the international action required to address an urgent international marine conservation issue.

and 60s laid the baseline that Pete Prince and others were able to build on. In 1976, during my second summer on the island, John Croxall joined BAS to head bird and mammal research. With an enthusiasm for seabirds and energy for fieldwork that sometimes left everybody breathless, he and Pete immediately formed an impressive research team and the South Georgia and Bird Island albatross populations have gone on to become among the best studied worldwide.

Conclusions from the Bird Island studies make grim reading, as populations of wandering, black-browed and grey-headed albatrosses have been decreasing since the late 1970s. The situation for wandering albatross is particularly alarming. In the early 1960s, when Lance Tickell made the first estimates, he calculated the South Georgia population as about 4,600 pairs. The 1984 census estimated 2,230 pairs, but in 2006 there were only 1553 breeding – a 30 percent decline in 20 years. Over the past 40 years there has been a 50 percent loss of nesting adult wanderers on Bird Island.

In the late 1970s scientists working independently on islands around the Southern Ocean were already becoming concerned about a slight but noticeable downward trend in albatross numbers. John and Pete were noting similar declines of wanderers on Bird Island, but without sufficient data, John could only write cautiously in 1978, '... it is even less clear what the ultimate causes may be'. Nevertheless, he was already aware of clues coming in from the findings of other seabird biologists. On Kerguelen and Crozet islands, adults were found dead from bill and face wounds, and disgorged hooks had been found scattered around nests. Evidence of commercial longline fishing as the most likely cause of albatross deaths mounted, and in the early 1990s it was openly blamed. As the result of relentless downward trend in breeding birds, wandering and grey-headed albatrosses are officially classified as Vulnerable (facing high risk of extinction), and the black-browed albatross is Endangered (facing a VERY high risk of extinction).

From the sea, the sight on a bright and blustery day of South Georgia's cloud strewn peaks, glistening snow fields and dark littoral skirt rising sheer from the ocean, has to be one of the most dramatic sights in the world. We leave Elsehul on such a day. The wind is strong and the sea a rolling swell of deep emerald green and icy blue topped with the streaks of broken waves. White-chinned and giant petrels whip by. Blue petrels, intermingled with flotillas of prions, are everywhere, their grey-plumage lost against the tones of the sea, but white-tipped tails marking their passage like undulating spots of light. A wanderer and a few mollymauks pass, and cape petrels come and go around *Pelagic Australis* as we head south-east down the island a kilometre or so offshore. Vast bays open up beyond passing cliffs and headlands. The piercing colours of icebergs grounded below steep cliffs show brightly against the darks shore and tussock hills. As we sail by – and so long as the weather stays clear – the ever-changing perspective of the mountainous interior shines magnificently.

With my painting kit spread out on an aft hatch-cover, I have everything strapped down and clipped tight. Not so much because of the wind, but the rolling swell would tip everything overboard. Braced against a rail, I work on, eager to capture as much as I can. What strikes me is the unique perspective I get on the ocean environment and the seabirds by being nearly at sea-level. On a large ship, the view is lofty and slightly

SOUTH GEORGIA FISHERIES

Since the mid-1950s, the waters around South Georgia have attracted commercial fisheries. But within 20 years, over-fishing meant some species became commercially unviable. Regulation followed and annual quotas were set for mackerel icefish, krill and most importantly, Patagonian toothfish which are caught on longlines. Fishing around South Georgia is now exceptionally well-managed, and seabird bycatch is negligible.

97 Passing down the north coast of South Georgia, October, 2009
30 × 42 cm · watercolour and pencil

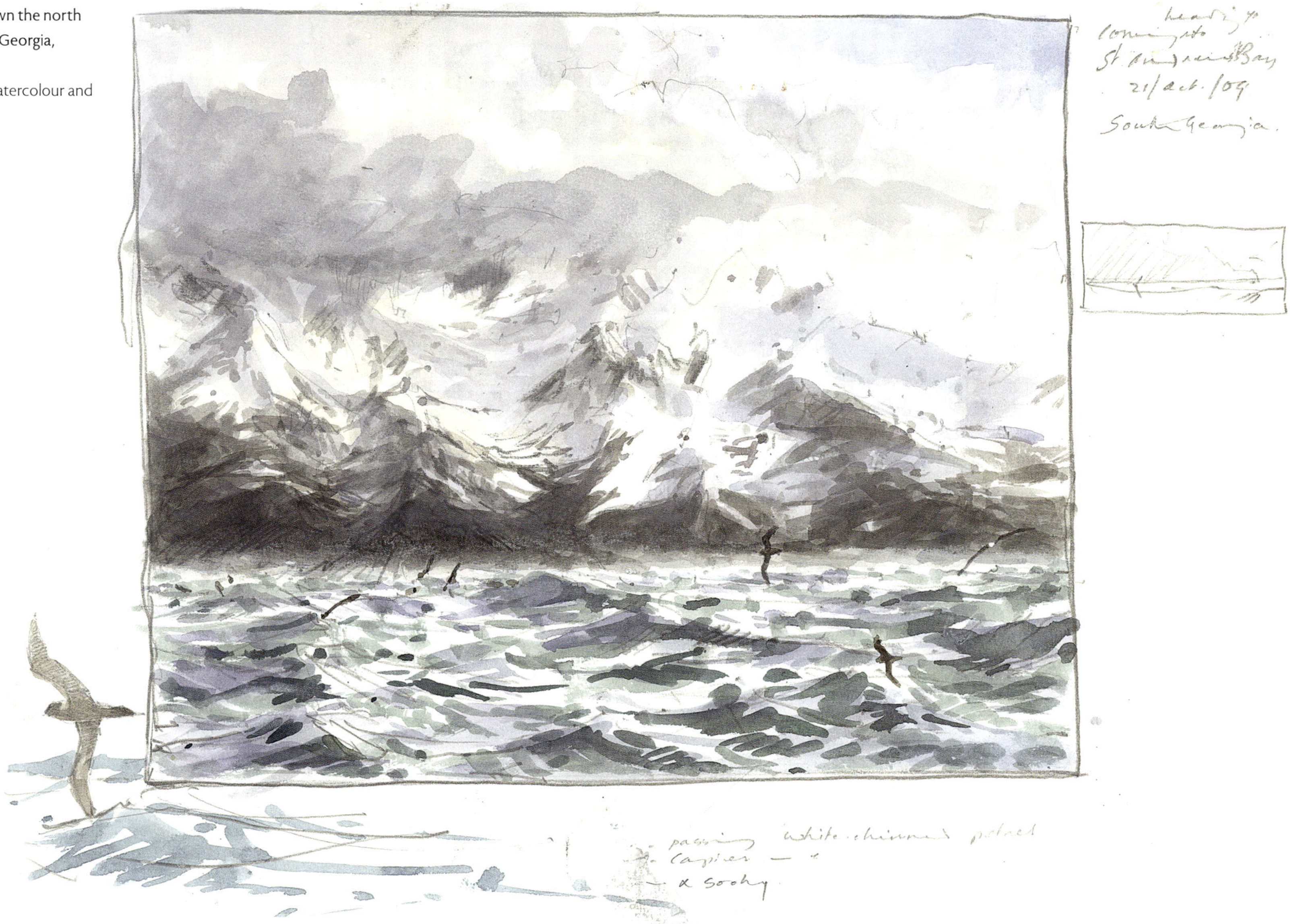

removed. A yacht offers a greater sense of connectedness with the sea and the birds. I am sketching a black-browed albatross skimming across the wind, rising and falling between waves. Under sail and heeling over, I feel we are moving together, and with no engine noise there is an elemental appreciation of the wind pushing us along.

South Georgia's position south of the Polar Front and in the track of a stream of depressions moving eastwards across the Scotia Sea generates a climate that is essentially cold, cloudy, wet and windy – and variable. The south-west coast and the mountains intercept the worst of the weather and the north-east side of the island is milder and drier. Snow and rain occur in all seasons but snow does not lie for long in summer. And the weather is capricious too: the driving rain and sleet of a stormy summer day will ease suddenly and the clouds roll back so it becomes warm, still and sunny, but equally rapidly, the weather can close in again, with even stronger gusts that lift the sea's surface into a frenzy of spindrift.

So for three weeks we cover the entire length of the island in every kind of weather, landing every day to walk and explore, and paint and draw. In Brandt Cove and Drygalski Fjord I unfold my painting kit at the snout of a glacier. In Moltke Harbour on the northern side of Royal Bay I watch in amazement as light-mantled albatrosses fly elegantly through ferocious gusts of wind that lift the surface of the sea. On a bright settled day in Stromness Bay, I tape together two large sheets of paper, lie them on the ground above the abandoned, collapsing whaling station at Leith Harbour, and work to try and capture the extraordinary sense of melancholy that pervades the landscape. And in the Bay of Isles I encounter wandering albatrosses again – not warming my hands under the belly feathers this time, or hooking a 'bodger' around the

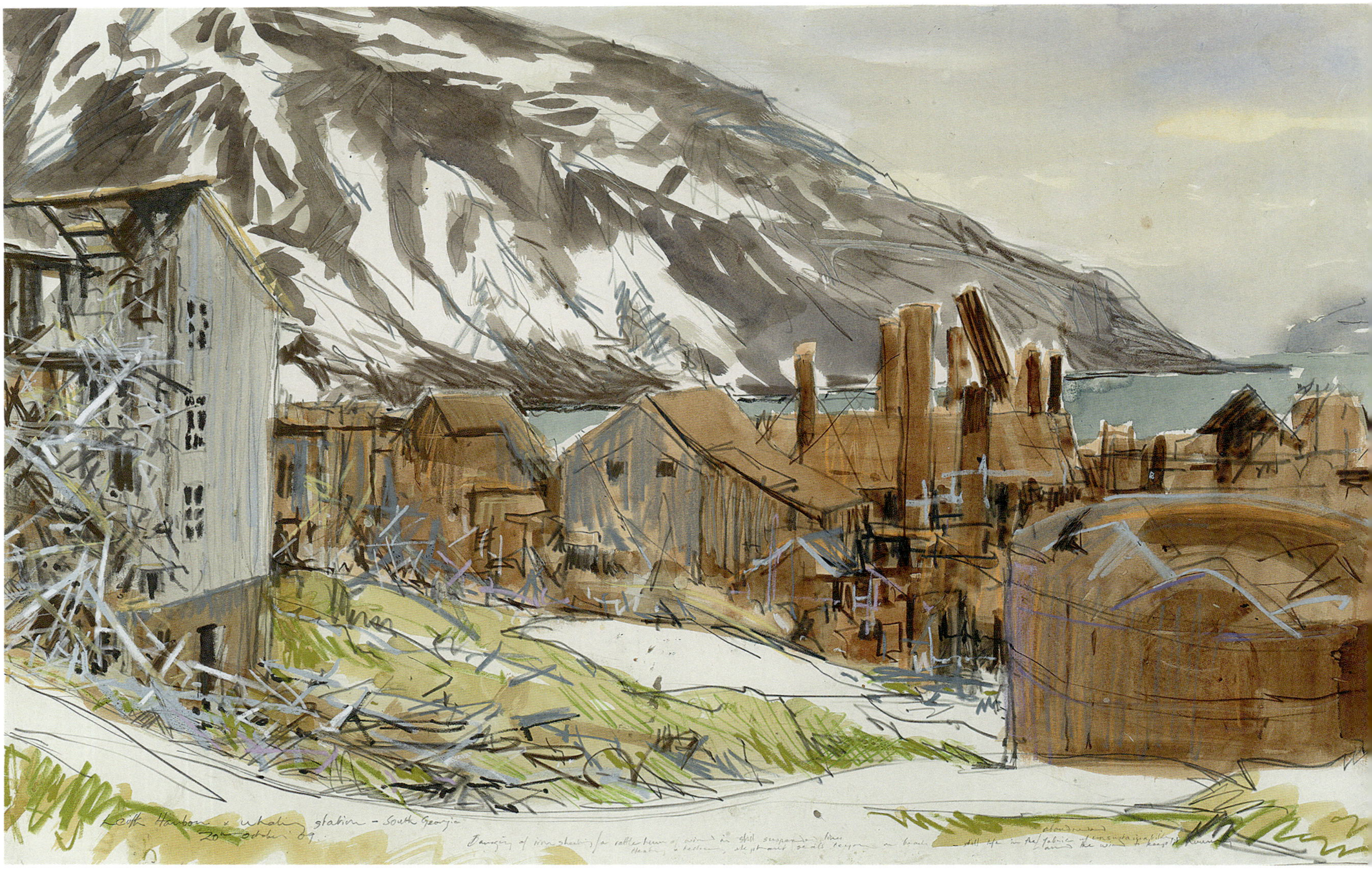

neck and checking the ring number but, just like other visitors to Prion Island I walk up the boardwalk at a safe distance from the nests.

South Georgia's wildlife has suffered not only from devastation of commercial exploitation. Invasive species introduced accidentally or deliberately have also wrought havoc among native species. Rats and mice were introduced accidentally by sealers and whalers. As well as feeding on insects, seeds and roots, and carrion, rats also take the eggs and chicks of small birds. Larger albatrosses and penguins are little affected, but the majority of smaller seabirds and the two endemic species – South Georgia pintail and pipit – are small enough to fall prey to rats. The main island has been all but abandoned by storm-petrels, prions, diving-petrels and blue petrel, and to lesser extent even larger bird species like white-chinned petrel. The endemic South Georgia pipit once bred throughout the island, but is now confined to rodent-free parts of the mainland and offshore islands and islets, like Prion Island.

The Bay of Isles is a jagged coastal scoop 14km and about 5km deep on the north-western end of South Georgia. Discovered and named by James Cook in 1775, the bay is filled with numerous islands – Albatross, Mollymauk and Petrel Islands among them. Prion Island was named by Robert Cushman Murphy in 1912. Because it is rat-free and has breeding wandering albatrosses, Prion Island is designated as a Specially Protected Area by the South Georgia Government. Disturbance is prevented by a strict permit system. Only two visits are allowed per day; and no more than 50 people are allowed ashore at any time, and no visit can exceed five hours. Visitors must keep to a boardwalk with viewing platforms which provides easy access and good views of the wanderers. It prevents erosion of fragile vegetation, and avoids trampling of prion burrows and South Georgia pipit nests.

The day is not good for making sketches – cold, wet air hangs in the breeze dropping a light dampness over everything. But I find a spot on the platform at the top of the boardwalk and settle down. About 30 metres ahead on a pile of compacted grass and is the beautiful folded

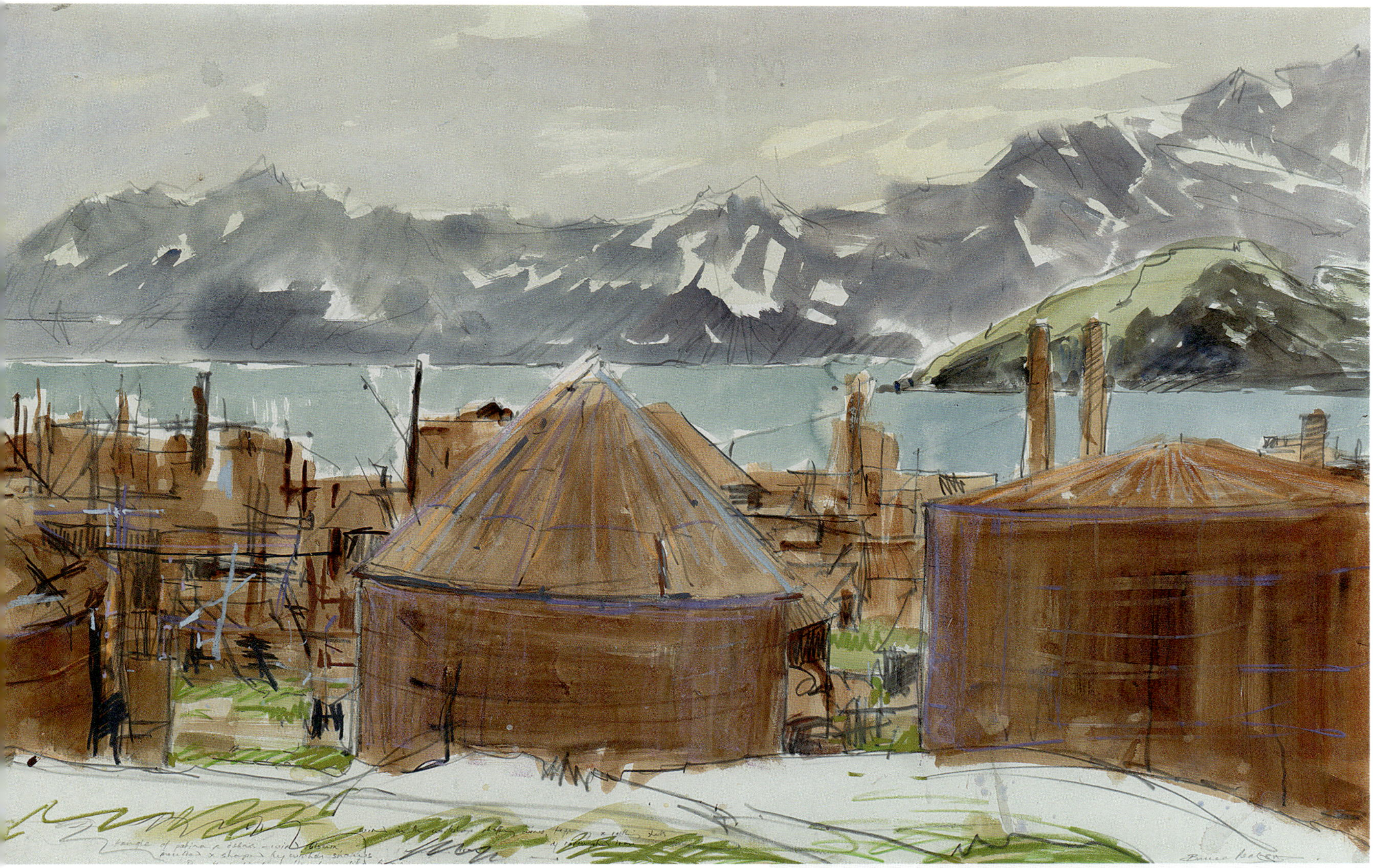

98 Leith Harbour whaling station, South Georgia, October, 2009
Diptych, each 76 × 122 cm · watercolour / mixed media

form of a young wandering albatross. I bury myself in the sketches and remember the last time I saw one on the nest. All these years later the sight is still impressive, and just as moving. After a while the young bird raises its delicate featured face and, with its enormous flesh-pink bill, begins preening. An albatross really is the most fabulous bird in the world!

When I walked up the boardwalk between the albatrosses, I began to feel my journey trailing them was approaching some kind of conclusion. The significance of the early intimate encounters had been the role of albatrosses as harbingers which positively shaped the nature of the work I would subsequently tackle as an artist. But now I see them more as omens. Either as portents of a future where marine resources are exhausted and the oceans devoid of their magnificent presence; or of a future where the challenge to protect the planet's marine resources is won and the slide towards extinction is reversed.

Perhaps it is Coleridge's epic poem about the Ancient Mariner and his slaying of an albatross that

WHALING LEGACY, AND ABANDONED WHALING STATION AT LEITH

The abandoned whaling stations on South Georgia fit well into the elemental aesthetics of a 'sublime ruin'. From a distance they seem to lean against the cliffs like great rusting ocean liners thrown onto the shore and left to collapse into rust-red symbols of unsustainability. Strangely picturesque, with their vast size dwarfing any onlooker, time is overwhelming these great works of man. In the gravestones of the whalers' cemeteries and the bleached bones of many thousands of great whales cast on the shore, there is gentle melancholy of loss.

South Georgia has a special place in the history of whaling. It was the centre for a major industry that destroyed itself in less than 60 years. In 1904 the Norwegian whaler and entrepreneur Carl Anton Larsen established the first whaling station which was so successful that a further six stations were established by 1913. Within a decade South Georgia had become the whaling capital of the world. The introduction of pelagic factory ships in 1925–26 allowed whalers to operate in the open sea beyond government control and whaling in the Southern Ocean became a free for all. The result was gross over-exploitation. In the years from 1904 to 1966 when the last shore station closed because numbers were too scarce for the industry to be profitable, over 175,000 whales had been processed.

Perhaps there is a link with the contemporary predicament of albatrosses – that unregulated maritime industries can play havoc with natural ecosystems. And that public pressure to exert control on an industry is worthwhile, even at the eleventh hour.

BLACK-BROWED AND GREY-HEADED ALBATROSS

There are about 15 principal black-browed and five grey-headed albatross breeding locations on South Georgia. Colonies are usually situated in tussock on steep coastal headlands and sea cliffs on both the mainland and offshore islands.

The magnitude of the long-term declines in breeding populations of these mollymauks has been dramatic. The 1977 numbers, from my last summer on Bird Island, were an estimated 124,332 breeding pairs of black – browed albatross for the whole of South Georgia; the figure for the 2012 season is an estimated 66,282 pairs. Almost half the population has been lost in the past 30 years or more, and the rate of decline has been much the same for grey-headed albatrosses,

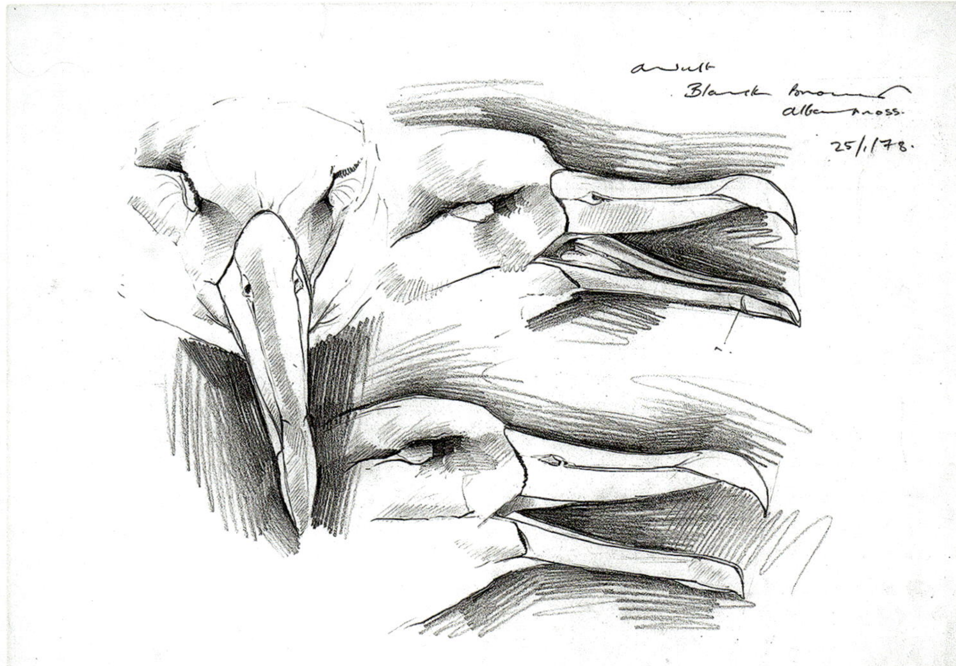

99 Specimen study, adult black-browed albatross, head and gape, Bird Island, 1978
42 × 59 cm · pencil

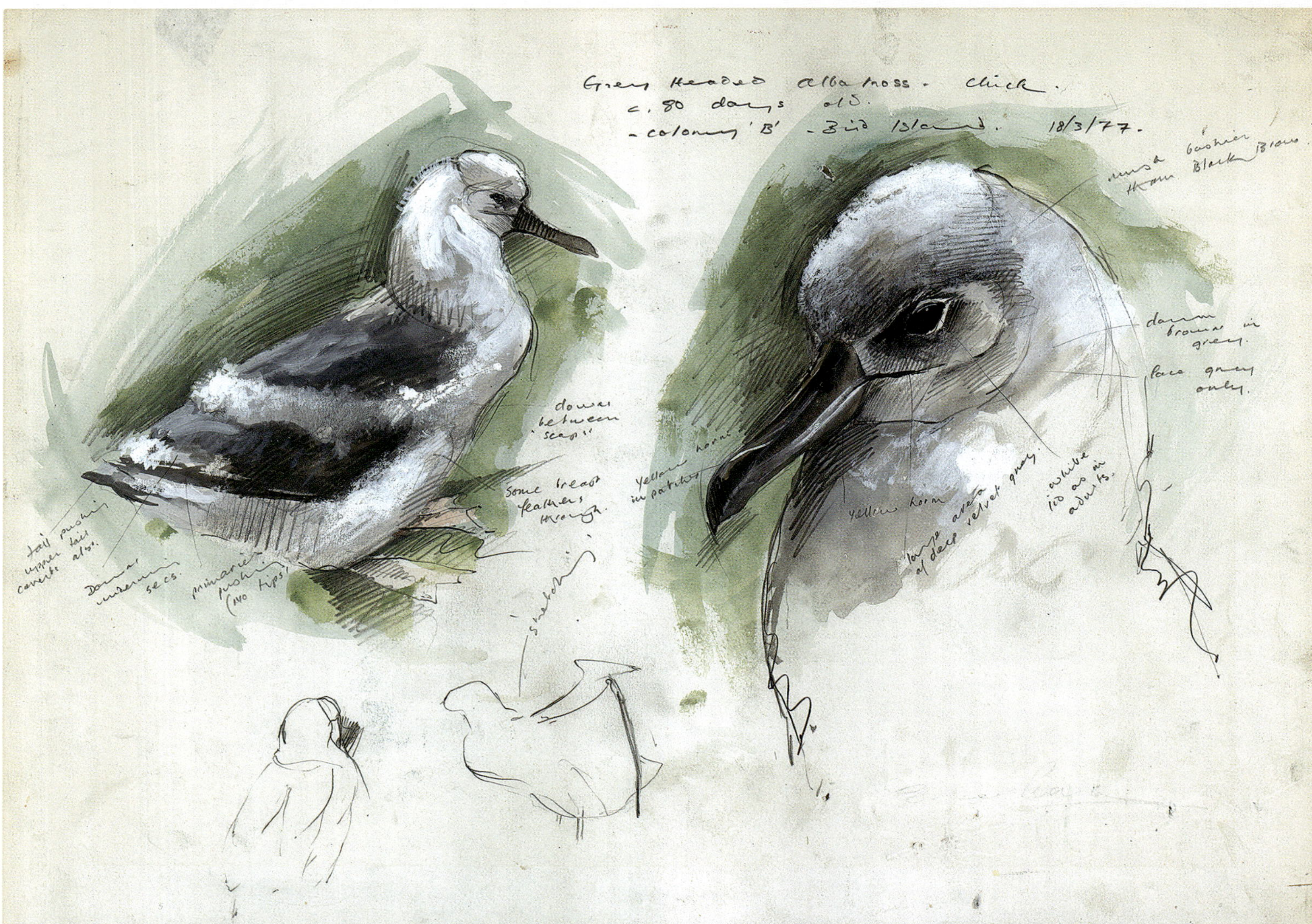

100 Young grey-headed albatross, 80 days old, Bird Island, 1977
42 × 59 cm · watercolour and pencil

has helped a bird which few people will ever see, become so familiar and symbolic elsewhere. Before the albatross is killed with a cross-bow, it is an omen of good fortune ushering favourable winds and leading the ship out of troubled waters. Having committed this mortal sin, the Mariner, with the albatross hung around his neck, is condemned to his own personal purgatory and forced to confess his sin repeatedly, and for all eternity. The albatross is now a bird of ill omen.

While I am on *Pelagic Australis,* I learn that there is a male wandering albatross – ring number 4039237 – nesting on Bird Island. Already an adult when he was ringed in 1956, this ancient mariner is well over 60 years old.

Within an hour or so the breeze quickens and swings round to the north-east sweeping away the mistiness and damp. There are pipits scurrying through the tussock and others overhead singing loudly as they dangle in the breeze. Prions are churring in burrows beneath the walkway and among the tussock mounds. Towards Albatross Island and across the Bay of Isles an adult female wanderer looking to land sweeps fast and low down the near skyline. I can hear the begging call of a wanderer chick start from over in that general direction. With wings dropped and feet trailing, she passes and circles to make a second approach. This time, with huge webbed feet extended to brake her descent, she lands and heads towards her nest and waiting chick. I was hoping I might see a feed, but my time is up and I head back down the walkway.

When I was drawing the last few pieces of the Troubled Waters story together at the BirdLife Secretariat in Cambridge, I attended a meeting of the Global Seabird Programme. Ben Lascelles, BirdLife's Marine Important Bird Areas Officer, presented an overview of the worldwide collaboration between seabird scientists in the Tracking Ocean Wanderers Initiative. Since it began in 2004 virtually all albatross satellite-tracking data have been gathered into a central database to better understand and highlight crucial areas for the conservation of albatrosses.

I watched the screen in absolute astonishment as lines of different colours representing different species began to meander out from their island breeding sites. The lines started slowly at first weaving thin scribbly patterns across the oceans but became increasingly animated as more and more data added energy to the display. Then the lines began to stretch around the birds' migration routes in overlapping ellipses and figure-of-eight patterns showing each species circulating between nesting and feeding grounds. The multi-coloured concentrations of bird tracks around the Southern Ocean breeding islands began to glow and flicker, and around the highly productive oceanic regions such as the Patagonian Shelf and the Antarctic Polar Frontal Zone the lines clustered into quivering forms, like organisms under a microscope. Crucially, they illuminated the upwellings of ocean currents where rich seabird feeding grounds overlap with fisheries.

It was extraordinary. On one hand I was looking at a powerful representation of the lives of hundreds of ocean wanderers condensed into a few minutes that showed the urgency of addressing the issues that have left 19 of the 21 albatross species under threat of extinction. And on the other hand, I was looking at a thought-provoking piece of contemporary art. Scientific data had been transformed into something purely aesthetic that in an instant showed the significance of our relationship with the oceans and its birdlife – but equally significant, connect us to the spirit of the ocean. This bridge between art and science through technology was totally unexpected; a fact which made it all the more striking.

Birders, scientists, conservationists, artists, writers and musicians, whose lives draw inspiration from the natural world, are beginning to come together to look at ways of developing a cultural agenda that supports conservation. The cultural value of birds and other wildlife is an idea for exploring new perspectives on our responses to nature. By looking at the oceans, its wanderers and fishermen, and by sharing their lives and exploring their perspectives, my aim in Troubled Waters project has been to explore these ideas. I have wanted to transform a personal passion for albatrosses and the whole natural world into a thought-provoking portfolio of work, something aesthetic that brings to life the open ocean, and which responds to the deep spiritual value of wildlife.

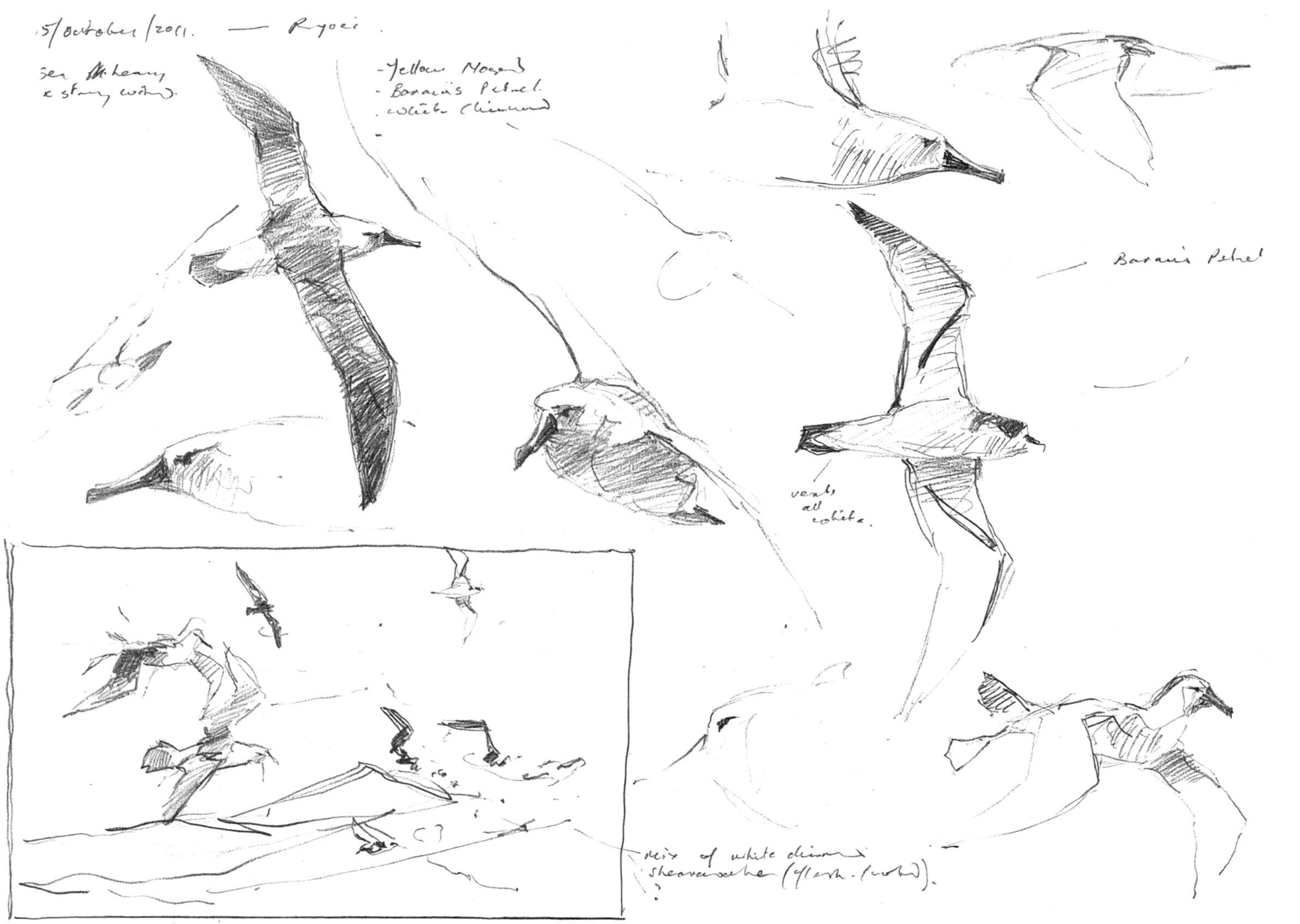

101 Seabird sketches, *Ryoei*, October, 2011
30 × 42 cm · pencil

TRACKING OCEAN WANDERERS

A major contribution to seabird studies has been the development of tiny electronic devices that are fitted to birds so their movements can be tracked over vast distances. They have revealed fascinating, and important, information about where and how oceanic seabirds feed, the routes they take, and how long they stay in feeding areas. Combining this information with the location of where world's fishing fleets are operating has provided unparalleled insights into the conflicts between albatrosses and commercial fisheries.

The British Antarctic Survey's work on Bird Island has been at the forefront ever since we tested an early and very simple device on a wanderer in 1976. All it did was record the amount of time a wanderer spent on water to get an idea of how long it spent actually feeding. Progress has been amazing. As well as tracking the birds by satellite, a recent joint-project with researchers in Japan attached miniature digital cameras to the backs of four black-browed albatrosses on the island. Incredibly, they recorded the first observations of albatrosses feeding alongside killer whales. Like gulls following the plough, they may be taking advantage of the orcas pushing prey closer to the surface.

Attaching remote tracking devices to albatrosses and petrels has meant scientists have been able to obtain a better understanding of how these birds use of the world's oceans. In 2004, BirdLife published *Tracking Ocean Wanderers*, with results revealing that albatrosses frequently travel vast distances (up to 2,000 km/day) in search of food for themselves and their chicks; making journeys which bring them into contact with a large proportion of the world's fishing fleet.

With the generous support of this pioneering group of seabird scientists, the tracking database has grown into a powerful conservation tool that enables the distribution of albatrosses and petrels to be overlaid on fishing effort data to highlight critical areas of potential conflict. As a result, mitigation against bycatch can be clearly focussed, enabling the most efficient and effective use of conservations resources. Since 2008 the data have also been used to ensure seabirds are factored into planning for Marine Protected Area initiatives worldwide.

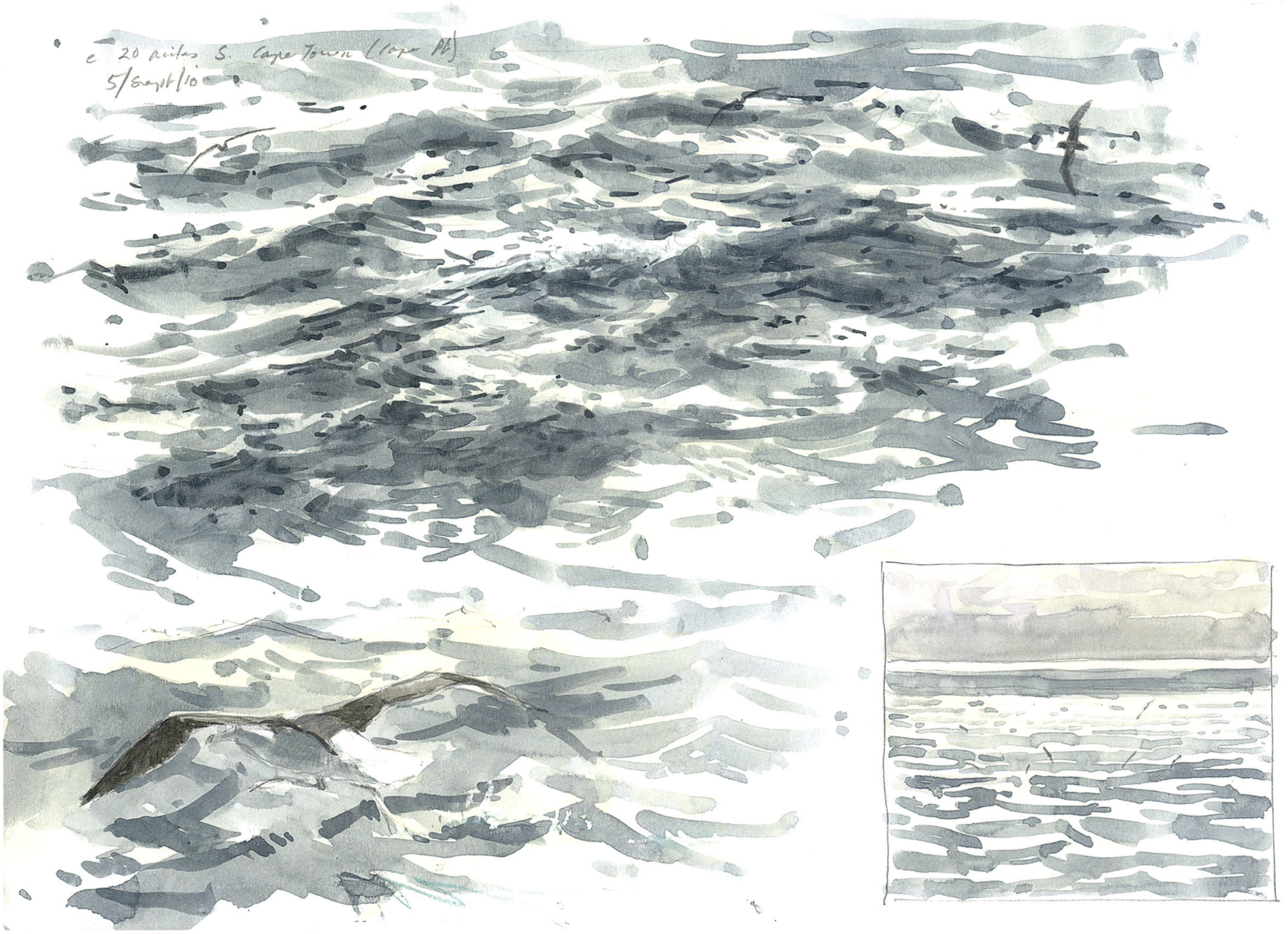

102 Twenty miles south of Cape Town, September 5th, 2010
30 × 42 cm · watercolour and pencil

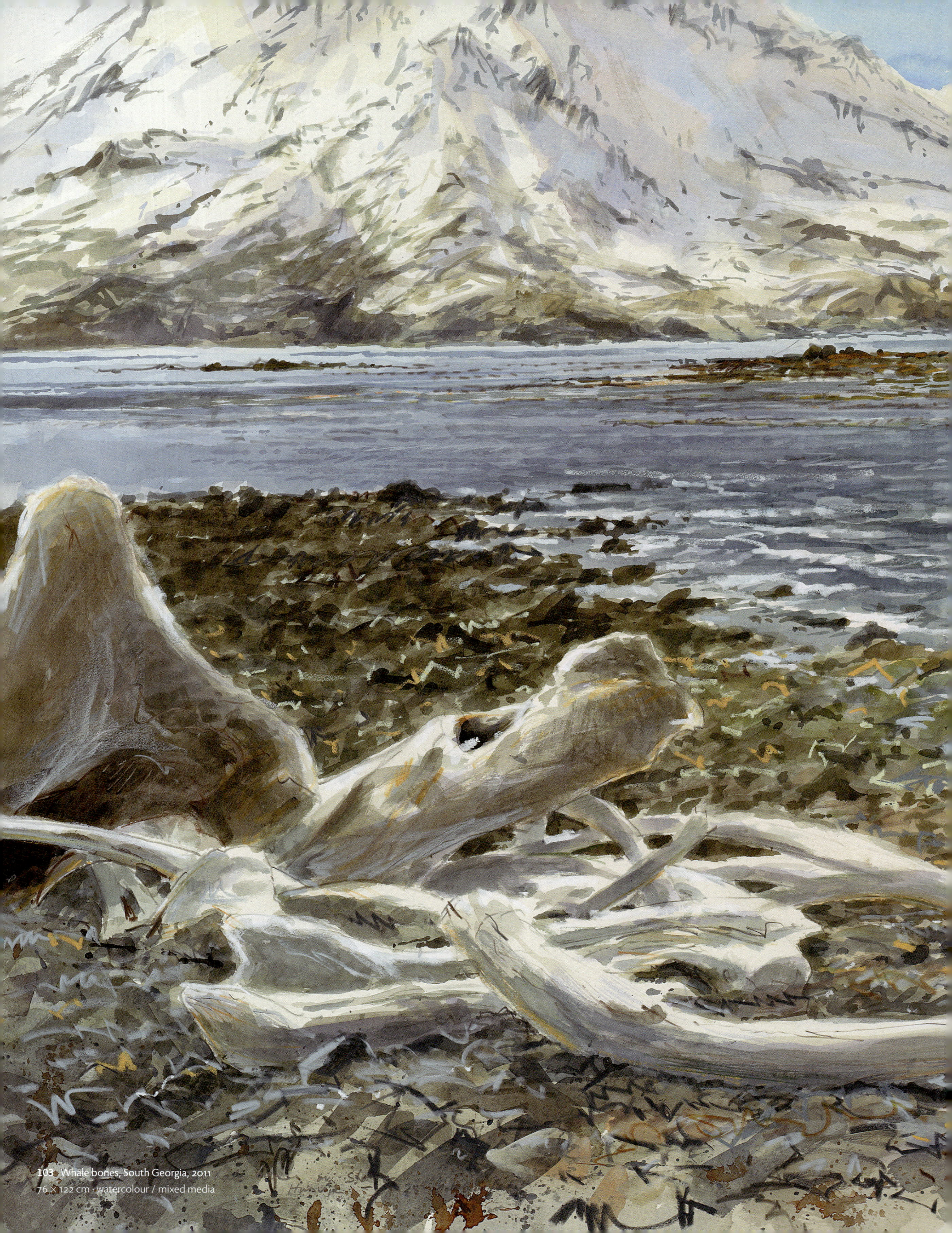

103 Whale bones, South Georgia, 2011
76 x 122 cm · watercolour / mixed media

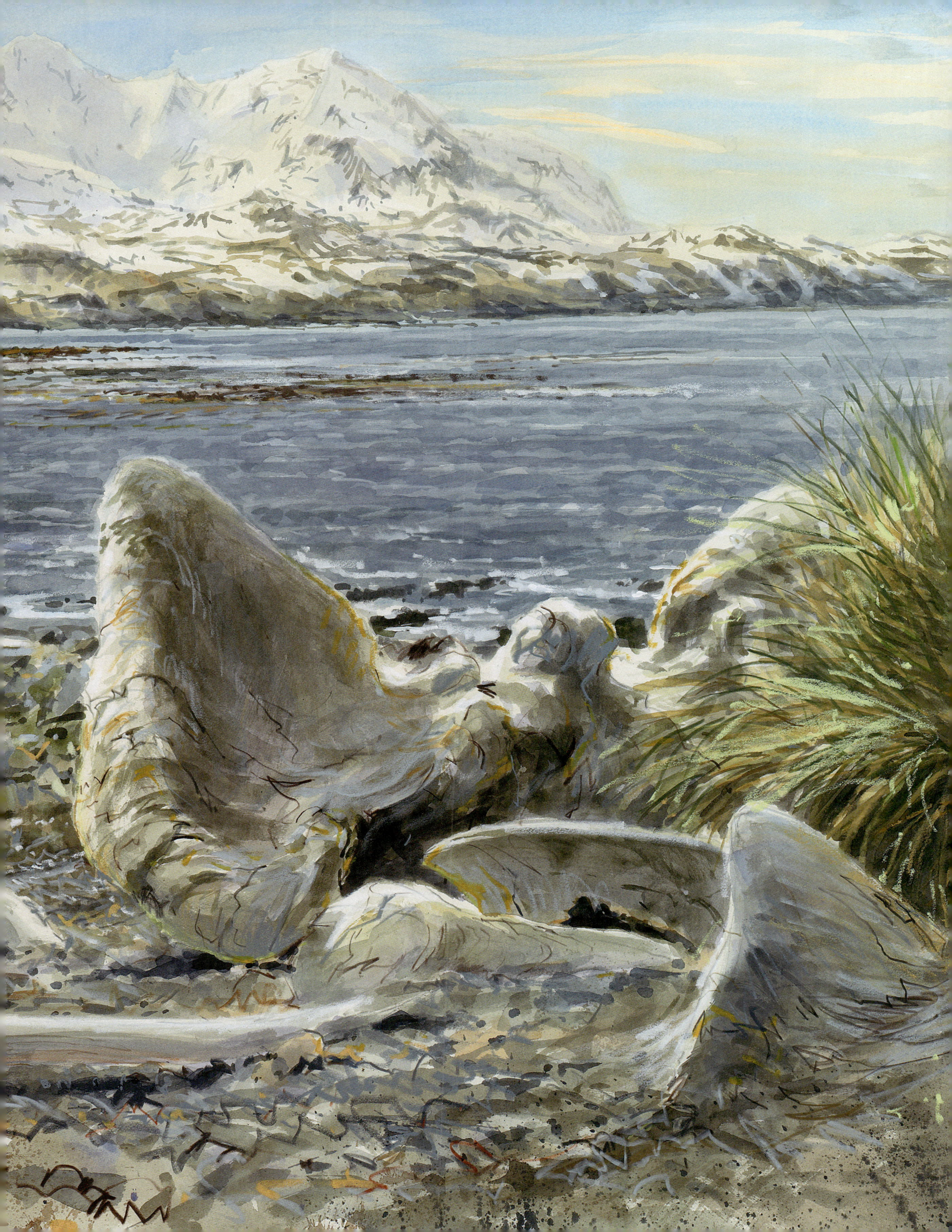

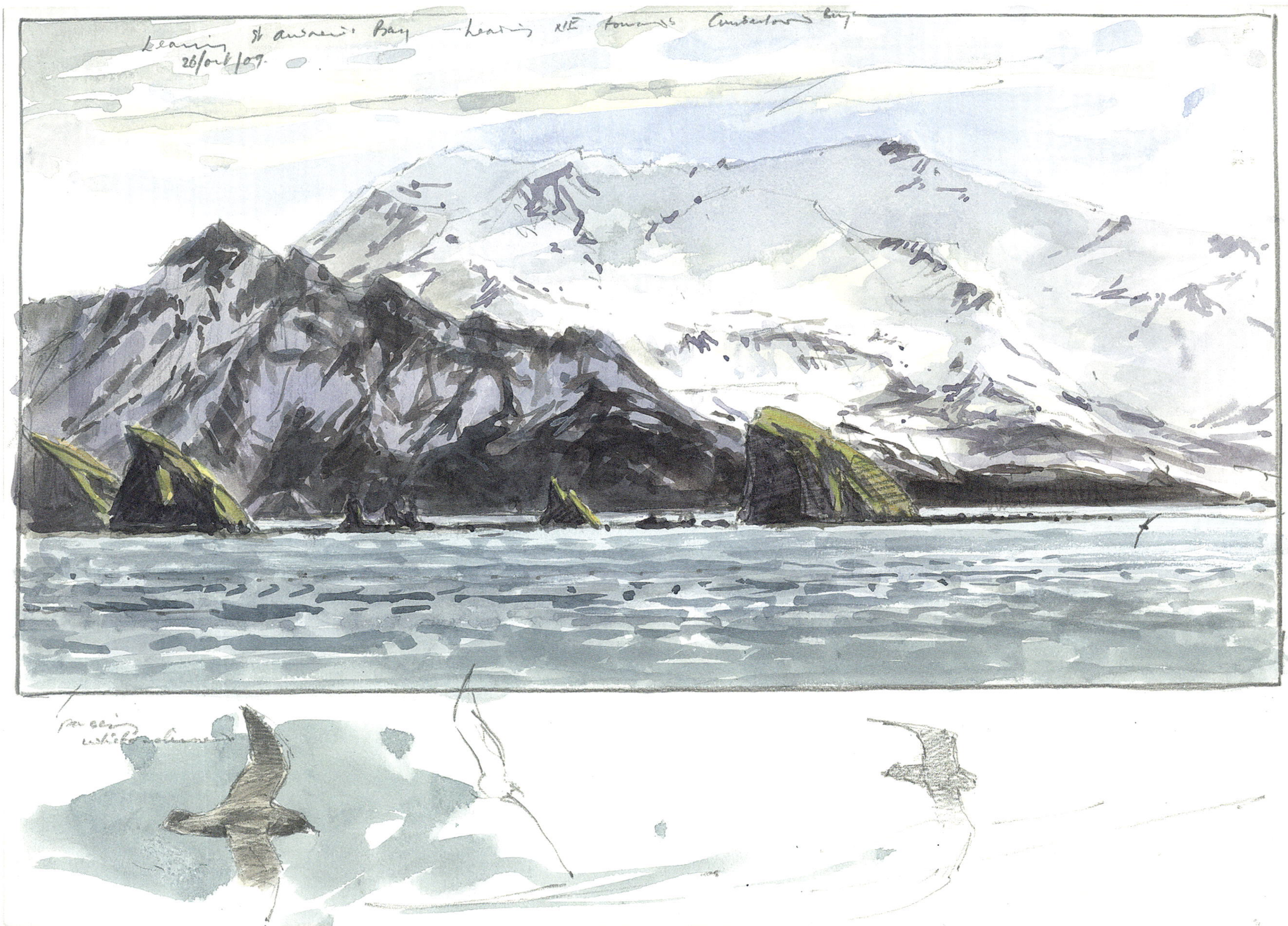

104 Passing down the north coast of South Georgia, October, 2009
30 × 42 cm · watercolour and pencil

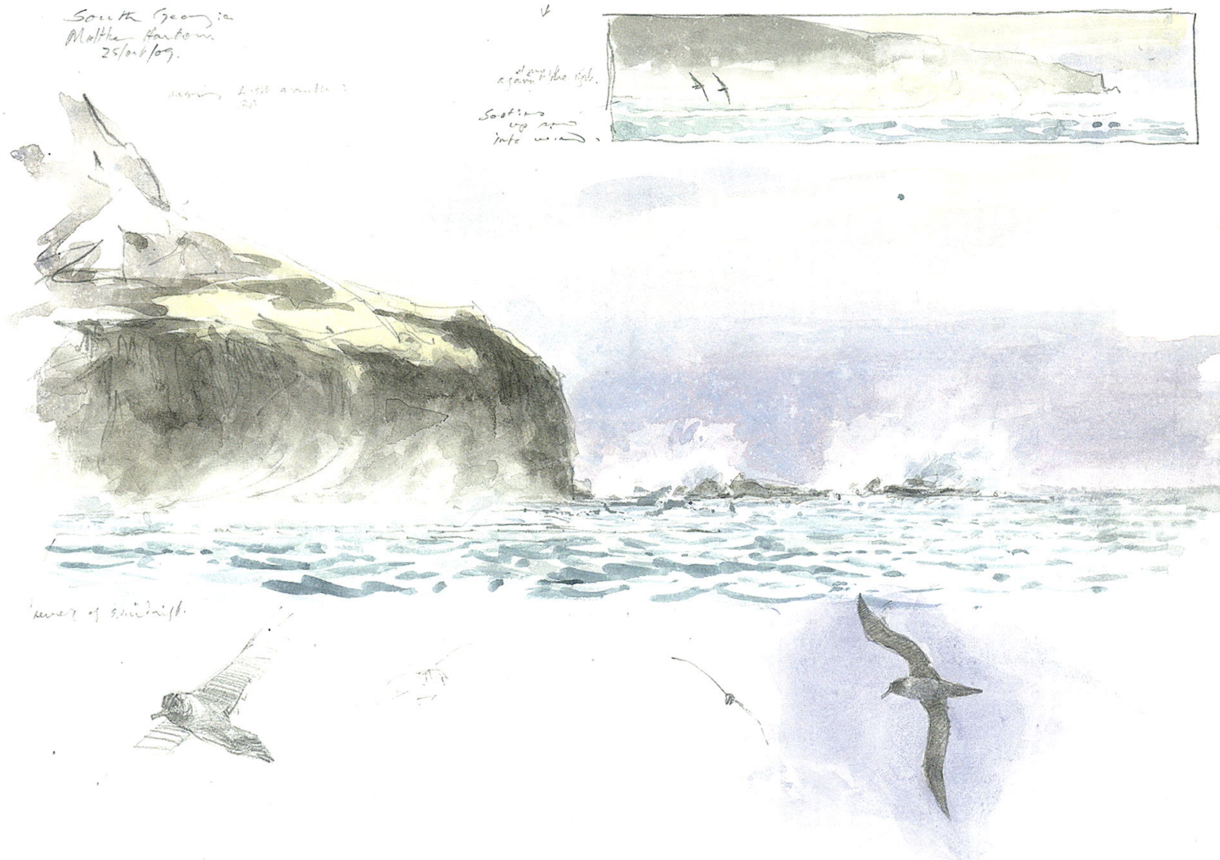

105 Spindrift and light-mantled albatross, South Georgia, 2009
30 × 42 cm · watercolour and pencil

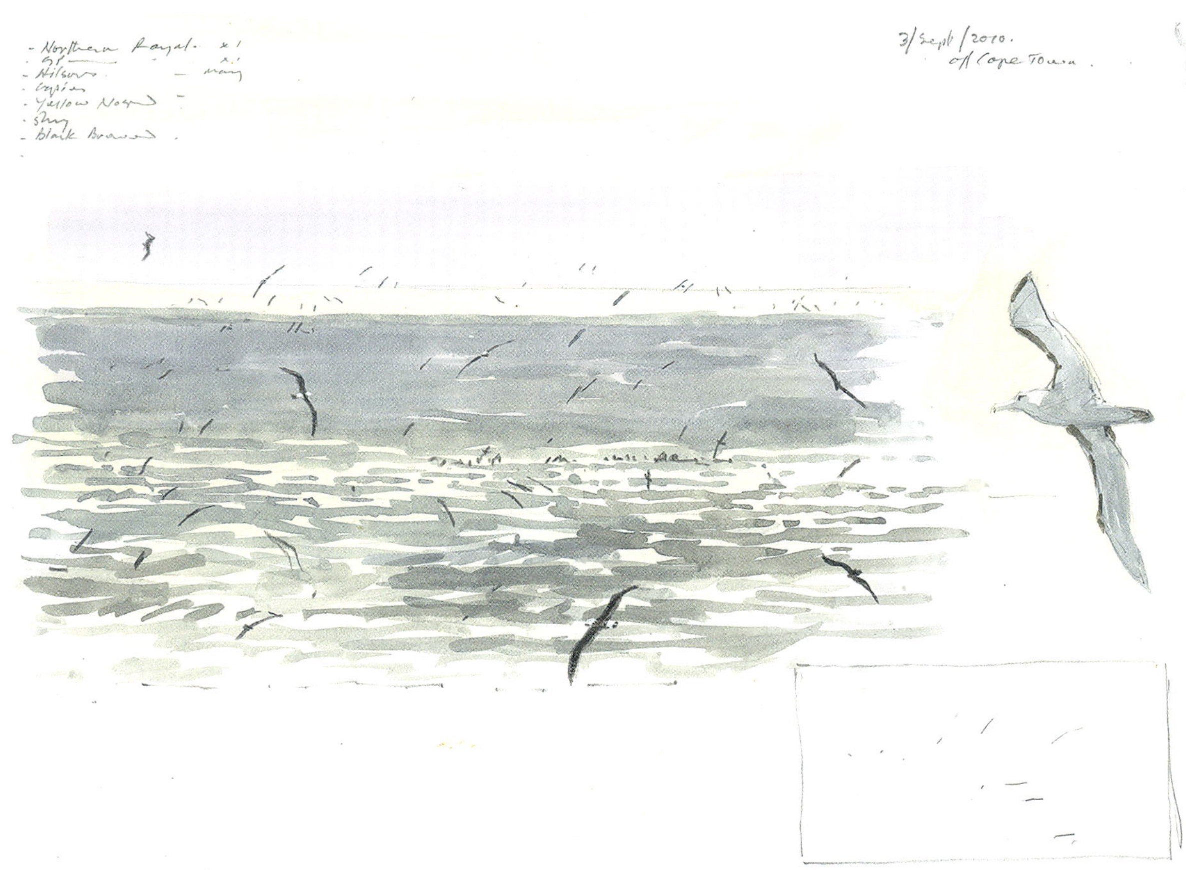

106 Birds at sea off South Africa, September, 2010
30 × 42 cm · watercolour and pencil

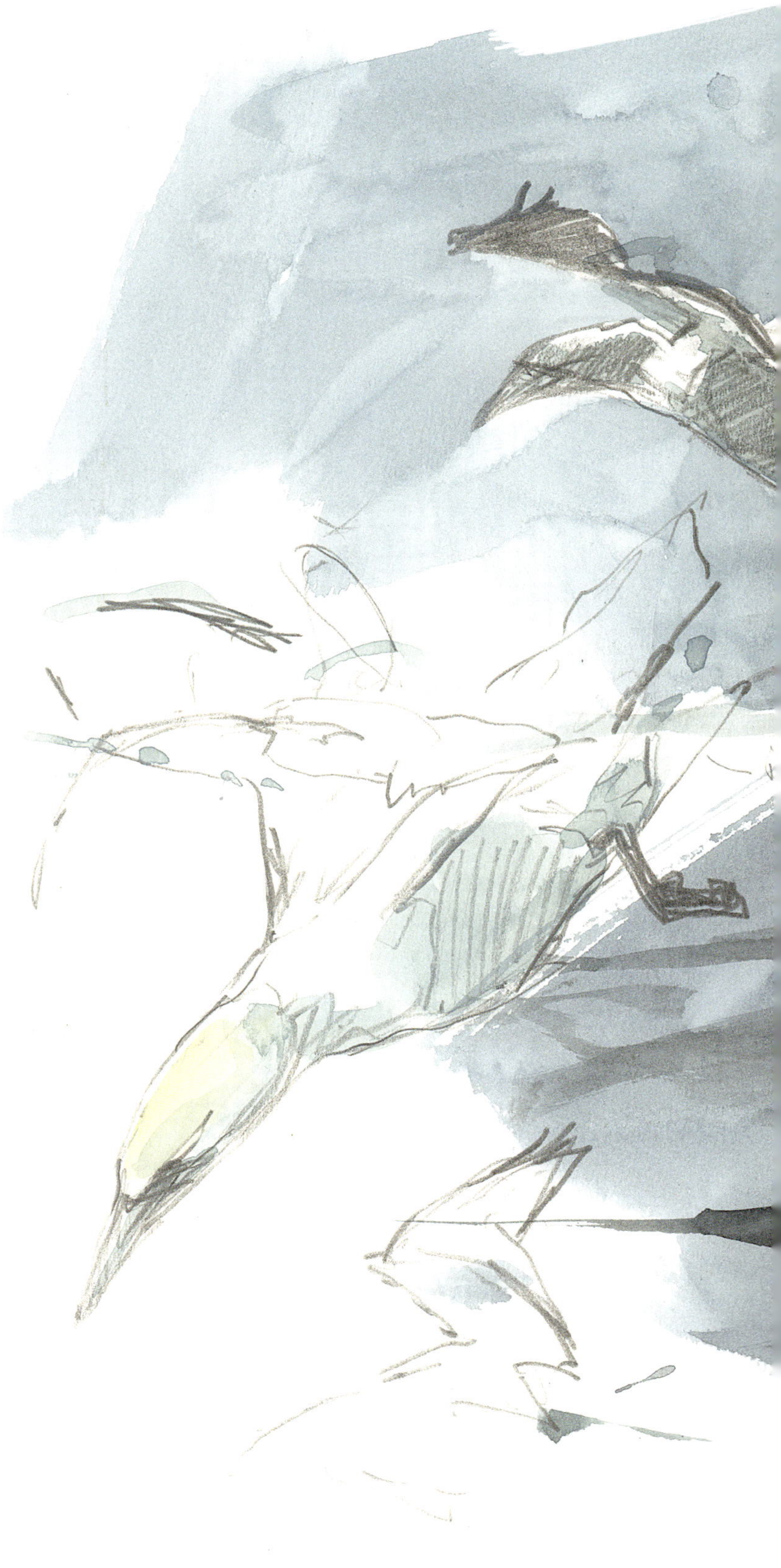

107 Shy albatross and cape gannet, September, 2010
30 × 42 cm · watercolour and pencil

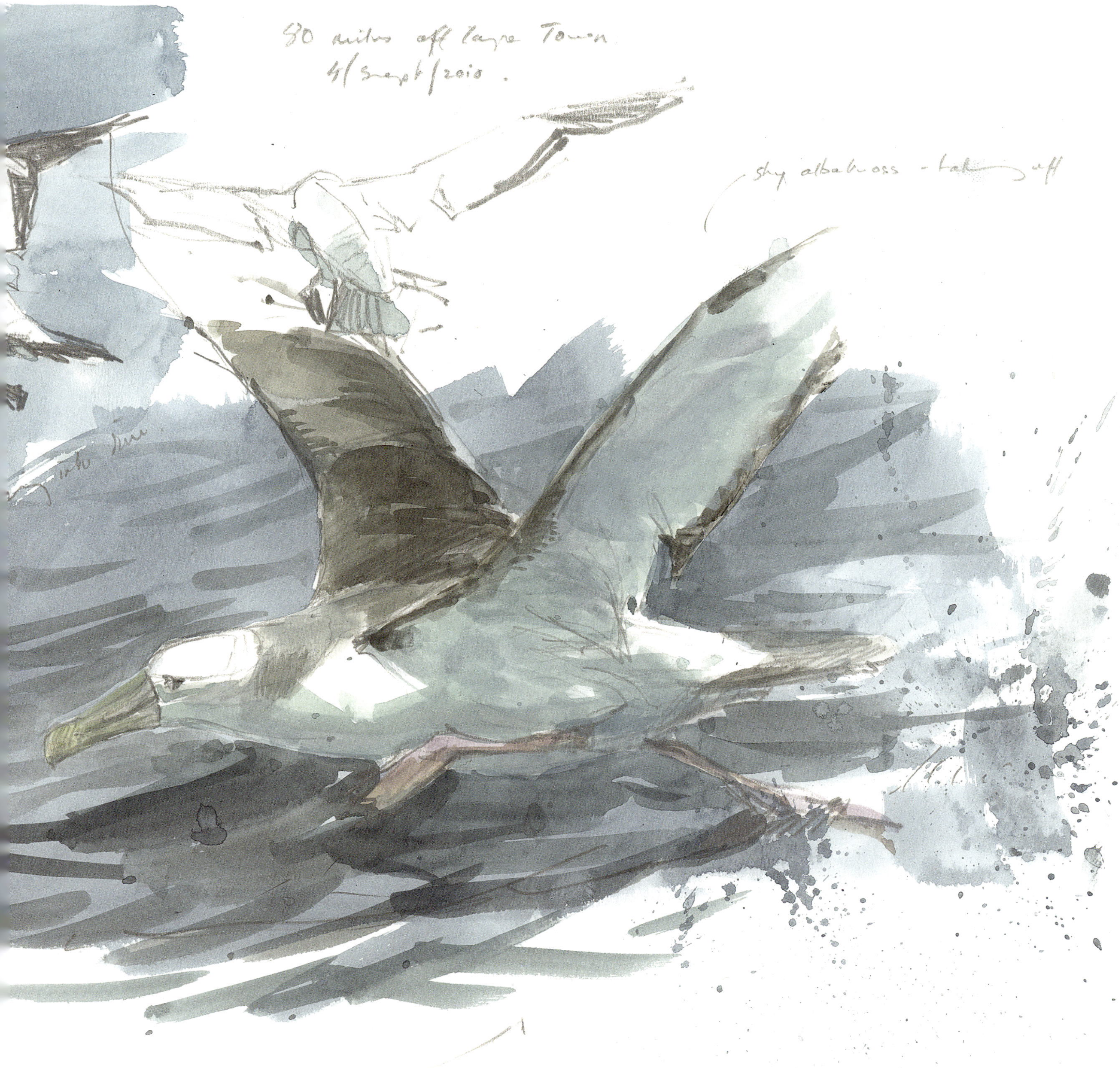
80 miles off Cape Town
4/Sept/2010.
Shy albatross - taking off

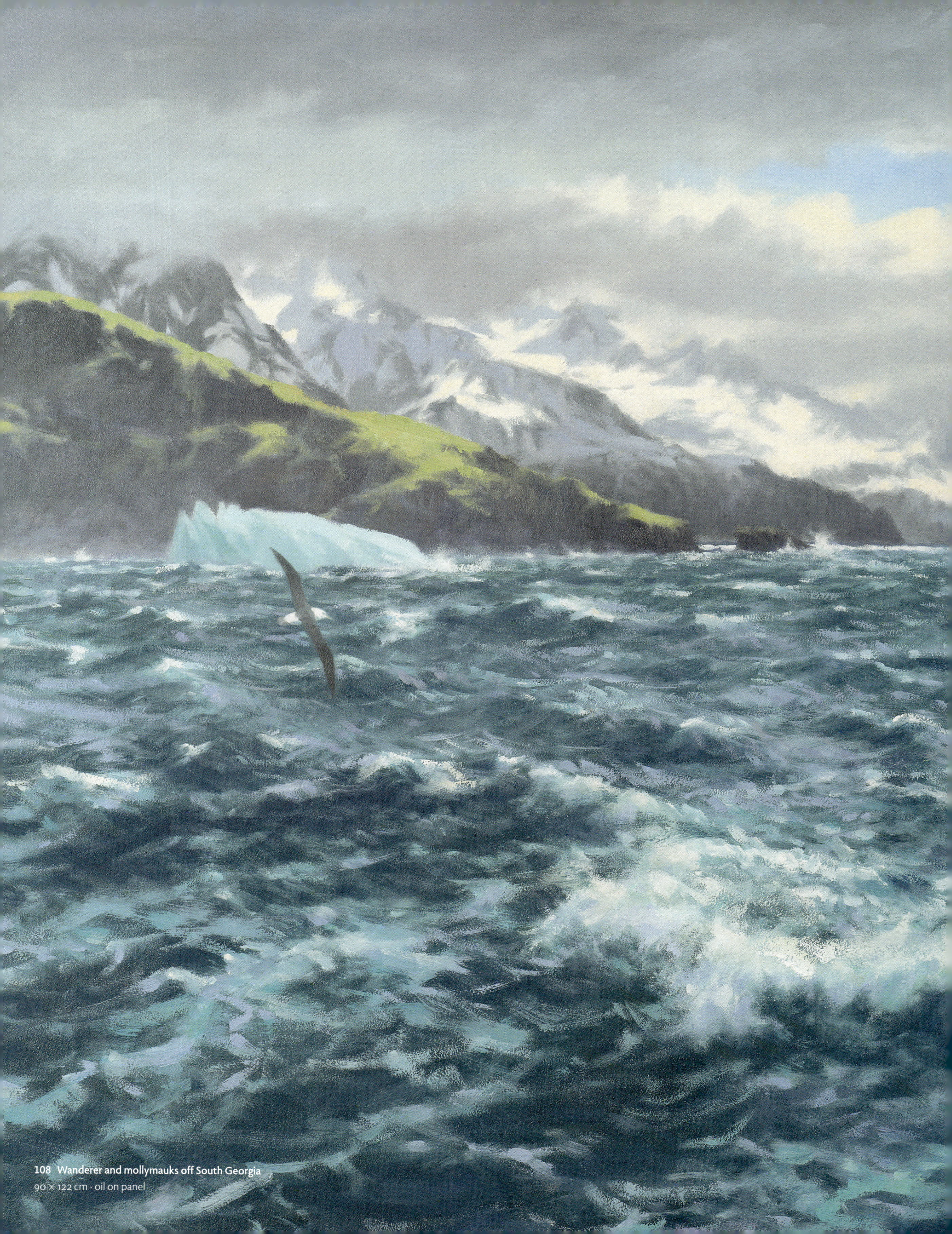

108 Wanderer and mollymauks off South Georgia
90 × 122 cm · oil on panel

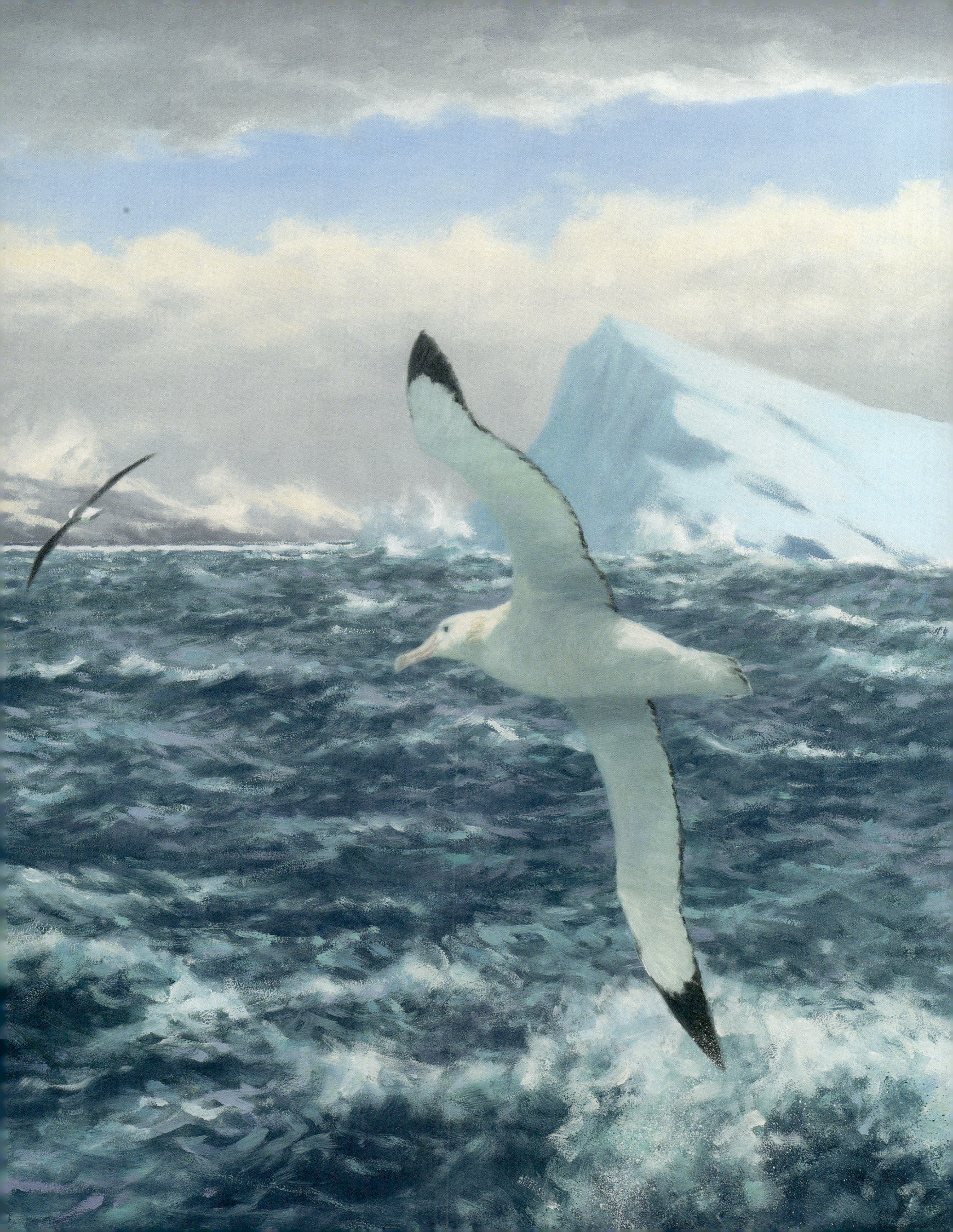

RSPB

Projeto Albatroz BRASIL

Aves Uruguay

CODEFF CHILE

albatross Task Force

BirdLife SOUTH AFRICA Giving Conservation Wings

Namibia Nature Foundation Committed to conservation

PRO DELPHINUS PERU

AVES Y CONSERVACIÓN BIRDLIFE EN ECUADOR

SAVE Brasil

AVES ARGENTINAS Asociación Ornitológica del Plata

Proyecto Albatros y Petreles URUGUAY

ATF CHILE

BirdLife INTERNATIONAL

Acknowledgements

The Troubled Waters idea goes back many years and many people have helped to make it happen. I would like to acknowledge their contributions and thank them for all the support, effort, guidance, advice and friendship they have offered throughout.

I am very grateful to Dame Ellen MacArthur for contributing a preface to this book. John Croxall gave the project his full support from the very beginning, and also graciously contributed the foreword. Lance Tickell sent interesting background papers that helped with fleshing out the early years on Bird Island and Richard Phillips at BAS helpfully provided historical and current albatross facts and figures. Simon Trapnell at Nature in Art supported an early funding proposal. Geoff Renner allowed me to share his cabin on a return visit to South Georgia, and Skip Novak and crew on *Pelagic Australis* made a more recent return very memorable. Dr David Wilson and Duncan Lawrie were free with their friendship and advice steering me towards Naomi Boneham at the Scott Polar Research Institute who arranged permission to use the sketch by Edward Wilson.

Ben Sullivan, coordinator for BirdLife International's Global Seabird Programme was extremely supportive, particularly of the requirement to get aboard a longliner and a trawler. In South Africa, Ross Wanless and Bronwyn Maree, and the team at the BirdLife office in Cape Town, enthusiastically welcomed me, arranged the voyages, and provided a great deal of background information. Meidad Goren of the Albatross Task Force in South Africa was a wonderful travelling companion and offered a lot of advice, comments and friendship; and Tshikana Rasehlomi helped answer many of my questions. SKN Tuna were extremely generous in allowing me to be accommodated aboard *Ryoei* where the skipper Jacques de Kock, First Officer James Chilongo and the crew made me very welcome. Back on shore, Jacques' wife Karolien and family offered great friendship and hospitality in the days we had waiting around on the quayside at Richards Bay. Also, Duncan Pritchard and Leonie Berning who befriended me and made my time ashore in Richards Bay so very special.

The publisher, Ian Langford, enthusiastically embraced the idea from the outset and was keen to publish the book, and support a special edition to raise funds for BirdLife's seabird conservation work. And without the creativity and professionalism of the designer Nye Hughes at Dalrymple, this volume would be the poorer. Martin Jenkins read through the manuscript. Fran Prince followed the project's progress and read through the references to Pete. And Sally Poncet and Andy Clarke were very helpful along the way.

Finally, I owe a great deal to John Fanshawe at BirdLife. We had been airing the idea of art and conservation working in a creative partnership for many years. We decided the idea of an artist being 'embedded' in an urgent contemporary conservation issue would be exciting and could possibly have interesting conservation benefits. Making it happen has required an enormous amount of effort and support from John, his BirdLife colleagues, as well as the generous support of the Wallace Research Foundation. Also, my efforts would have been much reduced without the support of Robert Burton as friend, travelling companion and fellow adventurer, editor, critic, and mentor – not only with the Troubled Waters project, but over the past thirty-five years.

BRUCE PEARSON · AUGUST 2012

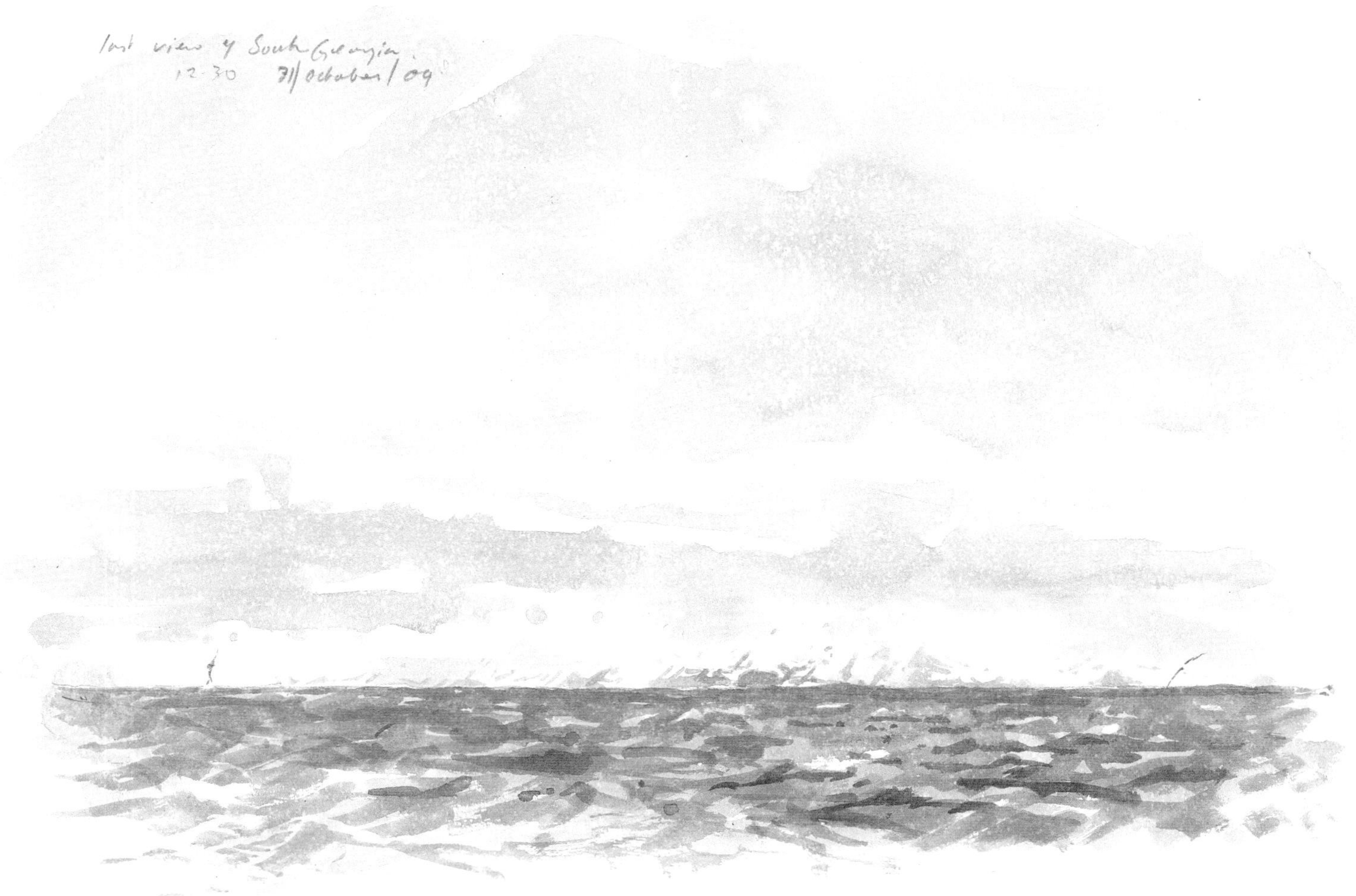

109 Leaving South Georgia, 12.30pm, 31st October, 2009
30 × 42 cm · watercolour and pencil